employee OWNERSHIP

Also By John Wiley and Sons

Employee Share Ownership Plans

How to Design and Implement
an ESOP in Canada

(ISBN: 0-471-64622-9)

employee
OWNERSHIP

THE NEW SOURCE OF
COMPETITIVE ADVANTAGE

CAROL A. BEATTY, MBA, PHD & HARVEY SCHACHTER

JOHN WILEY & SONS

HD
5660
.C3
B43
2002

John Wiley & Sons Canada Limited
22 Worcester Road
Etobicoke, Ontario
M9W 1L1

National Library of Canada Cataloguing in Publication Data

Beatty, Carol Anne, 1943-
        Employee ownership : the new source of competitive advantage

Includes index.
ISBN 0-471-64641-5

        1. Employee ownership--Canada--Case studies. I. Schachter, Harvey II. Title.

HD5660.C2B423 2001   658.3'225   C2001-903306-0

Production Credits
Cover design: Interrobang Graphic Design Inc.
Printer: Tri-Graphic Printing

Printed in Canada
10 9 8 7 6 5 4 3 2 1

Contents

Dedication

*To James, who has been a constant source of strength
and sanity for more than two wonderful decades.*
—Carol Beatty

To Seonida: mentor, partner and inspiration.
—Harvey Schachter

Acknowledgements

We are grateful for the assistance of a number of people without whom this project would never have seen the light of day. First and foremost, thanks to the wonderful students at Queen's University who did a lot of the background research: digging up the names of companies, making contact with the principals and getting permissions, interviewing and writing first drafts of the case studies, and summarizing a lot of the previous research on employee ownership. We are deeply indebted to Jennifer Hutchinson, Jennifer Mitchell, and Maureen Sterling for all of their fine research on this project. Thanks also to Mary Lou Coates who helped immensely with an article that served as a first draft for one of the chapters.

Thanks also go to the many people who granted us their valuable time for the in-depth interviews it took to get the flavour of the employee ownership experience at the ten companies profiled in this book. Their candour, humour, and memory for detail were much appreciated. In addition, we owe a debt to the school board trustee in Kapuskasing whose chance remark piqued our curiosity about the whole topic.

We also would like to thank Karen Milner whose vision and editorial acumen helped and encouraged us so much during the writing of the manuscript. Thanks to Martha Wilson for her attention to detail and many valuable suggestions to make the manuscript clearer and better written and to Abigail Brown, who kept us on track and on time.

Introduction

Not much attention is paid to employee ownership, in a world where stock market ownership and lone entrepreneurs are celebrated. Employee ownership is an orphan. It should have appeal to those who support capitalism, because it spreads the capitalist notion of owning an enterprise to more people. It should also have appeal to those who are jaundiced about capitalism, because it echoes some communitarian principles. Perhaps because of that appeal to both sides in that eternal political debate, it doesn't have strong appeal to either side, and its adherents are few. But it remains a notion that most of us have wondered about. Can it really work? Isn't it hopelessly idealistic? What does happen when the inmates run the asylum? Can employees be entrepreneurial? Do the employees make any money?

Like most people, we occasionally wondered about those intriguing questions when we encountered material on employee ownership in the course of our daily work—Carol Beatty as a business professor and director of the Industrial Relations Centre at Queen's University, and Harvey Schachter as a journalist, covering public policy and business issues. This book had its genesis when Carol was holding a fact-finding hearing in a collective bargaining impasse between the Kapuskasing Board of Education and its teachers' union. The dispute, as is common, revolved around salaries: the teachers were asking for a much higher percentage increase than the board was offering.

In an informal moment, the board chairperson remarked that the board could not afford what the teachers were requesting. She explained that the big local employer, the Spruce Falls paper mill, had been bought by employees and local townspeople, and was still on shaky financial ground. The future of the entire town was riding on the success of that new venture. The teachers would therefore have to wait and see if the mill became profitable before any significant raises could be paid them.

"But at least the employees are not stealing from the company anymore," she added. In this small one-company town, it was apparently common knowledge that many of the workers' cottages had been built from materials pilfered from the foreign-owned mill.

It was a throwaway comment—but Carol was fascinated. If employee ownership could turn such alienated workers into model corporate citizens, then the whole concept was worth investigating. Thus began this study of employee ownership in Canada, which extended over a period of seven years and branched out from cases of firms in crisis to other companies where employee ownership arose as part of the management philosophy.

Carol's students went into the companies to talk to executives and workers alike, and into libraries to research company histories and the wide-ranging literature on worker ownership. Harvey joined in later, going back to each of the featured ten companies to extend the research, sharpen it, and make the individual case studies compelling reading for a general audience. The more we looked, the more fascinating the study became. Our variegated sample of companies offered rich and often unexpected insights. And as we continued our study, societal interest in employee ownership intensified, as it became de rigeur for technology firms to offer employees shares to bond and bind them to the enterprise.

The majority of the ten companies were located in Ontario, with others in British Columbia, Alberta, Saskatchewan, and Quebec. Some are well known—three were part of high-profile buyouts involving the Ontario government in the recession of the early 1990s, for which this serves as the first definitive evaluation—while others are almost certainly unfamiliar to you. They extend into a wide range of industries with diverse employees: steelworkers, paperworkers, trucking industry employees, brewery workers, garden nursery personnel, geologists, computer engineers, and high tech manufacturing employees. And they include both unionized and non-unionized settings.

Significantly, we decided to include only companies with a comparatively large percentage of employee ownership—the initial cutoff point was around 30 percent—because studies show that the effects of ownership are more pronounced at higher levels. Our cases include examples of large and small companies, start-ups, spinoffs, privatizations, and threatened closures—including both forced and voluntary ownership situations. They contain firms in the new as well as the old economy. Some have participatory management structures, some do not. But more importantly, of the ten, only one has not survived to date. And of the other nine, seven have proven to be highly successful in various ways.

Towards a New Deal

As Canadian society enters a new century, a new deal may need to be struck between management and employees. The old psychological contract between them certainly seems dead: the basic exchange of security and decent wages for dedicated service and strong loyalty to the company. Yet companies are finding it difficult to achieve a new balance—one in which there is flexibility to meet the ever-changing challenges of competition and economic turbulence while maintaining at least a certain degree of commitment from employees.

Employee ownership is one way to balance this delicate equation. It falls somewhere in the middle of the spectrum between absolute corporate power over the workers and absolute worker control of the corporate agenda. It can offer a win-win outcome for both, providing higher compensation for employees while at the same time preserving excellent corporate financial outcomes.

Studies have generally shown that employee ownership has a positive impact on profitability, revenue growth, and productivity. Indeed, one Canadian study by the Toronto Stock Exchange found that companies with employee share ownership plans had a 95 percent higher profit and a 123 percent higher growth in profits over five years. The companies we studied exhibited, for the most part, very positive financial results for the new owners, although it was impossible to put a precise figure to the benefits, given the wide range of circumstances we were chronicling. But we were taken by the comment of a seasoned and tough-as-nails CEO, Tembec founder

Frank Dottori, that employee ownership gives him a 15 percent advantage over his traditional rivals. That gave us a theme for this book—and it should give anyone from a traditional workplace food for thought.

Five of the companies in our sample were threatened with imminent closure before turning to employee ownership. Of those, two became stellar success stories while two others continue to survive, although Algoma Steel is currently in trouble. Only one has closed its doors. It is clear that these companies, with the one exception, were in a much stronger financial position after their employee buyouts than before.

However, it is not clear whether this turnaround can be attributed to employee ownership, to other factors, or to a combination of both. Most of the five companies began their new life with a stronger balance sheet due to monetary contributions—in the form of both liquid and non-liquid assets—from parent corporations, governments, and employees and communities. That meant they could establish themselves financially with fewer debt obligations, begin operations with a minimum of capital investment, and secure a customer base and sources of revenue. A second crucial factor was the reduction in labour costs that accompanied the buyout arrangements. Those often involved wage and benefit freezes or cuts as well as downsizing initiatives, and were used in addition to or in lieu of employee-financed investments.

Improved business conditions in some of the industries also set the stage for profitability and growth, as did a number of strategic decisions by individual management teams. Finally, employee ownership itself acted as a selling tool: at Spruce Falls, for example, it helped raise customer confidence in the company, which had been plagued with high senior management turnover before the buyout.

So many factors were at play. Still, considering the fact that all five of these companies were in serious financial trouble before their employees bought them, their survival record is impressive. And it strengthens the case for employee buyouts of struggling companies, to reshape and reinvigorate them, particularly in any future recession.

As for the other five cases, all have been very successful, some making their employee owners quite wealthy over the period of our study. The standout among this group is Creo, a Vancouver-based company supplying technology to the printing industry, which allows it to turn a computerized image directly into a printing plate instead of going through an intermediate step. Revenues have grown about 40 percent a year since 1996, and employee growth has been almost as fast-paced, going from 40 in 1989 to more than 1,500 employees in 1999. Share ownership at Creo has also created some very happy employees. The July 1999 initial public offering of shares valued the company at $1 billion, giving the founders and early employees 160 times the value of their first shares. And in March 2000, as the company joined the TSE 300 index and acquired its main rival, Scitex Business, shares rose from $24 to over $75 in one day's worth of trading before falling back to the $30 range in late 2000. Not all of these five companies were as profitable as Creo, but they all were success stories in their own right.

The Power of Participation and Ownership

In theory, the success of employee-owned firms relates to improved employee attitudes and behaviours that in turn rest on increased trust, involvement, and participation in the enterprise. A number of studies of employee-owned firms in the United States suggest that their superior financial returns are a result of the powerful twin combination of employee ownership and employee participation. The National Center for Employee Ownership concluded in 1996: "Researchers now agree that 'the case is closed' on employee ownership and corporate performance. Findings this consistent are very unusual. We can say with certainty that when ownership and participative management are combined, substantial gains result. Ownership and participation alone, however, have, at best, spotty or short-lived results."

Our case studies, however, offer several examples of companies that have succeeded without a great deal of participative management, as well as others that appear to have used it to great advantage. For example, at SFG Technologies, a small software firm, employee shares did not come with any voting rights or positions on the board of directors. The lines of authority were clear: the president was the boss. Yet after struggling for a number of years, the company and the employees realized a large windfall when operations were sold to a corporate suitor. At the other end of the participation spectrum stands Creo, where employees have an extraordinary control of their own jobs, evaluate their bosses in the annual performance reviews that determine stock options, and blend socialistic notions, empowerment, and free-enterprise zest into a tantalizingly successful stew.

In the next ten chapters, you will read in turn about each of the companies—their struggles and successes, and what they believe can be learned by other companies from their story. Following those descriptions, we analyze what those cases tell us both individually and as a whole, and in an appendix look at the legislative history of employee ownership and what other studies have revealed. There is a difference in tone and style between those parts of the book, reflecting the journalist and the academic, as well as the specific content. But we trust that you'll find in both sections that we don't settle for easy answers.

If you are interested in the concepts of employee ownership, you may find some guidance from a case similar to your own situation. If you are a student of organizations, you may find these cases fascinating in their own right. What the school board chairperson pointed to with her offhand comment was correct: employee ownership can dramatically transform a workplace for the better. But it's not easy or automatic, as our stories show.

The Cases

The Cases

Revolve Technologies

&

Finding the Employee Ownership Balance

"When I was in my mid-thirties, this seemed a good thing to do. Now I'm in my mid-forties and I would really like to get back to owning my home, which I did prior to this, and having my RRSPs, which are all invested in the company, and start thinking about my future."

—Kim Sturgess, president and CEO

Employee. Owner.

For most people, those are clear concepts. But blend them together into employee owner and the result can become quite complicated. Certainly that's what the employees of NOVA Corp.'s Hardware Applications Group found when they took on the risk and uncharted territory of starting their own company, after NOVA decided there was no place for the unit in its strategy. Originally, they were given about a month to define their new role as employee owners before their new company was launched. But as it turned out, they needed almost a decade to sort through all the complications, from decision-making to recouping their investment.

Their odyssey began in 1992, when J. E. (Ted) Newall replaced NOVA founder Robert Blair as CEO and began to overhaul the pipeline and chemical operation. To cut costs in what was expected to be an adverse period, the company decided to focus on four core areas: Alberta gas transmissions, North American gas services, international gas services, and petrochemicals. Among the stranded operations was the Hardware Applications Group, which had been developing innovative magnetic bearings and gas seals for NOVA's pipelines and other companies that bought its consulting services.

The technology allows rotating equipment, such as compressors in a pipeline system, to operate without oil lubrication systems. Because of the knowledge and creativity required to pioneer in this field, the group had developed a certain degree of independence in the bureaucratic NOVA Corp. structure. It had a reputation for being "elite" and always getting what it wanted—indeed, often doing what it wanted and seeking permission later. "There was a willingness to experiment and try new things which I don't think was common throughout NOVA," says Kim Sturgess, then a manager with the group.

Assessing the Options

When the group officially learned in May of that year that it would be dissolved, about half the employees were frightened; the other half, however, were excited by the new opportunity. Three options were on the table: selling the group to an outside company, folding the unit and placing some employees back in other jobs at NOVA, or selling the operation to its employees. Just as employees were split, so was NOVA management, with some supporting an employee-owned initiative while others believed such a spinoff would take too much unnecessary time and effort.

But momentum started to develop for the spinoff from a band of employees who were committed to the technology and enticed by the possibility of gaining a more risk-taking environment. With luck, they could recreate their jobs in the image they desired—and help the country in technological development. "We are all strong believers that unless we do something Canada is going to slip in its position in the world, the standard of living will fall, and we'll become the fifty-first state of the U.S. We thought we were innovating and developing something," said Clayton Bear, another manager of the group.

The group's management began to discuss the shape of the spinoff with senior NOVA executives. It led to an odd series of negotiations, because the group's management was taking on a quasi-union role in representing the employees in those talks on their future with the company. Later, it would have to turn around and negotiate with those same employees on its own behalf about the new venture they were forming.

The idea of being totally employee-owned evolved over time. Initially, management wanted the venture to be one-third owned by an institutional investor, one-third by NOVA, and one-third by employees. However, outside consultants advised NOVA that if a parent retained some control or ownership in the spinoff, it would cripple the new enterprise, preventing it from finding its own path in life. NOVA was also worried about exposing itself to liability from the new company's activities. It decided early on not to participate in ownership.

A backdrop to the negotiations was internal opposition from employees elsewhere in NOVA who viewed the initiative as a dangerous threat. The more talk grew about the possibility, the more they feared a successful spinoff could become a model that would be used to eliminate other elements of the company. "People thought we were a risk to their jobs," noted Stan Uptigrove, another manager with the group.

Two sets of issues emerged as important. Agreement would be needed on what intellectual property from NOVA the employees would be able to take with them, how they would be entitled to use that property, and how the company would be compensated. As well, it was not clear what severance pay, if any, the employees would be entitled to, or whether those who wished to stay with NOVA would be permitted to. The employees had individual employment contracts with NOVA, but those were unclear on such vital separation matters.

It was not just the contract that didn't provide guidance. This was a new concept for everyone, with no handy models, which slowed negotiations. NOVA was also insistent that a credible business plan be developed demonstrating that the venture would be successful. As one of the employees, Geoff Clark, noted, "They had not done anything like this before. We had never done anything like this before. We were talking to people who were bureaucrats and we were bureaucrats ourselves. We had management consultants who really weren't experienced in this area either. Since we were the first, I don't think we could expect it to go faster, but it was definitely frustrating."

Tension grew as the negotiations continued. By late November—six months after the original announcement—it was still unclear what NOVA would decide. But a week later, in early December, the company announced it would give the spinoff its approval—and set January 1 as the date for launching the new endeavour. That gave just a few weeks to settle a host of complex issues between the new company's management and employees.

Power was at the top of the list. Some employees worried that the proposed plan gave the four-person management team too much power. They would be serving not only as the senior management but also as the board of directors—and, additionally, would be the four largest shareholders. While some people felt it was reasonable to have the top shareholders managing the company, others felt that would simply allow management to oppress employees.

The result was a big concession by management: the company would operate like a co-operative. It would have a Unanimous Shareholders Agreement requiring unanimous approval by shareholders for certain fundamental decisions and set out varying levels of approval for other decisions. Employee owners as a totality would hold the power, not management.

Resentment also flared over the non-competitive clauses that NOVA wanted in the shareholders agreement, to prevent employees of the new company from walking away with NOVA technology. But the employees wanted to retain complete flexibility for future employment in the event that the new company went under. Management was caught in the middle. Trust—which was not particularly high anyway—was eroding. As Sturgess notes, when the agreement was being forged, the employees "didn't trust that management would deliver on what was being written. They believed the words were written by a lawyer for the benefit of management as opposed to the benefit of the employees."

She also felt that employees were so focused on themselves that they were losing sight of the greater objective. The new company's value statement revolved around matters like employees' being respected, treated well, and having a say in what they did. All reasonable—but also, as she noted, self-absorbed. "There was virtually no value that had anything to do with the external customer," she said.

A New Company Is Born

In the end, employee concerns were addressed and an acceptable agreement was patched together. Eighteen of the 35 individuals in the group agreed to leave NOVA and become the founding employees of Revolve Technologies Inc. And they did so with a sizeable dowry from the company. Once NOVA gave its blessing to the venture, it was extremely supportive in helping Revolve get off to a good start. Clark, who was to become chief financial officer, called it "the sweetest deal ever made from NOVA."

Every employee joining the new venture was given a standard severance package from NOVA. That was a generous gesture, given that the next day they would enjoy employment in the spinoff that NOVA was helping to set up. It also meant that the employees, now suddenly richer, were in a better position to support their new venture.

NOVA also granted Revolve an exclusive licence to all the intellectual property that the group had developed. NOVA was to receive a small royalty but only after Revolve enjoyed a two-year royalty holiday. Clark noted that the "royalty to NOVA does not even come close to the actual value of what that intellectual property is. It's just a token."

The new company was given all of the furniture, tools, computers, and equipment its team had been using at NOVA for a fee of $1 a year. Clark estimated the value, conservatively, at $200,000. NOVA threw in complete title to two vehicles and free rent for 11 months. And it agreed to backstop any credit arrangement from early December 1992 to the day Revolve began operations. Although that could have been a large financial gesture, in fact it resulted only in guaranteeing the few thousand dollars spent to set up a local area computer network.

NOVA also became Revolve's first customer, continuing all the research and development programs that the group had been carrying out for it. An agreement that NOVA held with Pacific Wietz to market a dry gas seal worldwide was assigned to Revolve. That allowed NOVA to escape liability but also assured Revolve of some significant cash flow.

Together, the package enabled the company to begin operations with a minimum amount of capital investment, an initial source of customer revenue, and few financial obligations. That gave Revolve a window of opportunity to secure a customer base and establish itself financially. It also meant no institutional investor would be needed. Revolve could be 100 percent employee-owned.

Since payroll was expected to be the largest expense in the initial months, the company devised a formula to reduce the burden while building its share structure. The minimum that employees could invest in the company was set at $10,000—but 40 percent of that could be funded by salary reductions in the first four months of operations. That not only helped the company but also reduced the employees' taxable income in a year when they were getting a severance payment from NOVA.

Fortuitously, in early December, the federal government had tabled draft legislation that would allow individuals to put shares they owned into their RRSPs. Since a portion of the severance package was a retirement allowance that could be put tax-free into an RRSP, the new legislation allowed employees to invest that money in their own company's shares while reducing their taxes. The regulations, which weren't fully drafted, put a 10 percent limit on how much of the company an individual could own, so Revolve simply adopted that maximum in its own shareholder agreement.

Investments by non-managers in the company ranged from $10,000 to $50,000, (the maximum of 10 percent) depending on their financial circumstances. Each of the four directors invested $50,000, although they each made substantially larger investments in follow-on rounds of financing.

What Does Employee Owner Mean?

They were now employee owners. They had to begin the process of figuring out exactly what that meant. The first year was dominated by trying to live up to the egalitarian framework they had conceived and trying to make it work. Since important decisions were to be made only with unanimous approval, shareholder's meetings would be called at midday over the public address system to discuss crucial issues. Although it was egalitarian and participative, it was also inefficient and frustrating. From signing leases to forging contracts with suppliers, everyone would have to gather for a meeting.

For all the semblance of equality, management was still playing the lead role. It would advise the other employee owners of decisions it was intending to make and then ask for input. The issue would be debated and then eventually employees would offer assent. People who disagreed would generally relent—and then leave the meeting and complain. So although there was a tacit consensus it may not have been a real consensus. But it took time—and effort—even to make that work, and it diverted staff from other pursuits equally important to a new company.

It was also fouling up delegation and accountability. Everyone wanted to be involved in everything. At times it seemed nobody was responsible for anything. The assumption that everyone was an equal partner was making Revolve virtually unmanageable.

Accentuating the problem was the fact they now had a bottom line. NOVA had been a large utility and in its pipeline division—where the Revolve employees had worked—capital expenditures could be charged back to users on a percentage basis each year. Cash flow was assured under that arrangement. Now, suddenly, cash loomed as a critical issue for a small company fighting to grow. "I never did worry in my entire life about cash flow but it very quickly became a top part of my management style," noted John Sears, director of applications. "You have to ask whether we can afford to do something. Is there enough money coming in? It determines what opportunities you chase, whether it be long-term or short-term."

The employee owners also had to learn, in chasing those opportunities, that it was vital to be focused on customers. That was a slow, difficult transition. However, the company performed well in its first year, earning $1.7 million in revenue, of which about $700,000 came from sales to NOVA and $1 million from other clients. Overall, there was a small profit—$50,000—and the company also won a prestigious technology award. They could all breathe a sigh of relief, as Clayton Bear later noted: "At the beginning, I was sick to my stomach for weeks at a time, wondering if we were doing the right thing... Nobody except us believed this company could work, but we're over a year old now, and once you have survived your first year, you're real to people."

It was now time, however, to change the meaning of employee owner by terminating the unanimous shareholder agreement. Top managers were encountering trouble with business contacts, because they didn't have sufficient authority to make deals. The employee owners recognized that the system they had constructed was reducing the value of what they owned through the inefficiency it created. "People realized that the value of their own shares would improve if they just did their own jobs and let management do the job of managing the company," recalls Clark.

The shareholders agreement also created two other significant complications. It was impossible to bring on new employees unless they were shareholders, which was proving impractical. And the agreement barred outside investors. But it was becoming clear that for the company to grow it would need outside capital. Certainly no venture capitalists would get involved in a company with such an egalitarian decision-making structure.

The employee owners, therefore, delegated decision-making to their management. They began to focus on their individual jobs—the "employee" side of their role—and let management be accountable to them as shareholders in a more normal fashion. But they kept the structure flat, with just two layers: the directors, who worked as a team to run the company with one designated as managing director, and the employees.

That shift in mood intensified as they began to bring in new investors—mostly friends and family—who, of course, could take on only the ownership role. By April 1995, 28 months after Revolve's birth, the company had raised a total of $1.6 million and had broadened its base from 18 to 72 shareholders. The company was effectively semi-private: a private company of employee shareholders, with additional outside shareholders.

In that vein, Revolve formally reported to its shareholders as if it were a publicly traded company. It issued quarterly reports and monthly accounting reports in addition to the year-end audited statements. Shareholders were informed by letter of any significant decisions. An attempt was also made to bring employees together on a regular basis, to keep them informed of decisions and future plans. And annual employee surveys were conducted to weigh opinion about communications within the company and its direction.

Growth and Partners

But for growth, it became increasingly clear, greater fiscal and marketing clout would be required. The dry gas seal business was faring well but the magnetic bearing business was slower to develop than had been hoped and would need outside help to expand. In 1996, both the Business Development Bank of Canada and Ventures West provided additional financing. Getting venture capital was a new experience for the Revolve team and one that was to cause pain later, as outsiders gained a veto—effective control—on crucial issues like financing arrangements and key leases.

Moreover, even before that arrangement, managers realized that a partnership was needed with a global player who could help Revolve to sell its bearings worldwide. While mulling over that necessity, management was pleasantly surprised to be approached by SKF, a $5 billion Swedish-based operation. Of all the possible partners, SKF was certainly the best, but Revolve would never have considered approaching it because SKF had an investment in Revolve's chief competitor, S2M of France. However, that investment wasn't working out and SKF was scouting other opportunities.

It took two years to finalize a deal. In November 1997, SKF bought out the venture capitalists and took a 40 percent stake in the company. SKF's greater marketing and sales scope provided an immediate boost to Revolve, with revenues tripling in each of the next two years, as some large new customers were brought onstream.

The downside of the investment was that SKF wasn't interested in the gas seal business. Revolve had to sever that operation off. This resulted in two different businesses operating from the same location, with the same shareholder groups but headed by different managers with very different operating styles and strategies. The seal business was owned 100 percent by family, friends, and business associates. The magnetic bearings business—which quickly grew to become the large operation—was 60 percent owned by those same family, friends, and business associates, with SKF holding the remaining 40 percent.

SKF also had been granted the right to increase its ownership, which seemed convenient not only as an exit strategy but also because it potentially offered more capital for growth. While the gas seal business does not require much investment, the control systems for the magnetic bearings have to be changed every two or three years, to keep up with the latest microchip technology.

From the time the venture capitalists moved in, the management structure became even more traditional. Instead of the four directors sharing power, with a nominal managing director, Sturgess was named president and CEO to oversee operations. "They like a clear decision-making structure," Sturgess said of the venture capitalists. "And it has in fact worked a lot better, although we still have a more open decision-making structure than many other places. We ask for employees' opinions and there's lots of input. But I make the decisions."

In that new era, employees retained lots of responsibility and latitude themselves to carry on their jobs, in line with the modern notions of empowerment but as employees, rather than as employee owners. They attended regular shareholders meetings as owners and, along with the non-employee owners, selected a board of directors. All the board members were outsiders, with the exception of Sturgess. That ensured better advice than in a board comprising employees, she noted, but at times it also involved constraints if the board didn't agree with the internally generated plan of action.

Over time, the motivation that flows from being an employee owner wore off, Sturgess feels. Newer employees didn't invest as much—if they invested at all. "The *esprit de corps* is built around our technology, not our investment," she noted in 1999. "In fact, the investment is not talked about often at all except for those three or four people for whom it is a big investment."

After the better part of a decade, most people had managed to get on financially without their invested money and could be patient about when it would be returned. But as the biggest individual investor—owning 9 percent of the company—Sturgess found herself more hard-pressed, with the exit strategy a major preoccupation. "I want to pay my mortgage down. I have a lot of money in this," she said in that 1999 interview, six years after the company was formed. "When I was in my mid-thirties, this seemed a good thing to do. Now I'm in my mid-forties and I would really like to get back to owning my home, which I did prior to this, and having my RRSPs, which are all invested in the company, and start thinking about my future."

That opportunity was to come six months later, when, in stages, both parts of the company were sold. First, Flowserve—Revolve's dry gas seal partner, which had been building and developing a customer base for the dry gas seal technology while Revolve provided support services and engineering—bought that half of the operation. When it bought Revolve, employee ownership ended and the Revolve employees working in dry gas seals became part of a normal company, without shares.

A few months later, SKF made an offer to buy out the interests of the shareholders of the magnetic bearing business and that deal, after several further months of negotiations, closed in late September 2000. Revolve Magnetic Bearings Inc. became a wholly owned subsidiary of SKF, with Sturgess remaining as CEO. One executive left, but there were no other immediate changes in the workplace. It remained empowered as before, but with traditional reporting lines and no employee ownership.

Closure Comes

After leaving NOVA's embrace, a common term in the Revolve lingo about the past was "bureaucratic." Now, they were joining another large company, with the potential for bureaucracy. "It is something to watch for," Sturgess acknowledged. "But so far, so good. Clearly there is more bureaucracy. But at the moment there's also a trade-off. We had a different kind of bureaucracy [as an independent company] in dealing with a board of directors, banks, and things like that. So now we're dealing with an internal manager and an internal treasury department. So far, that doesn't seem to be a heck of a lot more time-consuming."

Did she and the others feel relief, after their long search for safe harbour? "Closure is a better word. There was a sense of closure. But the jury is still out on how people will react over the long term. And I expect additional changes in personnel."

Financially, the employee owners did not see fabulous fruits from their seven-year investment. Everybody got some money back, but there weren't the huge rewards that employee ownership has brought to other companies. Sturgess was able to pay back her mortgage and is where she began, with her house mostly paid down.

Would she do it again? "I wouldn't do it again, but I'm also a lot older. When you are in your early thirties, giving up everything is fantastic. When you're in your mid-forties, no. But I'm happy I did it. Heavenly days! We built a technology that is world-class. We have 50 people employed. We have kept this level of people employed—not including the dry gas seal people—for many years. We built something, made it grow, and I learned a tremendous amount about managing organizations."

Lessons Learned

Kim Sturgess has learned three key lessons about employee ownership from her experience at Revolve.

1. Make sure at the outset that you get top-flight input on structuring the deal—and similarly with any future deals to bring in outside investors. In particular, think about your exit from the very beginning. "People told me to do that and I said, 'Yeah, yeah.' But you have to think about the exit from the start," she stresses.

2. Tied to that is the necessity to maintain control. Revolve's team lost it twice: once to the venture capitalists and then again, on the magnetic bearings side, when it joined too closely with a major partner, SKF, giving it the right to buy up more of the company. That dramatically reduced any future negotiating power for selling the rest of the company. As a key customer and sales channel, Revolve was too dependent on SKF; when the buyout offer came, the employees effectively had no choice.

From the start, an employee-owned company must assess how fast it wants to grow versus how much control the original team wants to retain. Taking on venture capital can speed growth. But it comes at a cost. "The minute you lose ownership and voting control of the company you have your money invested in something that you don't control any more. That situation should be avoided at all costs. If you want to put everything in, you need to control," Sturgess stresses.

3. Finally, she warns against ever getting into a situation in which you are trying to manage by consensus in a group. "Never—ever. It sounded great and it fit with my views: I like to be inclusive and empower people. But somebody has to be in charge. Period, end of story," she says.

That means settling the tension between being employees and owners. "Employees are employees and owners are owners. When employees try to be owners and be involved in all the decision-making—well, certainly in our case it didn't work. Things got better when everybody agreed they were employees first and owners second," she says.

It has been a bruising experience for Sturgess. But the technology and the original team remain alive—albeit now in two other companies. What they achieved was in many ways heavenly, as she puts it, even if it came at the cost of what their financial investment might have made elsewhere during a time of booming stock markets. Revolve's growth curve is similar to those of other small companies—and particularly technology companies—so the lessons it provides are vital. The tensions that its employee owners have felt are not unique. Other employee owners will face them, as they struggle with decision-making efficacy, the demands of outside investors, and the need for capital in a technology business.

Algoma Steel

∞

Taking a New Path

"Employee involvement takes a generation to really create.
You don't turn people around in two, three, or four years.
They have 30 years of training and conditioning in how they
are supposed to act and react. We're trying to change that.
We're trying to change a culture."

—Steve Boniferro, vice-president human resources

When Steve Boniferro uses the word "we," confusion can occur. Sometimes "we" means the unions at Algoma Steel Inc. Sometimes "we" means the company. And sometimes "we" means the union, company, and all the employees at Algoma.

The confusion is natural, given Boniferro's history—and the recent history of Algoma itself. On July 27, 1998, Boniferro was the area co-ordinator for the United Steelworkers of America at Algoma, the man charged with representing union and worker interests at the company. On July 28, 1998, Boniferro—with the union's blessing—became vice-president of human resources at the same company, the man responsible for representing the company's interests in labour relations with that same union. That's an enormous leap, rare in the annals of labour-management history. But at Algoma, it was in many ways just a tiny step.

Since the 1993 buyout that gave employees majority ownership, Algoma has been working on the "we," trying to make workplace processes and decision-making a joint effort between management and employees. Boniferro has not only been crucial to building those new structures and practices, but also, with his change in status, became the human embodiment of that quest. For several years, he was co-chair with then-human resources vice-president Moe Thibault of the all-important joint steering committee, through which important operating decisions flow. More importantly, to get approved, decisions required the two of them—management co-chair and union co-chair—to agree.

The duo had to be in constant contact and to forge absolute trust in order to make that arrangement work. Instead of trying to sneak issues past each other, they learned to raise everything early, hash out possible problems together, and avoid any surprises—a total break with the tradition of adversarial relationships between management and union that had characterized Algoma in the past. "I knew everything he knew and he knew everything I knew," says Boniferro. Somewhere along the road, the "we–they" became "we"—and so when Thibault left to run an American company partially owned by its employees, who better could management turn to for his replacement than his alter ego, the union guy?

When he met with CEO Sandy Adam to discuss the job, Boniferro told him, "What you see is what you get. I'm not about to change my principles or think differently than I did before." His boss-to-be answered: "I don't expect you to. That's why we want you." And Boniferro says that despite the reservations he had initially, the job is in fact a good fit: "The issues Algoma has been struggling with over the years have become everybody's issues. We—the union and the company—came to some conclusions back some time ago: we need to have fewer people here; we need to find a way to do it that has the least impact on the people who work here; we need to change the way that we do work—and those are all things that we still need to do. I get a chance in this job to make some of that happen now more effectively than I could before."

At the same time, Boniferro is the first to warn about reading too much into Algoma's transformation. The company has been struggling financially, after a few strong years following the buyout, and in 2001 even was forced to seek court protection from creditors, as high energy prices, a slump in demand, and a flood of imports battered the North American steel industry, pushing at least 13 steelmakers into some form of bankruptcy protection. Decision-making can be slow at times. Old antagonisms still linger in some quarters. Training has been cut back, because of the financial situation, and the process of creating self-directed work groups stalled. "I don't want you to think we're a Fantasyland here. We have lots of problems of our own. There are days when you look out and you say, 'The system just doesn't work.' And then other days you say, 'Yeah, yeah, yeah!' You get to see the fruits of it," he says.

Some High Profile U.S. Steel Workouts		
CHAPTER 11 FILINGS	DATE	EMPLOYEES
Bethlehem Steel	Oct.15, 2001	13,000
LTV	Dec. 29, 2000	18,000
Wheeling-Pittsburgh steel	Nov. 16, 2000	4,800
Gulf States Steel	July 1, 1999	1,906
Geneva Steel	Feb. 1, 1999	2,600

Source: *Wall Street Journal*

The Struggles of the Past

Algoma is the third-largest producer of steel in Canada and is Sault Ste. Marie's largest private employer. The company has a fabled history, but until recently nobody would have compared it to Fantasyland, given the litany of problems over its first century. Founded in 1893 by Francis Henry Clergue, who aimed to use the Sault Ste. Marie location to seize the growing market for steel rails in the Canadian West, the company struggled because it had placed itself too far from the large markets for iron and steel in the Northern United States and central Canada, because it lacked a reliable fuel supply, and because it was initially equipped with inappropriate machinery and processes. In 1903, the company was unable to meet its payroll, hundreds of workers mounted a noisy demonstration, and the Canadian militia was called in. Finally, the Ontario Liberal government provided a $2 million loan on condition that the company reorganize internally. However, even after the restructuring, Algoma continued to be plagued with inconsistent management and by technical blunders, the vagaries of the steel industry, and employee unrest. As demand for steel rails weakened during the 1920s and 1930s, the plant was often shut down for months.

The fragility of the company, the isolation of the community, and cultural tensions between workers kept unions from being formed at the plant when organizing became commonplace elsewhere in the industry. It was only in 1943 that resentment at the plant flared into a complete walkout of workers and three years later that a first contract was negotiated. Over the next forty years, economic and labour-management tensions persisted. Tim Armstrong, who now sits on the company's board of directors, remembers that when he was deputy minister of labour in Ontario from 1976 to 1986, fears of a strike at Algoma always arose at Queen's Park, the seat of the provincial government, when a fresh round of bargaining commenced. The 1980s were not particularly kind to the company, starting with the recession early in the decade that cut demand for steel in automobiles, durable consumer goods, packaging, and heavy non-residential construction. From 1982 to 1990, the company lost money in seven of nine years.

In 1988, Dofasco Inc., the country's largest steel producer, bought 100 percent of Algoma for $560 million from its owner, Canadian Pacific Ltd. Since Dofasco had more rolling capacity than raw steel-making ability, the acquisition allowed it to balance production flows at half the cost of building a new facility. However, analysts were wary, noting that while Dofasco was a financially stable, non-unionized company, its new subsidiary had an uncertain financial position, was particularly susceptible to economic downturns, and had a history of chronic labour problems.

The analysts, rather than Dofasco management, proved prescient. In 1990, Algoma suffered a four-month strike during which employees demanded wage improvements despite a worsening recession for both Algoma and the rest of the steel industry. Competitive pressures were also intensifying with the surge in mini-mills, which produced steel from scrap metal using new technology in a low-cost, non-unionized environment.

It was all too much: by the end of the year, the company was technically insolvent, and unable to meet payments on $433 million in debt obligations, primarily to the Royal Bank, Toronto Dominion Bank, and Canadian Imperial Bank of Commerce. The company was given a three-month extension to re-evaluate operations. Talk centred on the possible closure of three or more operations at the plant—structural shapes, rails, and cold rolling—at the cost of 2,000 jobs. Others mused about an even more brutal restructuring, slashing the work force from its nominal size of 7,500—about 2,000 people were already on a layoff—to 3,500 within the next few years.

None of those options tempted Dofasco, which instead tried to wash its hands of financial responsibility for the company, including pension liability, by announcing a $700 million writedown on January 23, 1991. The impact would be devastating to the workers and the Sault Ste. Marie economy, wiping away 22 percent of local employment and 20 percent of local residents' personal income as the Algoma workers lost their paycheques. That blow to the local economy would also rob municipal, provincial, and federal governments of tax revenue of between $75 million and $185 million each.

Government Moves In

While the company sought protection under the Companies' Creditors Arrangement Act and began to develop plans to restructure its debt, Leo Gerard, then Ontario director of the Steelworkers, turned to government for help. He called for a crisis team to be formed of all the players and tossed the ball to recently elected NDP premier Bob Rae with the comment, "I think the quarterback of this exercise has to be the premier's office."

Well before Rae had taken office—back when the Progressive Conservatives were in power under Bill Davis in the early 1980s—Ontario had established a unit to oversee restructurings and capital investment projects that required government assistance. By 1989, this unit had evolved into the Strategic Investment Group, under an entrepreneurial-minded civil servant named Peter Tanaka. It was intended to attract investments into Ontario, such as auto plants for which government would have to offer some incentive. But when the recession hit a year later, the focus switched to restructuring and retention rather than luring new industry. And employee ownership was not a new concept in the unit: it had been considered in the mid-'80s when the Hamilton Firestone plant was closed, but union leaders were leery. "To come into vogue, it took a crisis—a recession. It also took a government like Bob Rae's, which was tied into the unions," says Tanaka.

The political crisis was actually twofold: it was not just at Algoma but also at Spruce Falls Inc., a paper mill in Kapuskasing, where 1,450 jobs were threatened in a town of 12,000 people. The northern community was organizing to buy the plant, demanding government help. The clamour was more muted in Sault Ste. Marie, Tanaka notes, perhaps because the town was larger. But both were in important political terrain for the NDP. The Steelworkers union was more disposed to employee ownership than the Canadian Energy and Paperworkers union, so its file moved ahead quicker. Indeed, Tanaka points to Gerard as the catalyst in the whole affair: "He took on a leadership role bigger than life. He came marching into Queen's Park on this one—to the premier."

But the premier was also to play a key role. "Bob Rae didn't have much respect or use for bureaucratic reporting lines," notes Armstrong, who was then deputy minister of industry, trade, and technology. "He took a positive, aggressive role in all of these restructurings. He would become heavily involved." Tanaka was also impressed by the premier, comparing the style of the social democratic premier to that of the then-chairman of TD Bank, Richard Thomson: "When big cases come in, he rolls up his sleeves. He took a personal delight in being involved. He was good at it, which may be why he enjoyed it. Maybe he felt it was tangible—it was something he could do and see the impact."

Rae called the Algoma union and management together for a meeting on February 1, along with four cabinet ministers, showing the importance his government placed on avoiding a closure. He limited the government's role at that time, however, stating it was "to make sure that people are all talking to each other." The two civil servants who would ensure that happened were Armstrong, who took personal responsibility for the file, and Tanaka, who, in a sign of the importance of his unit, reported jointly to both Armstrong and the cabinet. Armstrong chaired a 16-person task force set up to develop a solution, with representatives of all the affected parties, from the community to the banks.

Tanaka had been getting calls well before the Algoma crisis arose from banks about to call loans on companies and wanting the government to participate in a workout. That had led to four rules for government involvement.

His first rule was simple: "My job was not to turn the Ontario government into a banker." The second rule flowed directly from that: if government was to be involved financially, because of some compelling policy reason, it was not to bail others out and let them walk away unscathed. Everyone had to sacrifice: lenders, company, and workers. The third rule was that a viable business plan had to exist for the future—not a hope and a prayer. "Our job was to see if it made sense for the operation to go forward. If we propped it up, would it only hurt another company or industry in Ontario? Also, why did this situation happen and what evidence is there to believe the company can be turned around?" Tanaka says.

And that led to his fourth rule, with respect to the new creature being considered, employee ownership: it should be viewed only as a short-term solution. The idea was to nudge the company through the current mess and eventually into the hands of a player who could plunk in the robust investment needed for long-term security. At Algoma and Spruce Falls, the paths couldn't have been more different on that score. Algoma remains independent, having raised capital for investment through cash flow and sale of shares during the 1990s, whereas Spruce as part of the original deal found a healthy backer with a history of employee ownership itself in Tembec Inc.

**Tanaka's Rules for Government
Involvement in Employee Buyouts**

1. The government should not act as an investment banker.

2. All of the parties not just the government, must contribute.

3. There must be a viable business plan for the future company.

4. Employee ownership should be viewed as an interim solution
   until the company can be sold to a solid investor.

The Proposals Begin

The first proposal was to come from Dofasco/Algoma management in
May. It called for restructuring the debt and reducing carrying costs by
dividing ownership of the company between Dofasco, the four cred-
itor banks, union employees, salaried employees, the public, and the
pension plan. The workforce would be cut in half over the next four
years while the company focused on the sheet and plate business,
stopping production of structural steel, steel rails, and seamless tubu-
lar steel, and shutting down a mine and a sintering facility in Wawa.
As well, wages would be cut immediately by 20 percent (although
allowed to rise slowly again after 1992), pension indexing and cost of
living allowances would be eliminated, and the collective agreement
would be amended to permit no strikes until 1998. The Steelworkers
immediately rejected the plan, with one local president saying it
would "emasculate and eviscerate the plant, employment, and the
community." The bankers were only slightly more positive, seeing
their interest-bearing debt turned into non-interest-bearing common
shares and distressed preferred shares.

Now the ball was in the hands of the union, which had slowly
been coming to grips with the concept of employee ownership over
the years. Boniferro remembers attending a conference in the late
1980s with other union colleagues on worker empowerment and
worker ownership. The union had also been gathering data from
Sweden and Germany, looking at alternative workplace models, to see
if it should get involved in such ventures. But that was philosophy.
The Algoma situation was eminently practical. Gerard had been trying, without success, to find a buyer for the plant. The company's plan
was unacceptable. "It was employee ownership to survive, as there
was no other plan," says Boniferro. "It was a last resort."

The union brought together a team of financial experts, steel analysts, and trade lawyers to help it develop a deal. The trade experts were needed to ensure that any government assistance wouldn't be considered a direct subsidy that contravened the U.S.–Canada free trade agreement. The key advisor was Ron Bloom, a Harvard-educated investment banker whose firm, Keilin and Bloom, counselled American labour unions on buyouts.

Algoma had been scrambling for bridge financing of $50 million. To buy time and show good faith, the union offered to help, raising $10 million through a four-month, $2.89-an-hour pay reduction. "That was a tremendous sacrifice on the part of workers," said Bloom. But in return, the union wanted access to Algoma's books and to have an outsider brought in to both fill the vacant chairmanship post at the company and to serve as chief restructuring officer. It also wanted the federal government, provincial government, banks, and Dofasco each to match its $10 million. "We felt it was very important to establish the principle that everyone was responsible for saving the company. We weren't going to save it on the backs of the workers," said Bloom.

On June 26, Algoma was granted a three-month extension of protection from creditors by Ontario Justice James Farley, who was supervising the process. He told the company and union that they must exhibit "superhuman co-operation" in order to develop a successful restructuring plan by the new deadline. On July 31, oil executive Earl Joudrie, who had worked with many companies in financial distress, was named the company's new chairman and chief restructuring officer. Joudrie had been the union's candidate, since he didn't have any anti-union baggage. James McCartney, a partner with the McCarthy Tétrault law firm who was advising the company and later joined its board, notes that Joudrie's "objectivity, humour, and experience proved invaluable."

The next day, the union presented its own restructuring proposal, in which employees would become the majority shareholders of the company. The wage rollback would continue for another five years and 1,600 jobs would be cut through early retirement and attrition, but the company would continue to manufacture all its products and no mention was made of a shutdown of the Wawa operations. The proposal called for a $500 million capital expenditure program in coming years, of which $100 million would go towards a seamless tube mill. Bankers and lenders would trade their debt for distressed preferred shares and other equity. Dofasco, rather than wiping its hands of Algoma, would share in a $45 million environmental protection upgrade at the plant and pay $110 million of Algoma's $220 million pension liability, but would be able to claim a $75 million tax loss.

A key element of the union plan was the proposed framework for governing an employee-owned company. The union recognized the need for strong and independent management of the company, and so even though employees would own a majority of the shares, they would content themselves with a minority of positions on the board of directors. However, employees would be given the right to approve certain fundamental changes in future restructuring moves.

Several deadlines passed as the parties tried for the "superhuman effort" that might lead to success. The company embraced worker ownership, but its own business plan questioned the viability of tube mill production, given the volatility of the market, as well as the Wawa operation. It also felt the wage cuts weren't high enough but in its own plan simply made them permanent rather than confining them to five years.

The government offered a potential helping hand in November by announcing the Ontario Investment and Worker Ownership Program, to encourage employees to invest in struggling companies or those that required capital investment to expand or modernize. It provided a 20 percent tax credit on investments up to $3,500 a year for a person buying into an investment fund sponsored by a union. A matching tax credit announced by the federal government bumped the total to 40 percent. Companion legislation helped workers who were not unionized to be involved in the purchase of their employing company. They would receive a 20 percent tax credit from the province on the first $3,500 invested in the takeover and as much as 30 percent on additional funds invested, up to a maximum of $15,000 a year. Those incentives also applied to outside investors in such buyouts. The plan, ironically, was actually rejected by Algoma Steel once the buyout was complete, but it became available for other buyouts in the province.

The Deal Emerges

By the end of the year—four months after Spruce Falls workers approved their own buyout—the situation at Algoma was still unresolved. As Earl Joudrie noted, "The cattle were in the river but it wasn't easy to herd them out the other side." Armstrong was deeply worried, not convinced that Joudrie would be able to get the various parties to agree to a deal. He asked the court to appoint George Adams—a judge but also a former assistant deputy minister with mediation experience—to oversee an all-out negotiating session.

The banks initially resisted, claiming the court didn't have the legal authority to order the session, but when they realized the process carried the prospect for success, they decided to participate. Everyone gathered in Toronto's Park Plaza Hotel for what was termed "multi-faceted collective bargaining." Adams held general sessions with everyone at the beginning and end of every day and then met separately or in different combinations with the various groups between those plenaries, seeking consensus.

McCartney sums up the situation: "Everybody's reaction is that the other guy should get all the pain and I should escape. You have to convince them everybody must share the pain." Inevitable tensions occurred as everybody came to terms with that pain-sharing reality. McCartney remembers in the early morning of the final day scheduled for negotiations, at 4 a.m., hotel security investigated a noise complaint only to find three sober men in business suits. The offenders were Algoma negotiators, angrily debating whether a proposal from the union would be acceptable to Dofasco, which by then was the only dissenter to the emerging consensus. Later that day, the premier joined the discussions, helping to push everyone towards a successful conclusion. Bloom observes that huge disagreements arise in such negotiations on relatively minor issues that often have no real answer, such as whether the union should have 60 percent ownership or 62 percent ownership. In fact, he feels, "the real issue is do you want to work together and make a deal?"

In the end, they did. Algoma employees would take a permanent wage cut of $2.89 an hour with hourly workers accepting a comparable 14.5 percent cut, generating $200 million over the next five years. Holidays would be decreased by one week and the work force would be downsized by 1,600 over the next five years. In return, employees would get 60 percent of the common shares of the company, issued in slices over the next five years. But the shares would be held in trusts rather than by individual employees and would be available to them only when they retired or died. Algoma's creditors and preferred shareholders would hold the other 40 percent of Algoma.

Jim Garner, a financial advisor to Algoma during the negotiations and later director of corporate finance, noted that "the 60 percent figure emerged during the latter part of negotiations in early 1992. It was an important number to employees and ultimately was accepted by the other stakeholders who ascribed little value to the shares at the time. Many of the groups at the negotiating table were far from convinced of Algoma's viability post-restructuring and were protecting their short-term interests. However, some people involved in the process believed that the 60 percent allocation was too generous to employees, in relation to the proposed 14 percent wage and salary reductions, compared to the debenture holders taking a 40 percent haircut and the common shareholders writing off their entire investment."

Dofasco took the biggest hit, having its claim reduced from $224 million to $69 million in preferred shares, while also being asked to provide $30 million in loan guarantees. In return, it was allowed to claim $150 million in tax losses and was exempted from responsibility for pension liabilities. The province gave a $90 million loan guarantee (which in the end was never used), lowered freight rates on the Algoma Steel Railway that carried ore from Wawa to the plant, agreed to fund certain training, and provided an environmental waiver relieving lenders and preferred shareholders from liability for environmental costs in the event of default. It also protected Algoma directors and officers from personal liability arising from future operations. Along with the federal government, the province agreed to assume the costs of bridge pensions for those who could be lured into early retirement.

Included in the deal was a "negotiations protocol" for forthcoming bargaining and running the company that Armstrong likens to a Charter of Rights. It set out the terms for increased employee participation at all levels of the company and for a new organizational culture. That was confirmed when a new collective agreement was negotiated in May. Time clocks were eliminated and a justice and dignity clause created, stating that employees thought to be in violation of work rules were "innocent until proven guilty."

Issues Covered by the Negotiations Protocol for the New Algoma

The protocol sets out rules, processes, and deadlines for negotiating a new collective agreement and covers the following:

1. Workforce structure and management
2. Workplace restructuring
   a) Work design
   b) Participation programs
   c) Training programs
3. Restructuring plan
4. 1992–1996 Collective Agreements
5. The Employee Share Ownership Plan
   a) Statement of intent
   b) Corporate structure
   c) Issued share capital
   d) Algoma Employee Co-operative Corporation
   e) Composition of board of directors of New Algoma
   f) Employee equity trusts

The comprehensiveness of the document reduced greatly the potential for future misunderstanding and reinforced the equal partnership role of the union.

A joint steering committee, to be chaired by the CEO and the union staff representative, would deal with issues related to change in the workplace. Joining them on this committee would be the four local union presidents, three senior management members, and a representative of the supervisory staff. Three task forces were also established, under the auspices of the joint steering committee, to implement change:

- a training committee, to develop a comprehensive training plan;
- a problem-solving and cost reduction task force, to generate ideas from employees and involve them in reducing costs;
- a workplace redesign and technology task force, to assist workers in redesigning their workplace, through such initiatives as self-directed work groups.

The workplace was also to be dotted with Employee Participation Units, bringing together management and employees to figure out ways to enhance the effectiveness of each slice of the plant, in the same way as the joint steering committee would be doing for the entire plant.

"The interests of the employees are a more prominent factor in governance of Algoma than in the conventional business organization. The interests of the employees are right up front. It has its source in shareholding and is also built into the articles of Algoma," notes McCartney.

The New Algoma Is Born

On June 1, the New Algoma was born, after employees had voted three-to-one in favour of the plan. Two months later, a 13-member board of directors was established, with four representatives of unionized employees—two selected from the Algoma staff and two prominent labour officials from outside the company: Fred Pomeroy, president of the Communications and Electrical Workers of Canada, and Gerald Docquier, co-chairman of the Canadian Labour Force Development Board and a former national director of the Steelworkers. Murray Nott, a senior metallurgist, was elected to represent salaried workers. Seven independent directors were named, among them Joudrie, who was to be chair; McCartney; and two former provincial premiers: Bill Davis, and Allan Blakeney of Saskatchewan. The CEO would hold the final slot.

The steel industry is cyclical, and, as luck would have it, Algoma soon found itself on the right side of the cycle. The Canadian dollar fell by 15 cents, which also helped since North American steel prices are set in American dollars. As well, the supply of scrap metal for mini-mills dwindled as more came onstream, raising prices. That provided breathing space and a chance to get on with the major capital expenditures planned in the restructuring accord.

The company sought a new CEO, attracting Al Hopkins, a vice-president of Stelco and 30-year veteran of the steel industry. By the time he came on board, however—six months after the employee buy-out took effect—little change had occurred in work practices. He found a workplace that was frustrated and angry, doubting that any real change would ever occur despite the agreements and fancy words.

To address those concerns, he arranged 50 gatherings of staff that he jointly addressed over the next month with Jack Ostrowski, president of the largest local. The two would be in meetings from 7 a.m. to 11 at night—it became known as "Jack and Al's Dog and Pony Show"—answering questions and trying to convey that there was a different plan, different attitudes, and a different leadership. Perhaps the most important element was the symbolism of the meetings themselves: union and management working together, as equals.

"The steel industry is renowned for tough management which sets the rules and tells people what to do. I wanted that to be replaced by a participative model, with no unilateral decisions," said Hopkins. Among the people most affected, he knew, would be management and supervisors at the plant, whose authority would come into question and who would see the pace of decision-making slowed. "They had to be convinced that the consensus approach would ultimately produce better decisions, and that the process would speed up with time, effort, patience and dedication. Middle management felt the most impact because they were downsized with the new role of employees. However, the ones remaining were critical as coaches and facilitators, and had to learn how to help others make the decisions they used to make, while still keeping an eye on waste, yield, and productivity," he noted.

At the operating level, the principle of sharing begins with the joint steering committee, the hub of the operation. It deals with policy issues, staffing, hiring, and layoffs. It reviews capital expenditures and all of the annual plans that go to the board of directors as well as refereeing problems at lower levels of the company in the carbon-copy departmental steering committees.

On average, 14 to 20 people attend meetings. Although the CEO originally was a joint chair, now that role for management has passed to the human resources vice-president, and the CEO doesn't even attend unless something on the agenda requires his direct participation. Everyone found the CEO tended to be too powerful in such meetings: when he spoke to an issue, other managers tended to follow his lead rather than offer any contradictory views. As well, the CEO has a legal obligation to the board that may lead him on occasion to oppose a developing consensus in the joint committee or challenge its decisions later at the board.

At one point, all the senior managers for the company sat on the committee. But it became obvious that it was more important to recruit senior operating people instead, since they were the ones who had to implement the operational and human resource decisions the committee made. "We don't need the vice-president finance at the joint steering committee meetings—we can bring him in if we have an issue about finance—but we do need to have the general manager of the flat roll business there because we need to talk about what goes on in the mill," says Boniferro.

Is the committee truly joint? That's a simple question but it requires a complicated answer since it depends upon the definitions of "consensus" and "joint," which Algoma officials now realize are not as clear as they first appeared. The union and management readily agreed decisions must be made by consensus but had to figure out what that actually meant. Eventually, they decided for consensus to occur, at a minimum the joint co-chairs of the steering committee must be in agreement on a course of action. Ideally, everyone should agree but if only the two co-chairs are in accord that is deemed to be consensus, whatever the feelings of others in the meeting.

That means in some cases people can avoid supporting an emerging decision, knowing it will be taken anyway. "Some politics crawl into it," notes Boniferro. At the same time, he recalls only one decision where the two co-chairs took a decision without at least some modest buy-in from the rest of the committee.

The other difficulty was defining whether joint meant equal. Were the union and management equal—or simply working together? Over time, they have realized that decisions have to be taken collectively but the two parties aren't equal and have different responsibilities. When Hopkins retired and Sandy Adam replaced him in 1996, after holding executive posts at Toyota Motor Manufacturing Canada Inc. and Stelco, the new CEO was worried about decisions becoming terminally stalled in the joint process. He announced that if a decision wasn't being taken, he would make the call. If the union then disagreed with his judgement, its representatives on the board could ask for a review there. "I like that because it forces people to make decisions," says Boniferro.

In unravelling the meaning of joint, everyone has also needed to realize that they must refrain from needlessly interfering in other people's work. When Algoma became employee-owned, the widespread sentiment in the workforce was that since employees were ultimately the bosses they could now call all the shots. "People felt they could comment on anything," recalls Norm MacKay, union co-ordinator and president of Local 5595, which covers the tube division. "It caused a lot of headaches."

The union organized a one-day orientation session to curb that tendency. In two and a half years, it put 4,400 members through the workshop, reviewing the first 20 pages of the agreement between the union and the company and explaining the proper roles in the new ownership regime. "It doesn't mean you are the boss. It means you have the opportunity to have your say on certain major decisions," says MacKay.

Boniferro stresses that the union and its members can't replace the judgement of the people who have front-line accountability with their own ideas. "If the union doesn't like it, we can deal with it in another way," he says in an interview for the book, momentarily confusing his "we" as if he were still speaking for the union. When his lapse is pointed out, he notes that he has been consistent on this point whatever his position—union or management. "I say that now and I said that then. Because it's not a one-sided thing. There are some management folks who like to get wrapped up in somebody else's business just as there are some union guys who would like to tell the managers how to manage the mill. I say to both of them: it's not your job. He's responsible and will be held accountable. You can't tell him how to do it, as then he's not accountable."

To an outsider, the decision-making system may seem elaborate and complicated. But Boniferro insists it sounds more complicated than it actually is. And ironically, the biggest problems are when there aren't any tough decisions around, since that's when the temptation grows to micro-manage in other people's area of responsibility. On the other hand, when the iron ore mine in Wawa was closed in 1998, the decision was forged at the joint steering committee. "We did it together—the company and the union. We agreed it was the right thing to do," Boniferro says.

But they didn't stop with the closure decision. They went on to look at how to accommodate the displaced workers and established subcommittees to move those who wanted into new jobs at the main plant within a year. At another company, he points out, management would decide on a shutdown and then spend the next six months battling with the union over whether it was the right course of action before anything could be implemented. "We didn't do that. We sit down. We agree on the facts. We also closed the tube mill; we closed the structural mill. Those are decisions that are normally pretty tough to make and we made them relatively quickly and precisely," he says.

They also jointly agreed to build a flagship $400 million Direct Strip Production Complex that would offer state-of-the-art production of hot rolled coils at a low cost. It significantly reduces the work force by virtually eliminating product handling during the highly automated manufacturing process. It also lowers energy costs. The decision was taken together, both at the joint steering committee and then at the board. But Algoma experienced severe difficulties bringing it onstream, with production initially well below expectations. Inevitably, workers began to wail, "Who made that decision?" Boniferro's response: "We all made it. I may have been sitting on the union side then but I know the union and the company, together, sat down and went through everything. We agreed it was the right thing to do. We can't start pointing fingers at each other and saying, 'Jeez, I thought it would be done quicker.' We were wrong. But we'll get there. It was the right decision."

On the Work Floor

The Joint Steering Committee format is mirrored at the departmental level by the Departmental Steering Committees. Again, union and management representatives serve as co-chairs. The committees have to develop and submit to the joint steering committee an annual departmental plan, consistent with the overall strategic plan of the company. They direct the implementation of this departmental plan, oversee the application of human resource policies to the department, develop and implement training, and also generally deal with the quality of work life in that area.

The departmental committees are smaller and more focused. Some meet weekly, while others gather only monthly. Boniferro believes they are more effective than the joint steering committee because they all work in the same area and every decision they make affects them personally. "It's a bunch of people working in a place getting together to talk about how they can improve the place or deal with problems," he says.

Since many of the departments are huge, the co-operative model extends further into the grassroots through the Departmental Participation Units. Anybody can take problems or ideas for improvement to an Employee Participation Representative, who serves as a link to the wider unit by serving on the departmental committee. Most of the representatives are union members, who try to find a solution for the matter that has been raised. Originally they were provided with a special three-week course on problem-solving and decision-making skills. But that was too intense so training is now spaced out over a longer period.

Initially, the participation units opened a floodgate of suggestions for improvement from employees, with 900 ideas pouring forth for reducing waste, lowering operating costs, making better use of equipment, and improving product quality. In 1994, the ideas that were implemented saved Algoma $2.7 million. Employees can also take advantage of an e-mail suggestion program, entering ideas for consideration and then tracking their progress daily to ensure they aren't sitting at the bottom of some supervisor's "in" file. Whenever someone with responsibility receives a suggestion, he or she must log on and indicate who is taking accountability. In a typical year, the program will receive about 150 suggestions, with everyone guaranteed an answer. "It works reasonably quickly. And it pays no money—which is something I like," says Boniferro. "It's not designed to say, 'If you find something dumb happening we will give you some money.' It says, 'This is our plant and if you have an idea that can make it better, you ought to be telling somebody about it, and we should be making it easy for you to do that because if the plant does better we all do better.'"

Algoma also established some self-directed work groups in various departments to allow employees to take control of their work. Indeed, the first one formed in what was considered a "rabble rouser" area. But once given control of its own scheduling, crew alignments, and the ability to make decisions on capital equipment and work with customers, the unit became a model of co-operation—and productivity. Momentum in creating the self-directed groups halted, however, with about 20 percent of the work force in 40 self-directed teams. Part of the problem is political: a tussle for power between workers and supervisors. After the buyout, the salaried workers unionized, so now supervisors and workers on the shop floor are part of different locals in the same union. "They started to butt heads over turf and territory," Boniferro notes. As a result, the program lost its support and impetus. But the notion of having a more self-directed work force remains appealing to both management and union leaders, who are determined to revive those teams that are struggling and start new ones. The union even had the issue on its list for the last set of contract negotiations. "What we have to do is get it moving again," said MacKay, using "we" rather than blaming the failure on management in the pre-negotiating period. "It's we—joint. We both have to agree on what to do. Both parties need to be on-side for it to work."

Boniferro notes that self-directed teams have fared best, unexpectedly, where the supervisor was strong and a good communicator. Supervisors who weren't threatened by the team and, indeed, recognized the benefit that could come from handing over some tasks to the crew, freed themselves to tackle more important matters. "That was an eye-opener," he says.

**Design Principles for
Suggestion Programs**

To be effective, suggestion programs must provide a "win-win" outcome for both the company and the employees. At the New Algoma, the first flood of suggestions consisted largely of improvements that employees could clearly see were needed. However, nobody had ever asked them for their ideas before. Also, the employees were highly motivated to save "their" company. After this initial enthusiasm wanes, managers would do well to keep the following design principles in mind for their company's suggestion program:

1. Long-term success depends on trust, so ensure that the plan is administered scrupulously. Every suggestion should be taken seriously and should be given an answer.

2. Most successful plans are designed with the participation of employees.

3. The formula for calculating a bonus for contributing a suggestion, if one is offered, should be clearly explained and comprehensible to employees.

4. It should be decided up front whether the reward/bonus is based on individual or group suggestions, or both.

5. Top management support is crucial and should be visible.

6. In an operation that is already efficient, gains from suggestion programs may not be worth the effort. The paradox is that when increased efficiency and employee co-operation are necessary, trust is probably low and so the plan will be difficult to establish. That is why many companies start with health and safety or other "hygiene" issues first to build trust.

A New Approach to Training

After the buyout, Algoma intensified training for employees. The joint training committee maps out training programs that are published each year in a catalogue. In the past, training had focused on managers but now it's for both managers and workers—and often taken together, side by side. "Prior to 1990 the amount of on-the-job training I got was zero. And I worked 20 years," says MacKay. "So this was a big step."

Initially, the focus was on soft-skill training, such as communications skills, dealing with conflict, and problem-solving. In fact, nearly everybody in the plant took a problem-solving program, designed to ensure that when issues arose everybody was operating through the same process and using the same language. "We did that together—managers and union, it didn't matter what your job was. We did it by area and you went with your group," says Boniferro. Similarly, when the departmental steering committees were created, members were sent together for training on how to run meetings and work as a team.

Eventually, the focus shifted to job-specific training. It was a way of conserving cash as market conditions got rougher. But it also corresponded with the widespread feeling that the company had been saturated with soft-skill tools and now was the time to put them to work. Programs are established whenever the co-chairs for an area ask for a specific program for their work force.

The 1995 contract granted each employee the right to take up to 80 hours of training a year. The individual simply puts together his or her plan from available programs. Some have even used the opportunity to complete high school courses. But given the financial stringency, there is less focus on getting everyone to participate. "The go-getters did get 80 hours. But those who sat back didn't," notes MacKay.

Algoma, economically, has been rather biblical since the buyout, with years of plenty followed by lean years. After excellent years in 1994 and 1995, profits dropped drastically in 1996 and 1997, only to be followed by losses since 1998 due to deterioration in steel markets and the problem-plagued new Direct Strip mill. That facility was supposed to help Algoma cope through the steel market's cyclical phases but the ramping-up difficulties aggravated rather than alleviated problems. It took about a year longer than anticipated to adapt to the equipment, as employees needed to relearn their job in relationship to the faster speed of the equipment. "It was the difference between a Timex and a Swiss watch," says Boniferro.

The capital expansion was financed through internally generated funds combined with equity and debt issues. To help in that effort—and to pay off preferred shareholders—the union agreed in 1995 negotiations to have new shares issued that would dilute its own holdings below the 50 percent mark. Its holdings tailed off, in fact, to about 22 percent.

But in return, the union was offered further guarantees that employee involvement in corporate decisions would continue and, indeed, certain major decisions would not be permitted without employee consent. Algoma cannot, without approval of those holding employee shares, dispose of all, or substantially all, of its assets or businesses, buy another asset or business outside Sault Ste. Marie or Wawa, or amend the company bylaws relating to the appointment or number of directors if it detracts from the rights of the bargaining unit directors. A ceiling was also placed on the total number of shares—unless employees permit a new offering—and any major deviation from the strategic plan must be approved by 75 percent of directors, thus requiring at least some employee representatives to be on-side.

In the 1995 contract—negotiated in good times—employees more than made up for their $2.89 rollback. They also won benefits that didn't exist before, such as sick pay, putting the hourly employees on par with their salaried colleagues who would be paid when away from work because of illness. In addition, employees were each allowed to withdraw up to 300 shares out of the trust, which many did. Those who cashed in fared well, since shares then hovered around $12. Those who waited watched shares fall to the $2 range.

The sick pay decision—and to a lesser extent, eliminating time clocks—sparked considerable resentment, as some workers felt their colleagues were taking advantage of the system. The joint steering committee monitored absenteeism and, after it was determined that abuse was occurring, developed procedures to deal with it. Again, this wasn't a management-versus-union battle but a joint effort. "The union and the company said the policy is here for when you are sick and if you are abusing it, taking time off without being sick and getting paid, then you are defrauding the company and you will be disciplined," notes Boniferro. "It was signed by the company and the union. We had few disagreements on that issue—we had *some*, but not many."

The Difficulties of Building a New Structure

Algoma isn't a green field site, where new workplace procedures are being tested. And Murray Nott, who is in his third three-year term representing salaried workers on the board, feels that management has been too willing to concede issues to the union to keep harmony. In most cases, he argues, management has given the union concessions—be it no time clocks or self-directed work groups—without getting anything in return. Instead, he believes management should say: x will happen, if y happens. Then a trial period should occur, rather than full implementation. "You have to tie all their gains to corporate gains," he says.

Some people had felt that employee ownership would provide a more contented work force, which would then be more productive and profitable. But Nott insists that's a fallacy: "Profitability won't go up if everyone is happy. If a corporation is profitable, then people are generally happy. I didn't see the Hawthorne effect here—people starting to work harder as we have joint processes."

In particular, he points out the company has been slow to reduce the size of the work force. It's now down to 3,700 employees from the 6,891 on site when the original deal was signed (1,600 were on layoff at the time). That's a 46 percent reduction, but the reductions have come slower than expected—and are still not as high as necessary, Nott insisted even before restructuring talks—because the union has resisted amalgamation of jobs and cost savings. "We have more people here on site than we should have for the tonnage we produce. We're behind other companies on that," he says.

The lesson other companies should take from Algoma's experience, he feels, is this: "Don't go into this with altruistic views. Go into it as hard-nosed business people. After all, people don't change. If you had a reason for punch clocks before, don't assume it will magically change."

Boniferro is obviously more optimistic—and proud—of the achievements. But he also doesn't believe in magic, or Fantasyland: "Employee involvement takes a generation to really create. You don't turn people around in two, three, or four years. They have 30 years of training and conditioning in how they are supposed to act and react. We're trying to change that. We're trying to change a culture."

If he could do it again, he would reconsider the idea of holding employee shares in a block, since the impact of ownership would be felt more strongly if the employees had the shares at home in a dresser drawer. He also wishes union and management officials had been more specific in the original negotiations about what they wanted to accomplish in the way of workplace improvements—an ironic situation, since Algoma with its Charter actually went further down the path of imagining the future than most other companies in buyout negotiations. "We never clearly identified what the role of management and what the role of the union would be. I think we both accepted it had to change but we didn't talk to each other about what that meant. So the union had a view of what the management should be doing, and management had a view of what the union should be doing, but those views were very different from what each thought they should be doing on their own. And that has been a conflict to this day," he says.

Unions face a particular difficulty under worker ownership because they are neither fish nor fowl. The role can no longer be to fight management, since the union's task is now to work with management. For the union leader, however, that poses a particular problem, Boniferro notes: "How am I supposed to get elected? By standing up after three years and saying, 'I got along with management for three years?'"

MacKay says that's exactly what union leaders must do: "I'd say in an election, 'We have given you an opportunity—and will continue to have an opportunity—to have a say in the workplace. And I will work to enhance that.'" He believes that's a winning formula because "people don't want to go back to punching in and reporting to the foreman who tells you what to do."

Nott has his own sensitive election issues, since board confidentiality prevents him from keeping his constituency fully informed about some matters being discussed at the top. That was a significant issue initially but resentment has diminished over the years, after he patiently explained the need for confidentiality to employees in the union newsletter.

In Nott's first election, six people ran against him. Last time it was down to just two. He took a week's vacation to be free to wander about the plant and talk to colleagues about why he deserved their support. He also sent out his platform through e-mail.

Originally, he found it a shock to be on a board with two premiers and top business leaders. They would chat about prominent people who were their friends but only names in the newspaper—if that—to him. On the other hand, he feels he has more technical knowledge of the operation than most of the other directors and when the agenda shifts to those matters he can be helpful, asking questions—"not in a sniping way," he stresses, "but to alert other members." Besides, in the end, he has found that most board decisions are based on common sense. "The other board members have some extra experience, they share it, and you can assess it the same way as any other board member," he says. One of the toughest challenges is to remember that as a board member he must concentrate on the over-arching concerns of the enterprise: "If something is bugging me at my desk I have to leave it there because it's not a board issue."

McCartney has been happy with the board structure, combining union and independent directors. "It works partly because the balance has proven effective, but even more because the individuals who serve as directors represent their constituents effectively while advancing the interests of Algoma as a whole. A mutual trust and respect has developed over the past five years that has enabled the board to reach a consensus on some difficult issues," he says.

Armstrong, who joined the board at Leo Gerard's suggestion after he left government service, is torn in evaluating how effective the Algoma transformation has been. "I have a real difficulty determining if there has been a fundamental change in the culture there. There have been some improvements. But I can't get a real fix on whether the message has penetrated the rank and file to the extent we might have hoped. There have been some successes but it has been slow," he says.

In the late 1970s, as deputy minister of labour, he was working on new workplace democracy models with some progressive companies like Shell Canada Ltd. and Ford Motor Company of Canada, and he is not convinced that Algoma has even caught up to where those visionaries were then. "Based on my experiences, I've reached a conclusion—maybe it's a function of age—that employee ownership is not a panacea and not a necessary precondition for workplace democracy. The theory is that if you have a stake in the company, not only will you be listened to by management but also you will be more flexible. In fact, I haven't seen any evidence that that happens. When I look at the experience at Shell Oil and Ford, what drives people more is to say we each have our own roles, we'll have our disagreements, but in the meantime there are things we can do in the workplace to our mutual benefit. For us workers it will make things easier and for you management it will mean a better-functioning plant and higher morale. After spending 25 years thinking about this, I don't see any compelling case that as soon as you have employees owning the company you will have a sea change in the attitudes of management or labour," he says.

Armstrong also stresses that most companies and unions in worker ownership situations haven't thoroughly considered the implications of the new structure. While the Algoma board is informed, with union board representatives present, that labour negotiations are underway, it receives no detailed reports on the issues being discussed. The result has been that the board is essentially kept in the dark about this vital matter until negotiations are over because management feels it can't have a full strategic and tactical discussion beforehand with the other side at the board table. That leaves the board a rubber stamp on contract talks.

McCartney is more optimistic, however. He acknowledges it has been a struggle for all and much remains to be accomplished. "But we work together and respect each other. What we have now for Algoma and Sault Ste. Marie is better than the traditional alternative," he insists. And the key word in that sentence may be that two-letter word again: "we." It comes up time and time again, as people talk about the changes. Algoma has been struggling for several years and although company officials were optimistic when they sought court protection—CEO Sandy Adams stressed: "This isn't a bankruptcy. We've got financing in place to continue operations, so it is business as usual."—the reality is that the company will be restructured and that could lead to dramatic changes, including a sale. But jobs have been saved through the buyout and despite all the difficulties, the Algoma culture now has a greater sense of "we" than it had before.

Creo Products

ꙮ

Creative Individuality

"It's not just the shares. It's the way of thinking. I'm extremely happy here. It has been 10 years—I can't believe how lucky I have been."

—Lois Jacques, optical assembly specialist

When Lois Jacques joined Creo Products Ltd. on the recommendation of a friend in 1989, she was told something about shares and employee ownership but she didn't pay much attention. It was a new job in precision assembly, requiring somebody who could handle detail work, and her focus was on learning the new routine at the Vancouver company.

But there wasn't much routine, actually, and quickly she realized this was an unusual company. She was shown a few things, asked if she needed any tools, and then under the company's concept of unit presidency—every individual is the CEO of his or her own work—left alone. Occasionally Ken Spencer, the company's CEO, would wander in and ask if everything was OK. Did she need anything to help with her work? Since she worked alone, one time he asked if she wanted a radio, in case she might be feeling lonely.

Company meetings were held informally around the lunch table, with everybody sprawled about eating sandwiches. Communication was free flowing, with everybody kept informed. "I started to realize after a few days that this was a very different company. I felt listened to immediately. If I had something to say, I felt heard. I felt like I belonged and I could participate in the company fully," she says.

Before coming to Creo she had taken a parenting course and was taught that children want to do good things and be in harmony with their surroundings. Parents must allow them the chance to fulfill those needs, while teaching natural consequences and setting boundaries. She had trouble understanding that. But when she walked in the door at Creo, the light went on. "We're a harmonizing company, working together. It's not perfect. People make mistakes. But we're all trying," she says.

Creo was founded in 1983 by Ken Spencer and Dan Gelbart, who had worked together at MacDonald Dettwiler, and the company reflects their philosophy about people, work, and the importance of innovation. Both grew up in homes where money was tight and social justice was hallowed. The result when they formed their own company was a commitment to employee participation (long before empowerment became a buzzword) and a goal of having the company one-third owned by employees, one-third by the founders, and one-third by outside investors. They figured if their company did well, there would be more than enough money for everyone to share. And if it didn't succeed, they wouldn't regret giving a healthy chunk to others, since the shares wouldn't be worth much.

Gelbart, who was born in Israel, is a charismatic inventor. But he was distressed that the new products he was developing were being spun out into new companies by MacDonald Dettwiler, rather than being kept in the fold, because the firm wasn't interested in production work. Spencer had left Dettwiler in 1977 to become general manager of Glenayre Electronics, but as the two friends talked about the future, they were convinced that if they pooled their talents they could pick an idea, develop it, and build a successful company. They proved right, although their first idea—optical tape recorders—had to be abandoned because it wasn't fast growing enough. The second idea, technology that allows the printing industry to skip the filmmaking stage traditionally required before turning an image into a printing plate, has proved to be a big winner.

Revenue growth has been close to 40 percent a year since 1996, as the company installed more than 900 computer-to-plate imaging systems in 29 countries, twice the number of any of its competitors. Nine of the ten largest commercial printers have adopted Creo solutions, including publishers of such glossy magazines as *Time, Sports Illustrated, Newsweek, Glamour,* and *Scientific American.* Employee growth has been almost as fast-paced. Lois Jacques was employee number 40 back in 1989. By March 2000, when it acquired its major competitor, Israeli-based Scitex Corp., Creo had more than 1,800 employees—primarily at four sites in the Vancouver area—almost a third of them devoted to research and development, to keep the company ahead of the pack.

Creo's Solutions: Technology and Philosophy

Gelbart and Spencer picked digital imaging because they sensed in 1991 that it would be the future of publishing. They became the first to develop and commercialize a fully integrated, high speed, computer-to-plate system that has become the industry standard. Commercial printing is a mature industry, where margins and deadlines are vital, and customization is increasingly important. Creo's products help on all three counts. The worldwide market for pre-press imaging has been estimated at $3 billion. Computer-to-plate unit shipments are expected to grow by 25 percent in the next few years. Creo, now teamed with Scitex, maintains a strong association with the makers of the famed Heidelberg presses, Heidelberg Druckmaschinen AG, and is poised to fight off competitors like Agfa-Gevaert N.V.

Creo's solutions consist of a comprehensive range of products that transfer computer-generated images and text directly onto printing plates, eliminating many steps in the conventional pre-press process, including the expensive and time-consuming task of creating and processing film. The key component is a patented thermal imaging head that uses laser beams to precisely imprint heat-sensitive printing plates and proofing materials. Creo's thermal head splits the output of a single high-power laser into 240 separate beams—more beams than competitive products, because those require a separate laser to produce each beam. That thermal imaging head technology won an innovation award in 1996 from the Graphic Arts Technology Foundation. Creo believes it gives printers more accurate images, greater colour consistency, improved pre-press reliability, and faster throughput. In turn, that affords printers reduced print cycle times and more flexible scheduling of presses.

The CREO Philosophy

The Creo Philosophy is a 19-page document that all employees are familiar with. Here are some key points:

Creo's Core Values and Beliefs

Our Core Values and Beliefs are based on these "givens":

- We strive to be the best in the world at what we do.
- We care about each other, our customers, our suppliers, and our shareholders.
- We will do our absolute best to honour our commitments.
- We believe people are more effective when self-managed.
- We will strive to act always with integrity and fairness.

Thus,

- We will cultivate an atmosphere in which individuality and the expression of ideas are encouraged.
- We will be open and communicate within the organization everything that is practical to communicate.
- We will strive to maintain high morale, and to encourage a stimulating and enjoyable environment.
- We will treat everyone equally and impartially, and commit everyone to being judged on merit and contribution only.
- We will not tolerate politics.
- We will sustain an environment in which the individual can have an impact without fighting bureaucracy. We consider ourselves members of teams rather than hierarchies.
- We encourage decentralized decision-making, and make decisions with the teams affected. We call upon everyone to be completely in charge of his or her own job.
- We will be tolerant of mistakes, because without risking mistakes, no progress can be made.
- We will provide training to enable each of us to make continuous improvement.
- We will promote from within whenever practical.

- We will pay fair compensation in line with the market.
- We are committed to giving shareholders a fair return commensurate with the risk taken. Decisions will always be made for the long-term benefit of the company, providing the short-term is not put at risk.
- We will understand our customers' needs.
- We will treat our peers in the industry with respect and help local companies whenever practical.
- We will work conscientiously to keep our facilities safe.
- We will work conscientiously to protect the environment.
- We will treat others within the company with common courtesy and respect.

Importance of Accountability

Unit presidency does not absolve you of accountability to anyone. You should be able to explain what you are doing and why you are doing it. Other people may have valuable input or it may be important for your team leader or project manager to know how you're planning to meet your objectives so they can help knock down roadblocks and make sure everyone's plans mesh. Accountability is not one-way. Leaders would be accountable to their teams as much as team members are accountable to leaders.

Hierarchy

Creo emphasizes contribution over hierarchy. We don't want people looking at an organizational chart and trying to figure out how to move "up" one level. Everyone needs to work to maximize their contribution to Creo by doing their job well and developing themselves in areas where they have relative advantage and uniqueness.

To prevent an emphasis on hierarchy, we generally don't publish organizational charts. Naturally, Creo does have an organizational framework, but salary and other compensation are not based on your position in the framework. Instead, your compensation is based on market value for your skills and contribution to Creo.

On Guidelines

Creo has guidelines to capture what we believe is in the best interest of the company. Writing guidelines is beneficial because you can get input from a group of people about what should be done in certain situations so you don't need to get input each time an issue comes up.

However, if you see a case where following a guideline doesn't appear to be in the best interest of Creo, it may be that the guideline is out of date or that it didn't take into account a scenario like the one you're dealing with. Never blindly follow a guideline when you don't believe it's recommending the right course of action. Go back to the stakeholders and convince them that your approach is better. If the policy is wrong in general, you should initiate a change with the owner of the policy as well.

Always, in every case, regardless of precedent, guideline, or rules, do what makes sense.

On Politics

Central to our Creo Philosophy is the belief that we should not tolerate politics in our company. Political behaviour includes:

- Misrepresentation: Wilfully misrepresenting or not disclosing information in an effort to make someone believe something that is untrue.

- Selfishness: Putting one's own interests before those of Creo or others. This includes taking credit for other people's ideas or actions.

- Personal behaviour: Acting inconsistently with people of different stature in the organization. This might include being rude, abrupt, or dictatorial to "subordinates," while being polite and respectful to peers/"superiors." Evaluating an idea according to its author rather than content is political.

But Creo solutions are not just technological. Its founders developed what they call "The Creo Philosophy," a comprehensive set of workplace guidelines based on employee participation and a formidable degree of trust in colleagues. Combined with employee ownership, it has given Creo an unusually low turnover rate within the technology industry—about 3.5 percent—and an unusually high level of morale, despite the stress of rapid growth. Gelbart, interestingly, dismisses employee ownership as a source of motivation or productivity, not believing it provides either. He considers employee ownership helpful for attracting talent but supports it primarily because sharing the wealth created by everybody in the firm with everybody is morally right. Creo seems to have transcended employee ownership, however, and created a sense of job ownership. People feel they have control of their jobs. And, in turn, their loyalty to Creo soars.

At Creo, for example, no purchase orders are required for employees to buy anything they need for their work. Most employees have a company credit card and what they need, they buy—whatever the cost. But that doesn't lead to indiscriminate spending, as if every day were corporate Christmas. Employees have been taught that purchases are justified only if there is an appropriate payback. In most cases, that means the item should pay for itself in one year, and over a three-year period should return three times its cost in savings. If the payback is intangible, employees are expected to fall back on a second criterion: act as if you were the sole owner of Creo and decide accordingly. That second rule simply reiterates the basic, overriding principle that employees are told from their first day at the company: "Always, in every case, regardless of precedent, guideline, or rules, do what makes sense."

The widespread purchasing freedom would seem ambitious but acceptable when Creo first started and had only a handful of employees. But today, with more than 4,200 employees—counting the Scitex addition—all believing they can buy anything they need, the approach would frighten most managers. "In one sense it's scary," admits Gelbart. "But on the other side, it saves all the people you would need to approve purchase orders and it saves all the time waiting until your boss approves the purchase order. So maybe some mistakes happen as a result of such a system, but the cost of such mistakes is much less than the cost of slowing down the operation of the company by an approval process. We do spot checks and the amount of abuse is close to zero. Needless to say, you are fired on the spot for abuse, because the other side of a system based on trust and openness is that there can be no tolerance for abuse."

Colin Evans, another MacDonald Dettwiler refugee who joined Creo in 1988 and has served as a project manager, says that everybody works efficiently because they have the tools that the liberated purchasing system ensures. "Let's say a problem comes up in North Carolina and the client needs me tomorrow. It costs $2,000. I can just make the decision. I don't have to ask anyone," he notes. "Overall, there's a huge amount of money involved. It alarms some people. But the people in management must trust the process. If they don't, you get gatekeepers. Then, when there are too many hoops to go through in a purchase, people don't bother." He remembers standing in line at Dettwiler every time he needed a new silicon chip. At Creo, employees just go to the storeroom, sign a chip out, and return to work.

The Unit President

The purchasing system is just one facet—albeit quite a dramatic illustration—of the unit presidency concept. It flows from a belief that if you hire talented people, they should know their work better than anybody else should. Therefore, if each person behaves like the president of his or her own unit, acting in its best interests and the overall best interests of the company, everyone gains. By that process, everyone effectively becomes management. Raffi Amit, a professor of entrepreneurship and strategy at the University of British Columbia and until February 2001 chairman of Creo's board of directors, says Creo's policy is that "when it comes to authority, people—unless they are told they don't have authority—should assume they have it. This is our secret weapon. People are taking responsibility and moving the company forward."

Of course, business units are not generally isolated islands of one. Typically, a unit involves more than one person and the interests of one unit routinely intersect with other units. Employees are therefore taught that as unit presidents they each have the responsibility to determine who is affected by a decision and to build an agreement on the proper path with those colleagues. "If you don't involve the appropriate group of stakeholders, your decision may not be effective because you won't have buy-in from the right people," the Creo Philosophy warns.

On small projects, it's assumed the team is in regular communication, so individuals can figure out how their contribution as unit president fits with the bigger picture. But when projects become large and it's impossible for everyone to stay on top of things, team and project leaders become the central points of communication. They are responsible for ensuring the big picture is known and interests are integrated smoothly.

The Creo Decision-Making Matrix

IMPACT

		Small	Large
NUMBER OF PEOPLE AFFECTED	Small	Autocratic If affects only the decision-maker or if a quick decision is needed	Consensus Reached by meeting or e-mail using the "can live with it" rule
	Large	Democratic Majority-rule vote	Small Group Hammers out consensus with input from all affected stakeholders

All employees are familiar with a handy two-by-two matrix on decision-making styles that Creo follows, in which the key factors are the number of people affected by a decision and the impact of the decision. If the impact is large but affects few people, it is expected that those employees will adopt consensus decision-making. The consensus can be reached in a meeting or, for simple issues, through e-mail or voice mail. "Consensus means that everyone agrees that they can 'live with' the solution. It does not mean that everybody agrees it is the best of all possible choices," the Creo Philosophy stresses.

If a decision will have a large impact and many people are affected, consensus decision-making might be attempted but participatory decision-making is more likely. Everyone can give input but a small group, those most directly concerned, hammers out a consensus. The decision-makers must keep in mind the perspectives of the wider assembly and must communicate the decision to everyone who participated with enough time to object if they wish. That principle, of course, applies to overall stewardship of Creo itself or major decisions like developing a new mission statement or building a new plant.

If the impact of a decision is small but the number of people affected is large, democratic decision-making is recommended. Don't waste time: take a quick vote and move on. That rule is used for decisions like what food should be served at the Friday afternoon gatherings that mark the end of each work week or the type of photocopier that might be purchased in a work area.

The final decision-making style is autocratic, and it is appropriate when the impact of a decision is small and affects only the person making it. That person makes the decision. Autocratic decisions are also acceptable if a decision has to be reached very quickly.

It can be quite contrary to human nature to follow the principle that people are best if self-managed. But by all accounts, Creo has been successful in taking that now-common theme of mission statements and making it reality on the shop floor. Cindy Walters, who joined Creo in 1991 to work in accounting and now manages corporate travel, says, "I still don't know about unit president. But I certainly feel self-managed—from Day 1. I like to make decisions and I know my job better than anybody else, so I should be able to make decisions." A lot of her work affects other people, so she consults. But when a recent deal with an airline came together that was ideal for the company and a quick decision was needed to save money, she went ahead and made it herself. "It was a no-brainer," she says. The key, she stresses, is communication. And it doesn't come just from the top. For communication to work under a self-managed system, everybody must be communicating with everybody else.

Coming to Creo can be difficult, however, if you have been a manager elsewhere. "To be a leader, you are taught by society that you have to be in command. You need information as well, that must be fed up to you. Then you make the decision and it ripples down," notes David Brown, vice-president business strategy. Creo is careful in hiring to make sure newcomers fit its philosophy. Managers must learn, Brown says, "that you have to earn authority rather than get it as part of the position you hold. If you try to push and tell people what to do here it doesn't work. You can pull, however." But the system works, he insists: Creo deals with lots of hierarchical organizations and although sometimes it's slower to respond because of the requirement for consensus, generally the unit presidency philosophy and the lack of bureaucracy means that Creo is faster.

Performance Assessment and Share Options

Supporting the philosophy is an intensive and all-inclusive performance assessment carried out every October on each employee. But it's not the sole preserve of bosses to judge performance. Any employee can evaluate any other colleague. "I can do anybody I want; whoever I come in contact with," stresses Walters. "If I want to review Dan or somebody else in top management, I can do that. If a receptionist helps me during the year I can put her on my list and give her a pat on the back. In fact, they encourage you to do that."

But it's more than a pat on the back. Compensation is based on peer review. And while profit-sharing in the company is equal—everybody gets the same, from CEO to shipping clerk—stock options are determined by contribution to the company, as set by the peer review process. It begins with all employees naming whom they wish to assess and then assigning them numerical ratings, on a 1–5 scale, in six categories: teamwork and treatment of others; honouring commitments and self-management; quality; productivity; leadership; and overall contribution. The results are fed into a computer and the numbers are averaged, so no differentiation is made between evaluations from above, below, or alongside. Team leaders then meet to discuss the ratings of their respective employees and what the contribution of their respective units has been to Creo's success. Through that process, they determine compensation and divide the available stock options.

The system traces back to Gelbart's days at MacDonald Dettwiler when he noticed that the people management considered effective were not always the people their peers considered effective. Management interaction with employees came primarily through meetings, where some people excelled even if they were awful outside the meeting room. Management therefore didn't know the difference between who was contributing and who was simply talking nicely. Peers did.

The peer review system is also biased in favour of individuals who are co-operative and work well with others. If somebody is unpleasant, inevitably in a peer review system his or her score will suffer. Compensation therefore is determined not just by how effective a worker somebody is but by whether he or she is pleasant to work with. That may seem unfair or even counterproductive but Gelbart insists it's critical: "You want to drive your workplace in that direction of having people who are pleasant to work with. The reason is that it's never the work that makes you tired. You only get tired from interaction with people you don't like. One way to minimize that interaction is by applying social pressure. With peer review, people will try to be helpful to colleagues."

It brings Darwin's theory of natural selection to the workplace. People who help others at the expense of their own project will fare better on peer review. With management review, on the other hand, all that counts is your own project and that is ultimately counterproductive. "What matters to the company is the total benefit of all projects. It doesn't help if you did your project well but at the expense of other projects," Gelbart says.

The system works. At the end of the process, evaluations are discussed with individual employees. In addition to the numbers, employees are given feedback from the qualitative comments colleagues make. Employees change their behaviour when they see it costs them. They also recognize that the feedback is local—from the people around them—rather than just from the bosses in the inner sanctum.

Despite the pressure that the assessment system provides to be nice and get along, Raffi Amit believes overall it actually ensures the company isn't populated with Yes Men and Yes Women. "It's not a case that if your boss doesn't like you, you're toast. It's a consensus, based on all the people you work with."

Is it fair? "Absolutely," says Walter. "It feels very fair." She was a bit nervous before her first evaluation, but now takes it in stride. Most people have a gut feeling about how they are performing—if anything, they tend to be too self-critical—and generally team leaders give some warning so that nothing strongly negative comes out of the blue. Dave Baker, a tool and die maker, notes that employees are always reminded that criticism is intended to be constructive and intended to help rather than to seek revenge because you're mad at someone. He has received some suggestions about how he might change how he operates: "You don't see it until you get feedback on your habits. Then it gives you something to work on. Everybody wants to improve."

Despite the assistance of computers, it is a massive and time-consuming operation overall. Walters tries to keep her assessments down to about half a dozen. Team leaders might have 20 to 30 evaluations to complete, each taking 20 minutes to half an hour, and they then have to attend several days of meetings to divide up the stock options. In product development, for example, the various team leaders rank 300 employees from top to bottom, after considerable debate. Everyone must receive some options or otherwise the entire venture would be considered punitive. So a minimum is awarded to all and then options shoot up on a fairly steep curve according to contribution.

Executives who came up through the ranks generally fared well in performance ratings prior to joining management and since they are widely viewed as making a significant contribution, they still end up with top marks. But this is a chance for employees to think broadly about contribution to the company—and how it comes from all areas. "You might say, for example, that people in the shipping department make a low contribution," says Evans. "But if we don't get our latest machine to a trade show on time, we're out of luck. And it's not uncommon for them to work until 2:00 or 3:00 a.m. to make sure we ship. They only do that because they want to make a contribution. And they are recognized and rewarded."

Small-Firm Ways and Big Payoffs

Recognition comes between annual reviews as well. As Creo has grown, it has tried to retain some of the flavour of its small-firm days. Every Wednesday at 3:00 p.m., for example, work stops and everybody gathers in the cafeteria for cake, doughnuts and other goodies. In the old days, of course, that ritual took place at one site rather than many and was a chance to celebrate birthdays with a cake. Now it's a chance to snack and meet casually with your colleagues, so you can know each other better as human beings and develop ties that will translate into the rest of the workweek. "It's a tradition. It encourages people to socialize and to put a face to a name," says Walters.

On Fridays, at 5:00 p.m., the tradition of Happy Hour continues. Alcoholic consumption, of course, is moderate these days, but beer and wine are still available. And a sumptuous catered buffet is provided—at company expense—for employees to enjoy: chicken wings, ribs, sandwiches, salads, vegetables, and dips. In good weather, the event takes place outside and if a team is celebrating a milestone the members might put some hamburgers on the barbecue for their colleagues. "It's unbelievable. What other company would do that?" says Walters. "It's their way of saying thanks for your work."

When the company was small, Happy Hour was an intimate gathering of friends. But it still remains a pivotal time of the week for many employees. They'll stay until 6:00 or 7:00 p.m. rather than rushing home—even though this gathering is on their time—and then some will return to work, finishing projects. Working late at Creo is not unusual, as with most project-oriented and research and development enterprises. One employee interviewed began by describing his early days at the company as follows: "I started by doing what most people at Creo do: I got divorced." The company, mindful of that, pays for family counselling, insists employees take their vacations within 24 months of earning them, and has flexible hours, with employees able to take time off in lieu of overtime. "They believe that not everybody is creative from 9 to 5. Some people come alive in the evening. Some of my best work comes from 6 p.m. to midnight. You bank your extra time and then at Christmas take a few extra hours to go shopping, or, when a friend calls who needs help, you can take time off," says Walters.

Jacques, a single mother who has two children, bought a townhouse a few blocks from work so she can head home in the afternoon when they come back from school and then make up the time after dinner. She has also always felt comfortable bringing her children with her to work when necessary. "There's a lot of freedom here. If you're having a downright lousy day, it's OK to go out for a walk or leave early," she says. "On the other hand, when I'm driven to finish what I'm doing, no bell goes off at 5:00."

But the icing on the cake for Walters—and so many others—is the chance to own shares. Pay at Creo is at market rates. Profit-sharing is a plus. Share ownership can be a bonanza. It traces back to the beginning, when shares were given out directly (although now that the company is public it has had to switch to options, whereby employees are given the right to buy shares at a favourable price over a certain period of time). Given the track record of the founders, it was decided when they started that a proper valuation for the company would be $6 million. The July 1999 initial public offering of shares put the company's valuation at $1 billion, giving the founders and early employees 160 times the hypothetical value of their first shares.

For those who joined later, the return was still fabulous. In the early 1990s, for example, a share was worth $1. At the time of the IPO, after a stock split, that share was worth $70. "It's a 40 percent appreciation per year," notes Gelbart, proudly.

Although stock options and share ownership are now common in technology firms, they were not popular when Creo began. More significantly, the proportion owned by employees is much higher at Creo than in most companies. Prior to the Scitex acquisition, they accounted for 20 percent of ownership (founders and senior managers held another 20 percent), compared to the 2 or 3 percent held elsewhere. Although there was some dilution with the acquisition, the granting of stock options meant employees were affected less than other groups, and still retain an unusually high percentage of the firm. That results not just from the humanitarian instincts of the founders but also the fact that Creo was able to fuel its growth in the early years from within and didn't take outside investors until after seven years. So employees and founders controlled a larger pool of wealth before they were forced to share. Goldman Sachs, the well-known investment banking house, which first provided an equity infusion of $20 million in 1995, owns about 20 percent, with other investors holding about 20 percent and the general public about 20 percent.

Goldman Sachs may seem like an odd investor for a little-known Vancouver-based company, but it's a testimony to the strength and vision of the company. Amos Michaelson, who joined Creo in 1991 as managing director and succeeded Spencer as CEO on his retirement, believes in always starting with the best. When the company realized it would need a major investor in the mid-1990s, the founders initially thought of returning to the Federal Business Development Bank, which had given them $1.5 million in 1989. Michaelson, instead, approached Goldman Sachs, and to everyone's delight they came on board.

The company is tough-minded about investors. Institutional buyers, as expected, began to flood Creo with calls after the IPO to request meetings with management when officials were visiting the West Coast. It's a common ritual—adding some information and filling out their schedule. But it demands a lot of management time and Creo is a very practical (and lean) operation. So when the requests arrive, the practice has been for the investors to automatically be sent a note advising that Creo would be happy to meet with them but they should remember that every hour Creo management devotes to them is one less hour spent working on increasing the value of the investment. In most cases, the investors withdraw, telling Creo to simply increase share value.

A few years prior to the public offering, in anticipation, the company switched from giving employees shares to stock options, to meet security regulations. Beyond that, and the addition of an investor relations manager and assistant, Creo found it had to make surprisingly few changes when going public.

The company's policy of open communications internally has been maintained. "There aren't two sets of information—one set for the management and one set for the employees. All information is open to all employees," says Gelbart. "It doesn't mean all employees are aware of it. Most of them don't care. But every employee has access to all the information management has except for personal salaries. And if something important occurs, it is sent as a message to the whole company."

But as a public company, that raises sensitive questions about who exactly is an insider whose stock trading must be regulated. Is it everyone on staff? The company knows a potential conflict exists but for now is determined to continue with openness. It's also proud that nobody has taken advantage of that policy. Creo has never suffered a leak of sensitive information.

The other big change has been the addition of Scitex, which more than doubled the size of the company and added a pile of people not familiar with Creo ways. But six months after the change, Gelbart was optimistic: "We have converted Scitex to the Creo style of management." It was decided to begin by giving the Scitex employees significant equity in the company. That was accomplished through a stock option offering to all employees, whether they were ex-Scitex or traditionally Creo, which amounted to 8 percent of the company's equity, or over $100 million in shares. Revenues continue to rise—the run rate, or what would be achieved in a full year of the combined companies, is about $1 billion—and profit for last year was $60 million. "It's not a disgrace," says Gelbart, with pride.

Employees elect one of the nine directors, for a two-year term. Candidates need three nominations and campaign through e-mail rather than hats and balloons, sending out a statement of goals. Colin Evans, worried that some of Creo's original beliefs were eroding with growth, won election a few years ago on a platform of strengthening that foundation.

But after his victory, he had to confront what the role of a director actually was. "A senior manager told me I was not elected to be the Buzz Hargrove of Creo," he says of the high profile union leader "And I had to agree," he says. He realized that he was a director of the company, not an ombudsman or labour leader. Many of his concerns were also operational, rather than the normal fodder for directors' meetings. But Michaelson took him aside and suggested Evans join the operations committee where he could push his ideas. In the end, he found that not only a useful vehicle but also like taking an MBA course in management: "It was more valuable than sitting on the board." His successor also sits on the operational committee.

Principles behind the Creo Approach

- Every individual is the CEO of his or her own work (the "unit-presidency" concept). So employees should share in the wealth they help create.

- Each employee has the responsibility to consult with others who will be affected by his or her decision and to build agreement. On bigger projects/decisions, team and project leaders are responsible for communications and integration.

- Employees can be trusted to do what makes sense (but abuse of this trust cannot be tolerated).

- Employee ownership helps attract key talent, but is not by itself a source of motivation and productivity.

- Hire only newcomers who fit the philosophy.

- **Compensation:**

  o Base pay at market rates (helps attract the best people).

  o Profit-sharing divided equally among all employees (keeps everyone thinking of efficiency and needed improvements).

  o Stock options based on individual contribution as decided by a comprehensive review system (rewards and motivates outstanding contributions and co-operation with others).

- Employees are recognized in other ways besides compensation: Wednesday afternoon gatherings, Friday Happy Hour, flexible scheduling, representation on the board of directors.

- Communications are open and all information is shared with all employees.

At his first few board meetings, Evans says that he "felt like a fly on the table. I wished I were serving dinner instead of sitting there. It was extremely awkward. The other directors are powerful, wealthy people with great experience, talking about concepts I had never heard about. It took me a year to come up to speed." He would huddle before every board meeting with Michaelson and Gelbart, asking questions so that he could be better prepared. But eventually, he feels he was able to contribute through his knowledge of employees and operations, stressing to the other directors the importance of Creo's unique culture and the dangers of making changes that might turn it into a high-tech sweatshop. Today, the non-Hargrove sums up his experience as follows: "I protected the interests of employees by being involved in decisions and making sure the value of the shares went up."

Most employees view that appreciation in shares as a lovely gift—but something for the future, which they keep in RRSPs for retirement, or plan to cash in to buy a home or cottage. For engineers and other technology specialists, stock options have become de rigueur these days. But for those in shipping, accounting, or other non-technical jobs, it's not taken for granted. "It's like a windfall," says Walters. "What other opportunity in my life would I have to come into this kind of money?"

Jacques occasionally sells some shares, when there's something special she wants to buy. Prior to the stock being listed, that was accomplished through the e-mail exchange the company ran. It regularly listed blocks of shares that were up for sale, ensuring excellent liquidity. A few years ago, she decided to take her children on a Caribbean cruise. "I look at other women who are single and I'm very fortunate. This company has provided me with a good lifestyle," she says. But she stresses her satisfaction goes beyond money. She enjoys the weekly lunchtime seminars—dubbed Creo University—on technical matters, personal growth issues, or financial advice. And, of course, she appreciates the sense of job ownership: "It's not just the shares. Money wouldn't hold me. It's the way of thinking. I'm extremely happy here. It has been ten years—I can't believe how lucky I have been."

Pacific Regeneration Technologies

⊙⊙

Public Servants Grow Their Company

*"The first thing I learned is that everybody goes into employee
ownership with an altruistic attitude. I learned that was a
recipe for disaster in that it all sounds good—fuzzy and
warm—but this is a business."*
—Chris Worthy, vice-chair, PRT Management

In 1987, a troubled Charlie Johnson walked into the Victoria offices
of Coopers and Lybrand seeking help. The British Columbia government was preparing to privatize its forest nursery operations, where he
worked as director of silviculture, and Johnson was looking for some
way to buy it. He didn't have much money. He didn't have any business experience. But after fighting desperately within the government
to prevent privatization, he was determined to keep together the nurseries and the team he had built.

The Coopers and Lybrand branch manager quickly sized up the
situation as bleak but passed Johnson on to one of the consultants,
Chris Worthy, more out of politeness than a belief that anything could
be accomplished. Worthy listened to Johnson but also didn't sense
much opportunity until he became aware that Johnson in his despair
was repeating the phrase, "I want to keep the employees together."
Worthy had worked previously for PCL Construction, one of Canada's
oldest contractors, which had become employee-owned in 1977 after
the founding Poole family ran out of heirs to run the business.

Sometimes, happenstance counts. The fortuitous teaming of Johnson with Worthy rather than some other management consultant in Victoria and the words Johnson happened to reiterate led to the creation of what is now Canada's largest forest nursery company, Pacific Regeneration Technologies. The company has pushed beyond British Columbia's borders to Alberta, Saskatchewan, and Ontario, buying up and consolidating mom-and-pop nursery operations. Somewhere along the way, the civil servants learned how to be shrewd business operators. And nearly a decade after the company was started in desperation, it held a highly successful public offering, becoming an income trust, with the original employee owners getting more than 34 times their original investment back. They celebrated their success by recommitting to employee ownership, each plunking down 10 percent of his or her individual payout in exchange for shares in a new employee-owned company. The new company manages PRT for the income trust, an investment entity that counts on a steady income stream from some asset.

But nobody knew the story would have a happy ending when Johnson and Worthy started writing it. In fact, Worthy is still in awe at Johnson's pluck—at age 52, he put more than half his net worth into PRT, when, given his long seniority, he could have stayed on as a civil servant and lived out his years until retirement.

"How many people would sink a significant portion of their net worth into a venture where the participants had no business experience, where there were no financial controls, and where there was a debt-to-equity ratio of four to one? And one that started as a decentralized operation with assets across the province? Not me," stresses Worthy.

"It's not your usual success story. But he did really believe that there was value in all these nurseries, and that if we could keep them together, they would one day prove him right. In the end, he was right—ideas have consequence."

Moving to Privatization

B.C.'s forest nurseries trace back to 1929, when the provincial government established the first in Victoria. In the mid-1950s, the province introduced a system of tree farm licences obligating forest companies to ensure that any areas they logged were adequately reforested. But in the 1980s, the province was fielding requests for over 100 million seedlings a year and was struggling to keep up. The province initiated a private-sector nursery program and began contracting out some of the seedling requirements.

The biggest change came in 1987, when the Bill Bennett government announced that responsibility for the costs of reforestation would be transferred from the province to the major forest licence holders. Under that policy, no compelling reason existed for the province to be solely responsible for most of the forest nursery production. The government decided to hand it to the private sector.

Under the terms of the privatization program, any proposal from a valid employee group had to be considered before the province could open the bidding process to outside tenders. That was the opening Johnson hoped to seize, even if originally he wasn't sure how. Along with Chris Worthy, the other key individual in his plan was Ev Van Eerden, who managed the private nursery program and had intimate knowledge of operations and the markets. The final player was CIBC, which gave them $30 million. Since many of the employees were rank and file nursery operators, putting in relatively small chunks of money, the venture needed outside capital—and it had to come from somebody willing to accept a highly leveraged operation. "In this case, a bank took risk—more risk than it should have," says Worthy.

Gaining support, it turned out, required not just confidence from the leadership but also a willingness to display uncertainty. Employees seemed tense at the first few meetings. Finally, Sandy MacIver, a Coopers and Lybrand consultant helping with the process, suggested the difficulty was that the deal's proponents weren't addressing how scared people were. "I know it's important to appear confident," he told Johnson and Van Eerden, "but don't either of you have any doubts about this?" Johnson had none. But Van Eerden said, "To tell you the truth, I haven't had a full night's sleep since this privatization thing was first raised. I have full confidence in Charlie and you guys, but it's still a lot of money and I get concerned." Once he began admitting that hesitation at meetings, buy-in intensified.

The government rejected the first offer from PRT for six of the nurseries, claiming the bid was insufficient, and opened bidding to the public. That still infuriates Worthy, who believes the government was negotiating in bad faith. The proposal had become controversial, with some private nursery owners fearing a sweetheart deal for former government employees and hoping to perhaps pick off one of the nurseries for their own operations. "The political heat became too great for the government," says Worthy.

Starting a Company

In the end, however, nobody could match the PRT bid of $5.7 million, precisely because it was for a number of nurseries. As Charlie Johnson had foreseen, it made sense to keep the nurseries together: The larger scale presented economies to the ultimate purchaser, which in turn allowed a higher bid. And in the end, Worthy likes to point out, the nurseries were purchased for just about what had been offered in the original proposal. But there was a cost: In the interim, the market had started to change, and a tough challenge had just become tougher.

Forestry companies increasingly wanted their stock in containers but the six nurseries that PRT had just purchased were primarily traditional bare-root operations. That would require a dramatic and expensive restructuring of operations. In the first four years, PRT added 325,000 square feet of greenhouse space to meet the new demand, taking advantage of the capital CIBC had provided.

But at least the managers understood seeds, containers, and greenhouses—that had been their trade for many years. They now had to learn about profit and return on investment. They also had to learn about employee ownership—how to make it work. Fortunately, in Worthy they had a wise and patient teacher, who had carefully thought through the intricacies of such ventures and helped them to avoid some of the pitfalls.

A chartered accountant, he had been supervising the outside audit at PCL for Coopers and Lybrand in the early 1980s when the construction company persuaded him to take over the new role of internal review. Because of various internal problems—very serious legal problems that began just prior to his joining the company—he had to work closely with the chairman and other senior executives in what turned out to be a major reorganization.

"The first thing I learned," he says of those early days at PCL, "is that everybody goes into employee ownership with an altruistic attitude. I learned that was a recipe for disaster in that it all sounds good—fuzzy and warm—but this is a business." Employees may have been owners at PCL, but they didn't call the shots day to day. PCL had strong leadership in its executive offices. "The leadership was benevolent but it was leadership in a dictatorial form," he says with a laugh.

Why Privatization Worked at PRT

Before	After
Operations restricted to British Columbia	Company could expand to other provinces
Government operation could not keep up with demand	Rapid investment in greenhouses, laboratories, and technologies enabled PRT to meet demand
Financing had to come from taxes	Financing came from employees and private investors
Slow decision-making had to go through the political process	Rapid, flexible response to problems and challenges
No incentive for government employees to improve the products or services	Clear monetary incentives for improving the business
Operations vulnerable to political shifts and changes in governments	Operations subject to market conditions and rules of business
Little development of managerial skills	Managers learned business skills rapidly
Low risk/low reward climate	High risk/high reward climate galvanized employees

Worthy believes executives of an employee-owned company have a special role, whether they acknowledge it or not. It's not the same as a regular corporation, even in these days of more-empowered management. They have to be very tough-minded while also being very sensitive to the employees' needs. "The temptation is to be a little bit softer because it's an employee-owned situation," he notes. But they must have the strength of character to push on with what they believe is right for the company, even when colleagues around them at work—legally their owners—disagree.

That's hard to do, not just because of the practicalities of owner-ship but because of the unique bonds that can develop with employ-ee buyouts. They can quickly turn into a we–they situation—those who own shares versus those who don't.

At PRT, management ran the show, albeit with an open-door pol-icy. Charlie Johnson, who became CEO, had always been known for his people-friendly ways. Peter Richter, now regional manager for northern nurseries in British Columbia and Alberta, remembers when he was starting out in the early 1980s with the ministry, as a tempo-rary forest technician. He was in the middle of a field with a tractor when a convoy of vehicles arrived, along with his boss. He noticed some guy walking out to the middle of the field, towards him, which led him to fear he was doing something wrong. But the director of sil-viculture simply wanted to introduce himself and find out how things were going with the new job. "That little incident stuck in my mind ever since and has been a big part of why I am at PRT today," he says.

PRT experimented with having one employee on the board in the early years. He or she wasn't elected but appointed by management. However, the practice ended when it was felt the employee wasn't making much of a contribution due to a lack of the financial skills a board member needed. There had also not been any great enthusiasm for the practice. "I was probably more keen on it than the others," Johnson admits.

The Share Structure

For management to manage, Worthy believes it's essential they have the greatest number of shares. That means controlling the purchase and allocation of shares, since it's not healthy if individuals at rela-tively low levels own more than those at the executive level own. "Clearly while you want to see everyone rewarded to the greatest extent possible, the executives of the company are giving greater amounts of their time and energy and have a greater impact on the decisions of the company than a secretary, for example, could. That's not judgmental; it's a fact," he says.

At PRT, the key executives owned just over 50 percent of the stock from the outset, so they could drive the company. But attention was paid to ensuring that relative stake was maintained over time. And that required attention, because shares were never given away to employees—only purchased. "I learned that unless you actually pay for it and are at risk of losing it, ownership doesn't have any impact," Worthy says.

And shares are risks, Worthy stresses. Companies must therefore be completely candid about that aspect of employee ownership. Whenever an employee bought stock at PRT, he or she received a letter warning: "Please be aware this stock is a risky investment. There is no guarantee that you will earn a return on your investment or for that matter a return of your investment. This is not a public company and there is no market for the stock. The company is the only market and you might suffer a loss." The letter was so harsh that Worthy wonders why anyone would invest after receiving it. But the principals didn't want to be accused of promoting a stock. And it apparently didn't scare off too many people, since the stock issues were always oversubscribed.

Worthy's Do's and Don'ts of Employee Ownership

Chris Worthy has a very different approach to employee ownership than the leaders at Creo, for example. However, both companies were highly successful examples of employee ownership. We believe this demonstrates the robust nature of the concept and how it can be designed and adapted to different industries and environments. Worthy gave the following tips:

DO'S

- Do ensure that managers of employee ownership companies are both tough-minded and sensitive to employees' needs.

- Do give managers, rather than employees, the greatest proportion of shares, which is commensurate with their impact on the business.

- Do be candid about the risks of share ownership, not just the potential rewards.

- Do make adequate provisions for stock repurchase if the stock is not traded on a public stock exchange.

- Do establish a key man insurance program if the company is exposed to risk from a major shareholder's death or retirement.

- Do use conservative estimations and accounting practices.
- Do match dividend payouts to the growth needs of the company.

DON'TS

- Don't approach employee ownership with an altruistic attitude but with a business orientation.
- Don't let employees call the shots day to day. Leaders must lead.
- Don't give away shares to employees. Make them pay for their shares, even if the amount is small—otherwise ownership will not have as great an impact.
- Don't price the stock too high or employees won't be motivated or able to buy it.
- Don't use complicated valuation methods to price the stock or employees won't understand and may not trust the calculations.

The original shares had been set at $100. But it became clear that was too high, discouraging people from buying, so the stock was split 80 to one, coming down to $1.25 apiece. Since the only outlet for the stock was to sell it back to the company, the PRT board had to ensure that whenever an employee presented his or her stock certificate the company had sufficient funds to purchase. Any other situation would undermine confidence in the stock and its liquidity.

"That's something I don't think managers of employee-owned companies take seriously enough when they do their financial projections. What happens if a group of employees or a significant employee shareholder puts his stock to the company and the company is not able to buy it? That would be a dramatic negative event for the company and the shareholding plan. It just can't happen. So from a financial point of view, you have to plan for it," Worthy says.

That was particularly important for PRT, since it had a policy geared to retirement that required all shareholders when they hit age 60 to sell back their shares to the company in five annual slices. While some wiggle room was available, allowing the company to defer purchase each year until the shareholder hit 64, at that point it was required to catch up so that only the final 20 percent was left to be bought the next year.

Given that Johnson and Van Eerden, the two largest stockholders, were in their fifties when they started the company—and also to handle any unexpected death of a senior officer—PRT established a key man insurance program. That would have provided sufficient funds to pay back the shares of the deceased to the person's estate and also conduct a search for a replacement. The program was expensive, costing the company $250,000 annually in the early years when it was eager for capital to grow and not paying dividends. "It was a hardship to pay those premiums. Charlie Johnson and Ev Van Eerden could have said we would prefer dividends to that. But they were building long-term value," says Worthy.

In the end, PRT bought back very few shares in the years prior to going public. The company tried to follow a policy of issuing shares annually. The shareholders agreement decreed that the stock price would be calculated according to the audited book value of the company. "That was another thing I learned at PCL: keep it simple. Don't get fancy, bringing in an investment banker to throw around multiples of revenue or earnings. Most people aren't investors. Give them something they can understand and that makes sense," Worthy stresses.

He also insisted on conservative accounting practices for the company. A temptation always exists to show how well a company is doing but that can be dangerous, especially if there is some variability in revenues. While PRT is now a steady enough producer to be an income trust, it is essentially an agricultural business, susceptible to weather that could wipe out a crop. In December 1990, for example, a metre of heavy, wet snowfall caused the collapse of eight greenhouses at one of the original nurseries in Thornhill, B.C. Insurance helps to cover such calamities but not enough to wipe away the entire risk. Early on, the conservative accounting hurt the company with investors since it was accumulating cash but showing a loss. That meant everybody's shares were decreasing in value. "But it served us well because we kept the expectations of people down and we reinforced the notion that this is a long-term investment," Worthy says.

On the other hand, that violated one of the other lessons Worthy had retained from PCL, where substantial dividends had been paid out in the early years of employee ownership—sometimes three or four times the price paid for the stock. Very quickly, as might be expected, employee ownership caught fire. So tangible results from employee ownership, he believes, are very helpful in the early years. But PCL was a construction company that didn't need much capital to grow. PRT was a capital-intensive business and in the early years spare cash had to be directed to the expansion program.

Building a Team and Management Expertise

Those first few years began with Johnson and MacIver travelling to each of the nurseries to hold team-building sessions. The goal was to help the nursery employees realize they were now part of a "family," and ideas and resources should be shared. A newsletter was also started to keep everyone up to date.

"With government you had a budget and then you couldn't get the things you needed," recalls Denise Dionne, a grower at the Campbell River nursery. "We planted seed that was half dead for years, and we knew better. So the first thing PRT did was to get our own seed lab going and all of a sudden we were planting live seed, which was great. We got computers right away and blackout systems. With government we just didn't get anything; it was all labour intensive. When PRT came in, we all had a lot of ideas about things we wanted to change and we did it. Bang, bang, bang."

Randy Armitage, a grower at Vernon, in the Okanogan Valley, remembers the flexibility and freedom that was suddenly unleashed. "Individual nurseries could dig themselves out of a hole rather than waiting to be directed from Victoria or Surrey. If there was trouble with a crop, people could share ideas and try new things. Some nurseries are more aggressive in developing better cultural methods and the benefits could be shared."

The nursery operators had to learn how to operate a business. To help, annual corporate objectives were stated very clearly, without reams of documentation that might overwhelm staff. Nurseries, the civil servants learned, were now profit centres, responsible for meeting specific targets; performance bonuses were dependent on meeting or exceeding those goals. Each profit centre manager is evaluated annually on the basis of a short letter prepared the year before outlining a proposed budget as well as marketing, operational, and organizational goals. That letter must be submitted by November 1 and the goals are then negotiated with senior managers. The managers meet monthly with the CEO to discuss how they are faring.

"Business is a very disciplined lifestyle if you are going to be successful," notes Van Eerden, who succeeded Johnson as CEO after his retirement. "With all due respects to my former colleagues in government, some of whom are outstanding contributors to society, there isn't the same pressure there that you get from being financed by a bank or being owned by private investors."

He's quick to name what he had to learn most: return on investment. "When you spend money to buy a machine or a greenhouse, you have to be sure beforehand that you can get a sufficient return on investment. That can be predetermined. You won't be right 100 percent of the time. But you can make a reasonable assessment of what the investment will yield, either to your private investors or in our case now the public investors." Van Eerden, it should be stressed, is no slouch with the numbers side of the equation. He wowed Worthy, the accountant, during the negotiations to purchase the nurseries with the detailed spreadsheets he developed every night at home by hand, using a *Maclean's* magazine calculator he had picked up in exchange for a subscription.

The second lesson for Van Eerden was the importance of a company's market constituency. "If you work for government, there isn't the same pressure to perform. The marketplace is an incredible disciplinarian. That's very healthy—very positive."

The early years saw some labour discord. Money was tight. And some animosity lingered from the purchase, stoked by several of the civil servants who negotiated the deal for the government. They felt an asset of tremendous value was being given away to unscrupulous business people who would steal the value and leave nothing in return. Some of the PRT employees, even though owners, picked up that anger. Part of company lore is the story of two employees who at the end of one of the first years, in front of a bunch of colleagues, supposedly dropped their annual reports in the garbage can without opening them. Inside was a dividend cheque.

It was difficult to gain flexibility in the new contracts that were negotiated with the B.C. Government Employees Union for the privatized nurseries. And as PRT bought some non-unionized nurseries or nurseries with a different union, it only complicated the labour-management stew. Armitage, who negotiated on behalf of the union, remembers a love-hate cleavage building within him. The company was his, as the top executives kept reminding him in their pep talks. But at the same time, wages seemed to be falling behind and employees felt slighted. "I didn't see the good side of my leaders as a negotiator. So it was disappointing. They would say there was no money for raises but the boys in corporate could take friends out on a fishing expedition or find money for buying other nurseries," he says.

Johnson had hoped someday management could develop sufficient trust with its employee owners that they might break away from
the union. But it never happened. "A lot of people still want the com-
fort of having the union behind them," he says. "In the years I negotiated we spent as much money—and time, on the senior executives'
part—on the negotiations themselves as went into the salary increases. I looked upon that as terribly unproductive but there wasn't much
I could do about it."

Worthy Joins In

In 1993, Worthy decided that part of the reason for the discord was
that the management infrastructure was still weak, allowing rumour
and unsubstantiated opinion too much room to grow. He began a program of special management training sessions, improving information systems and hammering home the importance of return on
investment. He and Van Eerden also developed a program called
Improving Our Management Effectiveness, which delved into all
aspects of a nursery manager's operations, critically evaluating each
one's current practices and making suggestions for betterment. Some
grabbed it and ran with it. Some needed coaxing. But without exception, they all began to improve.

Worthy was like a firefighter. He was a board member, but his own
business affairs took him first to Washington, D.C., for a period, where
he was CFO for the eighth-largest construction company in the United
States, and then to Seattle. There he set up his own firm, Worthy
Capital Inc., to invest in companies. But PRT was always on his
mind—and close to his heart. In 1993, Johnson came down to Seattle
to visit and hash over things. One of his big concerns was PRT
Silvicare, an attempt to diversify the business base by establishing a
consulting service that would offer one-stop shopping to forest industry clients. It offered a full range of silviculture services including tree
planting, stand management, contracting, research and development,
harvesting, inventory, and environmental protection and enhance-
ment. But it was poorly managed and draining resources, both financial and emotional. CIBC had stuck firmly behind the company;
chairman and CEO Al Flood had even made three visits to this tiny
element of the bank's portfolio. But now the bank was expressing concern about a number of initiatives, including silviculture.

"Charlie was the real sponsor of this project. He could think strategically but his management execution didn't always match his strategic vision," Worthy recalls. So the longtime advisor volunteered to come in part-time and help. And then, as he began to rewrite the strategic plan for the silviculture effort, he realized that one of the investments he had been looking to put Worthy Capital money into was sitting right under his nose. So the man who had watched in amazement as the early investors gambled their savings—although he stresses that had he been an employee, he would have also invested from Day 1—now put his own money into PRT.

Eventually, however, the silviculture operation had to be shut down in 1996. That came after a tough meeting between the two men who had accidentally met a decade earlier, and grown to become friends and business associates. "When I told Charlie I couldn't support him any longer in this business and my recommendation to the board was to close it, I also told him, 'I do agree with your strategy. It's the right strategy. It's just that the market is not ready for it yet and I don't know how to implement it. Until we do, let's get out of it because it's costing us dearly.'" To his credit, Worthy says, Johnson supported the recommendation.

The company also became involved in two other projects aimed at the future. In 1989 it purchased Harris Cloning and Propagating Inc., which was developing new techniques for growing Saskatoon berries, Boston ferns, prairie roses, and hostas. The lab ceased operations in 1994 but the spirit of the initiative continued that same year when PRT signed a world licensing agreement with the University of Saskatchewan for a conifer propagation technique called somatic embryogenesis. That allows the cloning of large numbers of plants with improved characteristics by taking seed tissue and multiplying it in the lab with a hormone cocktail. The company has been experimenting so far with Douglas fir and other species, with promising results. The intention is to provide customers with genetically superior material so they can grow their plantations faster and practise more intensive forestry on shorter rotations and perhaps less land.

In 1994, PRT entered into a ten-year management contract with a pharmaceutical company, NaPro BioTherapeutics Ltd., to plant and maintain an exclusive plantation of yew trees designed to provide that company with a long-term supply of paclitaxel, which is thought to be a natural cancer-fighting agent and is being used in the treatment of ovarian cancer and other cancers. However, the U.S. Drug and Food

Administration gave NaPro approval to sell its drug in the United States only after 2004, which meant they didn't need as much material. PRT had been working to extricate itself from the contract, but NaPro's recent partnership with a major pharmaceutical company has led to a new contract and the first harvesting of paclitaxel.

Becoming an Income Trust

Those ambitious projects, along with the continual nursery expansions and the requirement to have money to purchase back the shares of the main owners when they retired, led PRT to seek a cash injection in 1996. Capital West was hired to find investors but the ones they came up with wanted 20 percent returns, so PRT declined. But through that process Capital West learned a lot about the company's business and was impressed by the information systems and financial accountability built up over the years. In March 1997, Capital West returned to point out that income trusts had become a hot investment and PRT was an ideal candidate—but it must act quickly before the market for such ventures changed.

The initial stumbling block was employee ownership, which didn't seem to fit the income trust model. And PRT leaders weren't prepared to jettison the concept that they felt had been key to growth. "We believe in employee ownership," says Johnson simply. Van Eerden adds: "You get buy-in. I really believe you have a special commitment from the employees."

But the investment bankers were nonplussed. "You can imagine their reaction," says Worthy. "What? The employees? How are you going to explain this to the public?" However, the more they discussed it, he says, the more apparent it was those feelings stemmed simply from the fact it would complicate the bankers' lives tremendously because of having so many owners and having to explain that novel element to investors rather than from any inherent problem with employee ownership. So PRT's officials remained steadfast. "We said we're going to have this or we're not going to have a deal," Worthy says. "After awhile, it became clear to Capital West that this was not a negative. This was actually a positive if it was sold properly to the public. What more could the investors want than an employee group with a vested interest in growing the cash flow of the public company because they would earn a percentage of that cash flow?"

So that was the basis for the deal. The management company was given a 20-year contract, with a set annual fee and an incentive payment geared to growing the revenue stream. It also kept control of the somatic embryogenesis project—since it was not an immediate cash generator—and the significant cash value that had accrued in the key man insurance program, which, like whole life insurance, returns some of the invested premiums to the company.

Van Eerden hit the road immediately, with black garbage bags full of seedlings, to sell PRT at small meetings with the financial community. "I'm a pretty down-to-earth guy," he explains. "I wanted to show them what the product is." He'd leave the bags at the back of the room and inevitably investors would soon start talking about a son or niece who had spent one summer planting trees. Then they would dip into the bag and take some seedlings for the house or cottage. "There we were on Bay Street, with all these guys in blue suits and white shirts and appropriate ties, and they were all going home with seedlings," he says.

It wasn't just Van Eerden who impressed investors. The years of training had paid off. Worthy remembers taking investment bankers to the various nurseries, where they would be astonished as the manager reeled off their return-on-investment strategies, gross margins, overhead objectives, and other sophisticated financial analyses.

The offering produced $56 million, of which $35 million covered the value of the company's employee shares and loans over the years. For the original investors, it was about a 40 percent annual return. Armitage, who bought only ten shares originally because he had a young child, is now naturally wishing he had bought more. But he still saw $1,000 become more than $30,000, which allowed him to buy a hot tub, take a vacation in Mexico, pay down some of the mortgage, and put some money aside for his son's college education—as well as purchase shares in the new management company. "It was found money—and tax free because it's a capital gain. I would say to anybody: own shares."

The trust and management company have overlapping boards, with some members sitting on both. Worthy was originally very apprehensive, seeing too many opportunities for conflict. But the members are experienced, and he now sees it as helpful, ensuring ideas are vetted twice. "At times there will be differences of opinion. You just have to be mature enough to work them out," he says. Johnson senses a greater sensitivity to risk now, given the need to ensure steady cash returns for the trust.

But Van Eerden expects—and is planning for—greater expansion down the road. Governments are pulling out of government-run nurseries. Many of the mom-and-pop operations can't compete with a sophisticated player like PRT, which has the latest technology in all its greenhouses, cost savings accruing from its size, and the ability to provide bundled services. The company can also offer its customers coverage in a variety of locales but with similar growing technology in each. PRT intends to be the industry consolidator in Canada—notably Ontario—and then push into the United States.

The somatic embryogenesis efforts are also being expanded: in 2000, PRT acquired a competing company in the field, Silvagen, and the combined teams were organized into a new company, CellFor. The interest in CellFor is now owned through PMI Investments Ltd., which includes long-term employees of PRT who don't want to cash out their shares in that venture on retirement, outside investors, and employees.

For all the ups and downs, a crucial thing PRT has is an esprit de corps. It's not just employee ownership, although that's a key part. As Reg Renner, production supervisor at the Reid Collins nursery in Aldergrove, B.C., puts it: "When I close the gate at night at our nursery, I realize that I own part of this nursery, but I also own part of the other nine." But it's also the fact a group of people everybody was prepared to write off—a bunch of civil servants—put up their own money and had the brains to build a highly successful company. "I think everybody wants to be a winner," says Armitage. "There were a lot of things going against us. But we proved we are winners."

Provincial Papers

&

War and Peace (and War)

> *"The board did feel that involving the employees was impor-*
> *tant but we simply failed at it, partly because we started late*
> *and partly because we couldn't get by the split in the work*
> *force between those who had the traditional adversarial view*
> *of labour and management, and those who wanted to carve*
> *out a new model."*
>
> —Jim Foulds, independent member of the
> board and ex-NDP MPP

Mike Matich likes to be positive. A maintenance and housekeeping worker at Provincial Papers, he tries to understand both management and his co-workers—and the business environment in which the Thunder Bay mill operates. So when a newspaper reporter was hunting for a comment from a typical worker on the first day of employee ownership at the mill in 1993, the ever-helpful Matich said that he was "cautiously optimistic."

The quote made the newspaper. And for much of the next four years—a period that included intrigue, infighting, and internecine warfare between management and union, and union and union—that cautious optimism remained Matich's guiding spirit. As a former teacher and entrepreneur, he feels sympathetic to management. As a union member, he understands and lives the workers' perspective. He tried to be positive. He tried to understand all sides.

But it's a measure of the turmoil and trauma of the brief experience with employee ownership at Provincial Papers that several years later, Mike Matich is deeply bitter. He feels betrayed. And he's not alone. Everyone seems wounded, still carrying the hurts and still struggling with the what-might-have-beens. Even though everybody acknowledges the positive elements of employee ownership—600 jobs were saved and a paper mill previously written off as not viable continues to operate successfully—nobody is wildly enthusiastic about the experience.

Employee ownership is supposed to bring everybody together. But at Provincial Papers, the divisions only intensified. They trace back, in some cases, several generations, to parents and grandparents who toiled at the mill. It's not just the classic gulf between union and management, but also union versus union—there were five in all, with notable lingering resentments between the two Canadian Energy and Paperworkers union locals, one representing production workers and the other trades. It sometimes seems that about the only thing that unites them all is an antipathy to outsiders.

Waiting for the Shoe to Fall

For a long time, Abitibi-Price was the outsider. The owner of three paper mills in the Thunder Bay area, it brought jobs to the region but also served as a convenient target for those seeking one. Provincial Papers workers always saw themselves as the black sheep in the Abitibi-Price operation, because they were producing a different kind of paper than the other plants and wondered how essential they were considered to the entire operation. The mill also fell behind in the boom days of the late 1980s when pulp prices soared to their highest level ever, but it was unable to increase its own prices to keep up with rising costs. Because of the inability of two of its machines to produce high quality paper consistently, many traditional customers were turning to imported paper. A strike in 1990 only exacerbated those problems, as the plant lost a substantial order by General Motors and saw other customers turn to alternative suppliers during and after the strike.

It was a vulnerable position as the global recession of the early '90s started to bite and demand faltered. At the end of 1990, with Provincial having lost $26 million that year, Abitibi-Price announced it would hold a meeting in the near future to inform the union and employees about the mill's future. And Provincial wasn't the only Thunder Bay mill on alert. To bring supply in line with demand, Abitibi-Price also indicated it would order substantial downtime in 1991. Although contractually obligated to allocate downtime amongst all its newsprint mills, the company mused that it might be beneficial to shut down one of them instead.

The first shoe fell at a plant other than Provincial, with the announcement that the Division Newsprint mill would be "permanently idled." It was an odd choice since Division had been the most efficient producer of pulp at any Abitibi mill in Canada within the previous 18 months. Initially, the news at Provincial was comparatively mild: The company announced in June 1991 that it would cut 83 jobs at the mill. But a company spokesman indicated more might be required and Provincial was considered in "survival mode." Indeed, it was more than Provincial that was in survival mode. A senior Abitibi manager, in a *Globe and Mail* article, described the company as "fighting for its life." Speculation was growing that Abitibi-Price would pull out of Thunder Bay entirely.

The company started shopping Provincial around but couldn't find a buyer. It became generally known that E.B. Eddy Forest products looked at a joint arrangement for the mill but decided it wouldn't offer a viable investment. Speculation and tension continued to build, along with various cutbacks, for another year, until October, 1992, when the company announced that it was intending to close or sell the Provincial mill within the next year, since it was not considered a core asset. The Division mill would also be formally closed.

By then, the community had accepted the inevitable closure of the Division mill but was horrified at the possibility of a Provincial shutdown. A study indicated it would drain $84 million out of the local economy and eliminate about 2,800 jobs, since three jobs would be lost outside Provincial for every one at the company.

Abitibi-Price set a one-year deadline for getting rid of Provincial. Forty buyers were said to have shown some interest in the mill but only four were continuing tepidly to pursue the possibility, with no firm offers having come forth yet. Although mill management preferred an outside purchaser, who could bring in new capital, that was probably unlikely given the state of the economy and the time frame.

Developing the Buyout

So management also met within a week of the announcement with the union executive to explore the possibility of an employee buyout. And again a deadline was set for an answer: January 1. The initial terms outlined at that meeting are worth highlighting. They not only set the framework for ensuing discussions but also turned out to be remarkably close to the final arrangement eventually agreed to, after four more months of twists and turns, deadlines set and deadlines missed. Some jobs would be cut to make the operation more economical. As well, salaried employees would take a 15 percent pay cut and hourly employees a 20 percent cut. In return for the salary reductions, shares in the company would be granted, with ownership split between management and employees. Abitibi-Price would pay $1.2 million in severance costs and also finance any cash shortfalls—up to a maximum of $20 million—that occurred until the end of 1997. Finally, the provincial government would be expected to provide a $15 million loan guarantee and assume shutdown and severance costs if the venture failed.

Employee ownership was not an entirely new concept for the five union locals. They had previously formed a group called the mill council that had engaged in general discussions with management on many issues, including other avenues to improve the business. As a matter of interest, council members attended an employee ownership seminar in Toronto by an association promoting the concept, where they heard speakers from a few employee-owned companies.

Their union brethren in Kapuskasing had recently participated in a buyout of the Spruce Falls mill and informal discussions were held with them. That buyout differed significantly from the proposal being considered now. The Spruce Falls employees had invested their own money in the company, whereas in Thunder Bay shares would be traded for a wage reduction. Spruce had also partnered with Tembec, giving it an infusion of new management and new capital. Glen Hallahan, the president of Local 239, and eventual leader of the coalition of unions in the buyout, remembers one strict warning he carried back from Kapuskasing: ensure the language of the agreement was tight and well understood by all parties, or additional problems could arise.

One other key figure from Spruce Falls was to be involved in the Provincial buyout: Peter Tanaka, the provincial bureaucrat who had helped to stickhandle both the Algoma and Spruce deals. Abitibi approached him when it recognized a closure could be imminent. And, of course, as the news became public and the Thunder Bay community reacted, the NDP provincial government—with its traditional northern base—was sensitive to the need to keep the mill operating.

When Tanaka met initially with the unions, they were resistant to a buyout. "They didn't want anything to do with employee ownership. They just wanted a job," he recalls. But Abitibi had convinced the onsite managers that an employee buyout was the only alternative to closure, so pressure was intensifying. And not just on employees: from Tanaka's perspective, Abitibi was cleverly using the employees to pressure the government into sinking funds into the mill.

The key, he therefore felt, was to get employees, rather than Abitibi, driving the deal. And they were starting to come onside, recognizing the reality. "My first instinct had been no," says Hallahan. "But it was either that or a shutdown. There was no buyer. We had no choice." Tanaka demanded a plan, to ensure there would be light at the end of the tunnel should the operation be kept alive. Each of the parties signed up consultants—Boston Consulting Group for the company; Keilin and Bloom for the CEP; and Ernst and Young for the government—and they began formulating strategies. Tanaka decided that with a general 20 percent rollback, a business case could be made for keeping Provincial alive.

The next stage was to negotiate an agreement. Two sets of three-day, around-the-clock discussions were held in Toronto in January, trying to meet the new, absolute deadline from Abitibi of January 31. But progress was limited, with Barry Ferguson, the director of employee relations, noting that "we're still not at first base." Abitibi-Price President Ron Oberlander warned employees in a letter posted in the mill on January 25 that if no headway were achieved by the deadline, the company would not grant an extension and would proceed with the closure of the mill on the weekend. Oberlander argued that the mill's employees were not accepting the reality of the situation. But Thunder Bay's mayor argued it was Abitibi that was not accepting the reality of the situation: "A few days is not very much time to finish a very complicated arrangement like this, and I hope level heads will prevail."

One of the big stumbling blocks was John Olsen, president of Provincial Papers and a vice-president of Abitibi. He wasn't particularly liked by union leaders even before the closure announcement. Now suspicions were growing about his motives. Many people viewed him as nothing more than a puppet for Abitibi and figured when the process was complete he would leap back to that company, where his loyalties really lay. "We felt his interests weren't Thunder Bay," says Bill Joblin, who was then vice-president of one of the CEP locals but not part of the bargaining.

Olsen and Ferguson were the sole negotiators for Provincial Papers. That left even other managers estranged from the process, increasing tensions (and subsequently creating problems, when the agreement had to be enacted by those other managers). In the end, the union coalition decided it would have to represent middle managers' interests in the negotiations. "There were about 80 of them and their futures were at stake but they had no say. We had a real problem with that," said Phil Poling, president of the Office and Professional Employees International Union, who was at the bargaining table. The unions fought successfully to gain them a representative on the board of directors.

Naturally, the most substantive issue was the wage cut. In an already harsh recession, with families struggling, employees were being asked to consider a one-fifth cut in their pay. Of course, that was probably better than having no job at all. For many employees, such unemployment might be long term since a shutdown would aggravate the local economic problems. Most of the employees were in their forties, and many had limited education; adjustment would be difficult as they lost their reasonably well-paid jobs. But psychologically, the severity of the wage reduction seemed to overshadow the positive effects associated with an employee buyout.

Another contentious issue was determining how many jobs would be eliminated—and from what areas of the operation. Eventually, negotiators agreed on 112 jobs—100 from the unionized workforce and 12 from non-unionized staff. But Poling pointed out that formula didn't develop through any systematic evaluation of operational efficiencies. It simply reflected the continuing "us-them" approach: after the magic number of 112 was developed, amounting to 17 percent of staff, it was then decided to cut 17 percent of "us" and 17 percent of "them." Moreover, the unions didn't feel that management was delivering a satisfactory list of who would be cut from its ranks since some of the people named had already left voluntarily.

Finally, management and the unions were at loggerheads about how to handle shares in the new company. Since the main objective of the unions was job security, they wanted an arrangement that would ensure longevity of ownership. Hallahan worried that if workers were suffering financially—and that was likely, after a 20 percent wage cut—they would be motivated to sell their shares to pick up some cash. If that happened, the workers could quickly lose their controlling ownership, leaving them working for less money without a substantial voice in the company.

Olsen disagreed, but eventually he would have to compromise. By the final agreement, unionized employees' shares could be sold only if they died, retired, or quit. The union also gained the right of first refusal: any employee tendering shares in those circumstances would first have to offer them to the group. Other provisions were also inserted to prevent the dilution of union shares. On the other hand, management and other non-unionized employees would be allowed to sell their shares after three years if a mechanism was available for that purpose.

As the deadline neared, the parties found themselves locked up in a Toronto airport hotel with veteran mediator Vic Tasse, whom Tanaka brought in to help bridge the differences. It was high-stakes negotiation time. Tanaka even remembers at one point an Abitibi official saying that the corporate plane was on the runway to fly up to Thunder Bay and close down the mill. He laughed at the threat: "The union may have resented it. But it was ludicrous. You don't need a plane to shut it down. You can pick up a phone. A lot of pressure tactics were being used by all sides."

On Friday, January 29—two days before the deadline—the management and union teams were able to agree on a broad outline of how the mill should run. That was an important breakthrough, since the workers would have a controlling share. In a climate of historic distrust, it was important to delineate the role of management and workers for the future. The shareholder agreement would state that management had the right and obligation to manage the employee-owned company under the direction of a CEO, who would respond to the board of directors. The employee owners could voice their concerns at the shareholders' meetings or through the board of directors.

Abitibi's deadline expired without a final agreement and without the threatened plant closure. Employees continued to report for their shifts. The focus now turned to negotiating the actual purchase of the mill from Abitibi and winning financial support from the Ontario government in order to seal a deal. As Tanaka remembers it, all eyes were on him: "Management was looking to the government for financing. The unions were looking to government for financing. The banks were looking to government for financing. And Abitibi was looking to the government for financing."

But he was looking to Abitibi-Price. He reminded them that it would cost the company money to shut down the plant. His team put it at $32 million and the union at $40 to $45 million. Abitibi never disclosed its calculation), but when company officials met with Tanaka they came up with a figure close to his own. He persuaded them to direct some of that money into launching the new company, reducing what the government would have to contribute.

The company agreed to provide $15 million to fund operations and an additional $5 million if more employees were laid off in the next five years. The company would also transfer over all assets and liabilities of the mill to the employees for $1. The government would offer a $6.5 million direct loan and an $11.5 million loan guarantee, as well as ensure a 20-year supply of wood fibre. Tanaka viewed the loan guarantee as primarily for optics: "If Abitibi's money and our loan was used up and the business was going south, then the business was probably over. But if they only needed a few million more, we would have given it."

Otherwise, the deal—announced on February 4, 1993, just after the deadline—resembled the initial proposal. The employees would take a 20 percent pay cut and agree to lose 112 jobs. The mill—New Provincial Papers—would be 75 percent owned by employees as a group and 25 percent by management. Shares were distributed to non-management according to pay levels: an employee making $30,000 a year got 30,000 shares while somebody making $45,000 received 45,000 shares. But management's portion was divided in two. They would receive 15 percent of the total company shares immediately, according to salary levels. The CEO would give out the final 10 percent as bonuses over the next four years, depending on performance evaluations.

Finding a CEO

Tanaka was concerned about that management. He suspected Olsen wouldn't hang around in the new operation, given the resentment that had developed towards him. And he was also leery that Dennis Bunnell, who had been brought in as general manager the previous year, might also decide to move elsewhere. Provincial, after all, was still a shaky operation, without an ability to pay huge salaries or offer much scope for management advancement.

As a safety valve, when recruiting board members, Tanaka tapped Ian Ross, who had impressed him while serving on the Eastern Ontario Development Board. Ross had previous experience in the pulp and paper industry. A lawyer, called to the bar in 1968 but who never practised, he had worked in export financing before joining Ottawa entrepreneur Rod Bryden's holding company in 1979, to help take Bryden's prized Systemhouse Inc. public. But on Ross's first day on the job, Bryden announced they were heading to Trenton, where he had just bought Trent Valley Board Paper. Bryden had invested $500,000 and advised Ross, "I made the commitment; you find the money." Instead of helping to finance a computer company, Ross was now in the pulp and paper business. They built that business, through acquisitions, from $12 million in revenues to $1.5 billion in about eight years.

Ross was therefore a handy man to have around on the Provincial board. Just how handy became clear on May 29, when John Olsen didn't show up at the official signing ceremony at the mill to mark its transfer from Abitibi to the employees. The expected new president was remaining with Abitibi-Price. And although Bunnell became acting president, board members found themselves unable to pin him down for signing a contract. Soon they found out the reason: he would leave as well, in the fall.

New company. New board. New operating concept. And no CEO.

Finding a new one would be difficult. At best, it would take four to six months to recruit a new leader. And could the company attract someone with the right stuff to Thunder Bay, to run a relatively tiny operation? Indeed, management staffing would be a problem in general, because some of the skills supplied previously by the corporate parent would now have to be handled by senior staff at the mill, who would be expecting salaries commensurate with their greater responsibilities.

That's when Tanaka took Ross out for a drink in Toronto. Ross didn't feel the board should let Bunnell stay until September but should ask him to leave immediately. And Tanaka didn't think the company could wait for the fall for new leadership, given its precarious position, because it could die.

"That's when he looked at me," Ross recalls. "I said, 'Don't even think about it.'"

But they did. And Ross agreed, reluctantly, to consider taking the job. The next step was a telephone conference call among the three independent directors of the board: Ross; Jim Foulds, the long-time NDP representative at Queen's Park, who had been asked by the union to sit on the board; and business executive Bill Bodenhammer. Ross, who was working at the time as a consultant with small technology companies, realized he had the flexibility to take the post and was the only hope for an immediate leader.

He flew to the mill to talk to the employees, who had never met him. He was blunt: "I'm not sure we can turn this around, but I'll do my best." And they were blunt. The second question was, "When will you move to Thunder Bay?" It was a classic test from those suspicious of outsiders. And Ross gave the answer they didn't want to hear: "I'll move to Thunder Bay when all our customers are in Thunder Bay—and I suspect that will be in a long time. I'll be where the sales are, in Montreal, Toronto and the Northeastern U.S. But you'll see more of me than you want to."

The New Strategy

To his mind, boosting sales was the key to the future. And in the end, deals with major clients revolved around the CEO, who had to be in contact with senior officials at companies like Quebecor, Maclean Hunter, and the Transcontinental Group. He also knew he had to bring harmony among the sales, manufacturing, and marketing teams. The previous sales manager had lived in Chicago and visited the plant only once a month. That distance led to typical departmental sparring, with sales claiming it could sell the product but the mill couldn't make it, and production claiming they could make plenty of it but sales didn't know how to sell it.

Ross wanted a more market-focused company. He hoped to shed some of the customers who were too expensive to satisfy. He also wanted to bring new products onstream, opening up new markets. The company had three paper machines but one was idle so Ross needed to find something to produce on it. He recruited new managers of sales and marketing; he overhauled the sales force, converting them from order takers, selling on price with no concern about cost, to a team whose compensation depended on the bottom line.

The product development team was unfocused, with over 100 possible new products under consideration. Ross transferred responsibility for that function to marketing and reduced their scope to two products. The first was wet-strength label paper, which can be put in a cooler with ice yet still stick firmly to a beer bottle. That wasn't a popular product for larger mills because it needed specialized equipment as well as slower runs. It also offered higher margins, another big attraction for Ross. In 18 months, Provincial would capture 37 percent of the North American market for wet-strength labels.

The second new product was a matte paper for textbooks that could be produced on the idle machines. That was developed in association with a friend Ross had at Simon & Schuster publishers. But the quality of Provincial's product was not the best and it was harder to grow that market.

Unionized employees had elected two employees to the board of directors: union coalition leader Hallahan and Dolores Maki, a quality control tester who had previously been on her union executive. But it would take time for them to get familiar with board procedures and for their constituency to become familiar with the limitations of employee ownership.

"It was like an implosion at the start," Hallahan recalls. "Everyone felt, 'It's my mill—management should listen to me.' But you can't listen to 700 people. Then they would look at their workmates and say, 'He's not working as hard as me.' They'd continually bitch."

Although changes had occurred in senior management, on the mill floor nothing really changed when Abitibi-Price left. It was the same work and the same managers—but with less pay. Matich saw his own income drop nearly $10,000, from $45,700 in 1992 to $35,000 in 1993, the year of the transfer, and $38,550 the next year, as some overtime kicked in. His mortgage was paid and his expenses minimal, so his lifestyle didn't really change and he continued to take an annual vacation. He could remain optimistic.

But others weren't as lucky. "The 20 percent pay cut was traumatic," recalls John Brophy, then head of manufacturing. "When you've got a family and you are probably mortgaged to the hilt and your whole financial structure is based on wages, a 20 percent pay cut can destroy your family. And I think in certain cases it did."

Employees were told to be proud since they owned the plant. But for some, it was at a significant cost personally. Brophy says that was reflected in the workplace, where workers never displayed any significant improvement in productivity or attitude. "When your home life and outside pressures are stressing you out, it's pretty hard to be positive at work," he observes.

Struggling with Employee Participation

Additionally, the advice from Kapuskasing had not been taken. No procedures had been developed in the negotiations for making employee ownership at Provincial Papers translate into employee participation.

Recipe for Burnt EO Stew
à la Provincial Papers

Ingredients:

- Twenty years of adversarial union-management relations
- Five different, competitive unions representing different employee groups
- One set of unrealistic deadlines for negotiating buyout conditions

Instructions:

Mix the above ingredients well, then add several paragraphs of vague and poorly written clauses in the buyout agreement. Fold in no interested investor or partner, and sprinkle liberally with resistance to change, refusal to heed other companies' experience, and confusion over roles. Bring to a boil over the heat of conflict until the stew reaches a high temperature and burns on the bottom.

Serves only a buyer or investor with a strong digestive system.

Worse, the managers who dealt with employees daily had been shut out of those negotiations and had no idea how to translate the goodwill of the Toronto agreement into goodwill in overseeing the mill. "We should have been part of the negotiations," insists Brophy. "When the union leaders came back they said, 'You weren't even there. What do you know?' So it didn't start off well. It was like starting off in a big hole and trying to work your way out of it instead of starting off nice and fresh on a level playing field and going forward."

Management met regularly with the union coalition, allowing them input. "It wasn't co-management but it was participation to a great extent," Ross believes. But that's not how it was necessarily seen by the rank and file. The view grew that union representatives were simply in cahoots with management. There was also a lot of anger that employee board members often couldn't report on critical matters because of confidentiality requirements.

Suggestion boxes were tried, but the company found too many of the ideas were submitted without much thought and proved unrealistic. It cost a lot, in time and money, to investigate each proposal, and so that initiative waned. New work systems were tested but the company never committed fully to them, Brophy says, because it couldn't get enough mutual trust between management and the unions to go further.

A 16-person team drawn from all areas of the mill visited other employee-owned operations to scout alternative work systems. But nothing ever resulted. Ross remembers employees turning on the union representatives for partaking in the tour: "They said, 'You guys were just going out of town for fun. We know what to do here. We don't have to learn from elsewhere.' They said that to their own representatives."

Hallahan remembers it differently—management refusing to implement any ideas it received because that would mean giving up power. "Nobody wanted to change," he complains. That includes union members, about two-thirds of whom, Foulds estimates, preferred the traditional adversarial relationship with management to the new co-operative form that their coalition leader was championing. A revolt brewed. Finally, fed up and determined to give more time to his family, Hallahan stepped down from his posts. Bill Joblin emerged as a powerful force, with a much harder line.

He was furious that the management that had brought the mill to near bankruptcy was essentially still in control. And worse, those managers had taken a smaller percentage pay cut than union members while getting a bigger share of the pie individually. He was appalled at front-line supervisors; he considered them still stuck in the 1960s, yelling and using intimidation when the employees needed education. And he wasn't any fonder of upper management as a group, viewing them as recalcitrant and operating from a very different perspective. "We had to battle for everything. Put pressure on. Create animosity," he says. "We aren't like the managers. We can't go anywhere else to work. We don't have the university degrees. We came from high school, went into the mill, and this is all we have."

Joblin also wasn't happy with the union's board representatives, believing they lacked the skills to take on management. "It's pretty intimidating to come off the industrial floor and go onto a board of directors. Things no doubt are confusing and the hand doesn't go up because you're intimidated." He originally had wanted the union to nominate a renowned local labour lawyer for one of the posts and back its representatives with legal and accounting consultants who could help them grapple with the challenge.

Dealing with the unions while also trying to heighten the company's marketing efforts was, Ross says, like climbing a mountain with a steamer trunk on your back. He claims the unions were so divided that the coalition leader, Conrad Fournier, even had to get approval of agendas from colleagues before being allowed to meet with management. "I concluded their involvement was a necessary evil," he says. "There wasn't a willingness to take accountability. They seemed to want a right of veto but there was no willingness to make decisions together and live with the consequences."

He believes that employees never truly understood the difference between being a shareholder and being an employee. "If you own stock in Bell you don't run into [BCE CEO] Jean Monty's office every day and tell him how to run operations. At Provincial, all the individual owners thought they had the right to do whatever they wanted." And the union, he insisted, was willing to play either the ownership card or the adversarial union card, depending on which would offer the best results at that particular time.

He considers employee ownership in a manufacturing facility an oxymoron, because when an employee owner enters the mill to do the daily job, he or she must necessarily assume the role of employee. The ownership role, on the other hand, must wait for monthly performance results. That tension and lack of clarity in roles negatively affects morale, he believes. On that score, at least, Joblin fully agrees, not believing employee ownership can work: "You have to put on two hats. It's very hard to be a member of a union and an owner. It's almost contradictory. One hat wants shareholder value to go up and the other wants security."

Tanaka also has reservations about employee ownership, despite having negotiated several deals. He believes it can work only in non-unionized operations. A union executive inevitably runs into conflict between its mandate to fight for job security, clear work rules, and equal pay for employees versus the new ownership role of promoting flexibility and greater profits. "It can work," he concedes. "But at Provincial there was too much history—too much animosity."

And the history they were writing wasn't picture perfect. The plant made a profit just two months after the new regime began; the next year management was even able to provide employees with shoe subsidies and a few other modest monetary signs of good faith, given that wages were frozen for two years. But Provincial Papers was still a high-cost producer. As management continued to tackle that issue, it became

Role Confusion about Employee Ownership at Provincial Papers

The anger and divisions at Provincial Papers demonstrated in the following arguments reflects a role confusion that was never suitably sorted out.

- It's my mill. Management should listen to me.

- It wasn't co-management, but it was participation to a great extent.

- Union representatives are simply in cahoots with management.

- Management refused to implement any idea it received because that would mean giving up power.

- We had to battle for everything. Put pressure on. Create animosity.

- I concluded their (union) involvement was a necessary evil. There wasn't a willingness to take accountability. They seemed to want a right of veto, but there was no willingness to make decisions together and live with the consequences.

- All the individual owners thought they had the right to do whatever they wanted.

- You have to put on two hats. It's very hard to be a member of a union and an owner. It's almost contradictory. One hat wants shareholder value to go up and the other wants security.

- The board did feel that involving the employees was important, but we simply failed at it—partly because we started late and partly because we couldn't get by the split in the work force between those who had the traditional adversarial view of labour and management and those who wanted to carve out a new model.

- The team that wins the Stanley Cup has the best chemistry. We didn't have it. We were always fighting.

clear to them that more layoffs would be necessary, particularly as margins were cut in 1996 and the company started to lose money.

The union executive was unwilling to swallow that prescription. Ross remembers being told by one union leader that it would be better to keep 700 jobs for two more years than to have 600 people working at the mill indefinitely. "I told him, 'You might as well just drink the Kool Aid now, like in Jonestown,'" Ross says.

Buyout, Again

Consultants had searched for new investment but had come up short. Another owner would have to be found. That was the escape that Tanaka had always envisaged anyway, believing the buyout could only be a bridge to a sale. Now a private consultant and a member of the board, he felt new owners were urgently needed given the increasingly inflammatory situation at Provincial. "Management was getting beaten down psychologically and emotionally by the constant negativism. I felt if we didn't sell the sucker, it would go down," he says.

Management was talented and marketable—and would soon eject for a less hostile working environment. Ross could easily move on. And Brophy had already turned down several offers; the board managing to retain him despite being unable even to give him any bonus. "We tapped out on goodwill with him," Tanaka says. "It gets to the point where it's simply not worth it for senior management—the pot of gold at the end of the rainbow is too small."

One person who was devastated at the prospect of a sale was Jim Foulds. To him, employee ownership may not be a panacea but it is definitely a moral beacon—a way for workers to gain some control over their lives and work. "I was ideologically committed to employee ownership, and I found it very difficult when it became apparent that it had to change. It's not too melodramatic to say I was heartbroken. Ordinary people have very little access to the levers of power and employee ownership is one of those," he says. "But you have to be practical. Hateful as it is, you have to operate within the international capitalist market."

Employee ownership requires a change of culture that never occurred at Provincial. Foulds accepts his share of the blame for that: "The board did feel that involving the employees was important, but we simply failed at it—partly because we started late, and partly because we couldn't get by the split in the work force between those who had the traditional adversarial view of labour and management and those who wanted to carve out a new model." Another factor: as a small company Provincial could never overcome the extra overhead costs required to have its own senior managers in areas like finance, marketing, and sales rather than count on the resources of a larger parent. "When you're on the borderline where $200,000 can make the difference between profit or not, just one of those positions can make the difference," he notes.

Ross had expected a sale from the start: "The strategy had to be to turn it around and steer it to safe harbour. As an orphan mill it couldn't last indefinitely; the industry is too cyclical." Indeed, when management had been seeking outside financing, a study ranking producers from high to low cost found Provincial twenty-sixth from the bottom— a comparatively high-cost performer.

RBC Dominion Securities was hired to find a buyer and found 20 expressions of interest. Four companies toured the facility, but when it came to the next stage, signing a letter of intent, only one remained in the hunt: Rolland Inc., a leading manufacturer of coated and uncoated specialty fine papers and de-inked pulp, which is 73 percent owned by Cascade Inc.

The initial offer was $24.5 million, but RBC Dominion Securities managed to ratchet that up to $26 million, which Ross considers very lucky since there were no competitors. In effect, the plant the employees had bought four years earlier for $1 was now worth $26 million. The employees could share in that lucre; it would amount to about $30,000 for senior workers, roughly making up for the lower wages they had endured due to the pay cut.

But there was still a major obstacle before the deal could be confirmed. Management had not fully received the 10 percent of the shares that during the buyout negotiations it had decided to put in a special pool for incentives. And the union leadership insisted those shares be put back in the general pie. Management resisted.

Tanaka was horrified. "I told the union, 'you aren't on the moral high ground here,'" he says. "If I had been a union member, I would have been ashamed. It was ethically wrong. The contract was there. Management's share was small compared to the work they had done."

But the dispute escalated, with employees viewing it as a battle between their receiving money and the managers'—notably Brophy and Ross—receiving money. "From their perspective," says Ross, "I was just an interloper there to line my own pockets anyway." In the end, unsure how the union membership vote on the Rolland deal would turn out—it appeared likely to be very close—Ross advised the board to concede the point to the union, even though it would cost him a significant amount of money. "I said, 'I'm not smart enough to know whether if we hang tough the deal will go down. This is too important to everyone; we need this deal,'" he says.

Many workers still saw Ross as an outsider but he had won some fans. Maki recalls being told by a fellow union member when Ross's appointment was originally being considered that he was so nice that you just wanted to pretend he was your dad: "He has a heart. That may have hurt him; he could have been stronger. But given our situation, he did a wonderful job." Hallahan concurs: "Ross worked his buns off. I have nothing bad to say about him. He kept us going." Foulds says a CEO had to be close to customers but Ross would have fared better if he'd had a home in Thunder Bay, even one he hardly ever used. "There was a perception that he wasn't a Thunder Bay person and didn't understand the work force. That perception was misplaced. Ian was a good CEO and did his best to understand the workforce. I know at times he felt equally frustrated by management and employees and buoyed by them. He's a genuinely decent and nice man."

Assessing the Experience

The deal was overwhelming approved, with well over 90 percent of union members supporting it. But at the same time, doubts lingered over the price and resentment over having to sell. Of course, Hallahan stresses that there were still people who at that point insisted the original buyout was wrong-headed, arguing either that Abitibi-Price had been bluffing or that it would have been better to simply shut down the plant. "It must be in the drinking water," he says of the negativism. "I can't fathom it." Dolores Maki blames gender: "Men sure can be bastards to each other. It's really unfortunate when people's egos come into play."

Matich had been an optimist throughout. He had felt moderately closer to management during the period of employee ownership. "I was trying to think of us as family. We were all working for the same goal, to survive. I didn't think confrontation within the family would help. You don't get anywhere by beating each other up," he says. That meant becoming widely known amongst colleagues on the shop floor as "the management man," but he refused to buckle under, uncomfortable as it was, trying to stay objective.

That objectivity now led him to believe the plant had been sold for too little. He had heard valuations of $37 million to $57 million for the plant. A new paper machine, he notes, can cost $500 million.

Here Rolland was picking up three paper machines—and a trained work force—for $26 million. "I felt betrayed when I heard the number $26 million. All along I supported the management but in the end I feel we got taken by Rolland. I feel the top management sold out," he says.

Maki, now off the board, supported the sale but also felt burned afterwards. Consultants had previously told Provincial it needed to invest $36 million in new equipment; since that would take too many years to generate from profits, a new owner was essential. But in fact after the sale she learned that Rolland simply allocates capital to a mill from the profit that mill itself generates, so any new investment at Provincial must come from Provincial. "I feel we were deluded in the sale," she says.

Rolland, which officially took over on May 1, 1997, streamlined the operation, introducing badly needed computerization of operations. Brophy was appointed general manager and Ross left, since Rolland's CEO would take over stewardship. Management was cut by 25 percent and an early retirement incentive was offered to downsize the union workforce by 20 percent while keeping younger people. Bill Joblin, of all people, says, "Rolland did everything we should have done. They cut the fat and were disciplined. The team that wins the Stanley Cup has the best chemistry. We didn't have it. We were always fighting."

Ironically, revenues improved almost from the moment Rolland took over, and, as the mill started to rebound financially, the employees saw some of that in their own pocket since Rolland has a profit-sharing plan. Rolland also threw $200,000 on the table to adjust some union wage rates upwards. And a new five-and-a-half-year labour agreement was signed, giving an annual two percent wage hike and making allowance for up to another two percent, depending on cash flow generated. But the plant workers still lag behind their counterparts at sister plants, as a result of the 1993 pay cut. "We'll never catch up," says Joblin. "Our sister local at Bowater is making $8 to $10 more an hour. At one time we were on par with them."

Yet, despite all the problems, he still views the period of employee ownership as a success. "I still have employment. I still have security. Thunder Bay still has 600 people working at a good wage. We saved our jobs," he says. Ross views the experience as one of the biggest challenges of his life—one he hopes never to repeat. "But we succeeded. We put out new products and made money. There was a dedication, funny as it seemed at times. We fought because we were family. It was schizophrenic," he says.

The main lesson to be drawn from the Provincial experience, obviously, is that management and union must from the start develop harmony and some sense of how they are going to use employee ownership. "Vague will kill you," says Hallahan. In forced buyouts, generally with the clock ticking, it's difficult to settle those matters. But it's harder to do on the run, afterwards, particularly when the climate changes. Joblin recalls that even at Provincial there was a love-in atmosphere at the start. But it collapsed pretty quickly, as old rivalries re-emerged: "If you want to be a skeptic, there are a lot of bullets to put in your gun. You don't have to look very far."

Maki believes it's important to clarify the role union board members assume. Do they represent the union or the members? What happens if there is conflict between those two roles, with the board members feeling the union is not really representing the average worker?

Often employee ownership draws people to the new board who have never served in such a post before. Maki and Foulds found themselves in that situation and believe training must be provided rather than expecting such individuals to learn on the job. Maki remembers initially being confused over terms like "generally accepted accounting principles." At the same time, they both stress that those handicaps can be overcome, because the main role of a board member is to use judgment. "I thought I needed to know everything, but that's not so," says Maki. "It's due diligence. You look for what is amiss and ask it be looked into. You're the overseer, not the person doing the work. But it took a few meetings to learn that."

Stan Kuzmich, manager of operations, has supervised the workforce under employee ownership as well as two different parent companies. With employee ownership, he found more politics—horsetrading and compromises—in decision-making. It was also harder to maintain discipline. The union contract became just a guideline; sweetheart deals were always being worked out, with leniency the norm. More people, for example, would be allowed off in peak vacation periods, stretching the rules. "It became almost voluntary to run on a statutory holiday. You had to take a vote," he observes.

He also compares the inability to cut the workforce under employee ownership with the downsizing that Rolland achieved: "You can take a harder line [with a regular ownership]." On the other hand, employee ownership guaranteed there would not be any work stoppages. Despite the politics, decisions could be made more quickly since they could be taken on site. When an issue arose, union and management could meet, reach a settlement, and sign off. Now they both have to check that the settlement is aligned with policies at other mills. And he felt there was a greater pride of workmanship under employee ownership. "You got more buy-in under employee ownership. It made my life easier," he says.

As for Matich, his advice for those contemplating employee ownership is simple: "Try to work together. Try to find the positive and eliminate the negative. Try not be cats fighting amongst yourselves."

Integra Geoservices

&&

Through Thick and Thin

*"People saw the only way to make money was a one-time
sale of the company and lost sight of having control of their
own job or the feeling of ownership."*

—Jan Dewar, senior processing geophysicist
and board member

When the Calgary office of Houston-based Landmark Graphics spun itself off as an employee-owned company in 1994, it had to find a new name to symbolize the new venture. In the end, they chose Integra Geoservices, to highlight the integrated nature of the seismic data processing solutions they offered the oil and gas industry.

But when people at Integra talk about their brief, four-year interlude with employee ownership, there are a surprising number of divergent views. All are agreed on one stark fact, however: without employee ownership, the company would likely have folded in 1995, when it hit a rough spell in just its second year of independence.

Employee ownership kept people focused. They stayed with the company, rather than leaving. And they worked harder than ever—at a company already known for hard work—to make their company and their investment successful. "It's different when you have a major chunk of money on the line. You'll do what it takes to keep the company growing," says Henry Leong, a seismic processing team leader. Jonathan Downton, vice-president of geosciences, concurs: "When we went through tough times it kept the company together. In other companies, when you have tough times, people vamoose."

But in part because of that memory—and the fear of someday having to scramble again to save their investment in the boom-bust industry they serve—Integra employees decided in 1998 to cash in and return to the bosom of a large company. Employee ownership brought many advantages and several significant disadvantages. In the end, the prime factor was that it involved financial ownership—being an entrepreneur, and putting your cash on the line. "We worried about whether we could weather bad times again. Would we have to work like dogs again to dig ourselves out? There's an advantage to just being an employee," notes Leong. With a chance to get back ten times their investment after just four years, it was a fairly easy decision to sell their shares and become employees again.

From Inverse to Integra

Integra started life in 1981 as Inverse Theory and Applications Inc., an appropriately academic name for a venture founded by three graduate students and professors at the University of British Columbia. The company developed geophysical algorithms from which it produced software that it sold. Although initially located in Vancouver, it set up a sales office in Calgary in 1985 and within four years the entire company had relocated to that oil centre.

The firm's strength was that it developed one of the first interactive seismic data processing workstations. Instead of having to rely on mainframe computers, geophysicists were now afforded a hands-on opportunity to play with data at every stage of their analysis. The company sold the software and associated hardware, and also offered a general data processing service.

Inverse met with success and grew rapidly, to the point that in 1990 Landmark made an unsolicited offer to buy them out. The idea was to combine Inverse's geophysical integration software with mapping software that Landmark had acquired from another company in Austin, Texas. Initially, the plan was for everyone in Calgary to stay put, providing the full range of service from research and development to customer support. But two years later, the research and development team was relocated to corporate headquarters in Houston, where they could work more closely with their counterparts. That left Calgary as only a service operation, under manager Mark Klingbeil.

The Landmark years were not hugely pleasurable for the former Inverse crowd and in 1994 they hit a crisis when head office decided that the Calgary service operation was not contributing enough revenue to the company—a fair assessment given that its revenue covered

Choosing a Course

As they considered options for their unit in the wake of its difficulties within Landmark, Mark Klingbeil and the others in the Calgary office saw four options:

1. The operation might be sold to another company.

2. The operation might simply be shut down, with the staff left unemployed.

3. They could attempt a management buyout of the Calgary office.

4. They could attempt a broader, employee buyout of the Calgary office.

If they wanted to preserve their current work environment, those four options quickly dissolved into two: the alternative methods of buying the operation from Landmark. And of the two, a management buyout on the surface seemed preferable. It was smoother and less complicated. Management was a smaller and more homogeneous group than the entire 21-person office. Indeed, the financial advisors brought in to help structure the deal pointed out that 80 percent of money in employee buyouts generally comes from the 20 percent of staff who are managers, so it made sense to confine the effort to managers.

But there was a powerful counterargument that won out. The office was a service operation, dependent on the skills and enthusiasm of its employees. Motivationally, it made sense to bring as many people in as owners as possible. With an employee buyout, Jonathan Downton noted, "everyone would share in the success of the company or have an opportunity to share in the success of the company. Everybody would be committed and would be trying to make the company succeed. It would be a joint effort rather than the effort of one or two people."

only 50 percent of overhead. A burst of changes occurred in quick succession as they tried to fix the problem, but the realization soon set in that the Calgary operation would always have difficulty meeting Landmark's goals. Landmark decided to exit the service end of the business.

After deciding on employee ownership rather than a management buyout, the next difficulty was learning more about employee ownership. They searched for a Canadian company that had gone through a similar experience and came up empty. They found a few magazine articles and picked the brains of a benefits counsellor, but without any significant success. "It was really frustrating," says Klingbeil. "Basically we had no models we could look to. Our information was really limited."

Employees were also divided. It was a traumatic issue: should they gamble by investing money to keep their current company alive and thereby retain their jobs, or should they gamble by letting it shut down and count on finding other jobs reasonably quickly? Neither option was one that the employees wanted to face—and neither was particularly appetizing, except for those with a natural entrepreneurial bent.

Moreover, the base for a buyout was shaky since employees held a healthy level of distrust towards the management group. But overall, the prevailing sentiment favoured a buyout, for four different reasons, depending on the individual evaluating the prospect: the investment opportunity; the control, which would be greater than under a large company; continuity; and security. People knew what their current jobs required and were comfortable with the technology they were selling. It made sense to stay together, if possible.

Ron Tinline, manager of special projects, who had previously owned a business in Denver, was actually quite optimistic since he knew the company had a strong infrastructure and talented people. "It takes quite awhile to build a good infrastructure—generally three years —and we had that. So I wasn't worried about the immediate future." But Tom French, who was central with Klingbeil in negotiating the deal, feels that the dominant motivation was security: "A lot of people bought jobs rather than buying for an investment. They bought for the wrong reasons." Buying for security, he argues, is not negative but it's also not positive, since when the immediate crisis disappears, the motivation for being an owner fades. Indeed, management throughout the discussions tried to discourage employees from acting out of a job-saving impulse. But that was like trying to stop Niagara Falls from running. With closure of the office a possibility, security was just too powerful a force.

Negotiating an agreement between the employees took about a month. One major issue was whether a new company could pay sufficiently high salaries to attract quality people. The result was a variable compensation scheme, in which employees would be guaranteed a certain base pay and then—whether owners or not—share in a large chunk of the profits. That would allow pay to balloon in good years and retract in bad years. The profits would not be shared equally but be allotted according to merit.

Although some employees didn't favour this system, the majority felt it was a clever way to structure some of the risk ahead. However, that meant everybody was forced to take a cut in regular pay. In some cases, that would amount to only 10 to 15 percent. But for other people, it rose as high as 40 to 50 percent, increasing the venture's entrepreneurial risk.

Another fundamental issue was the disbelief amongst many employees that this new project would actually succeed. "Geophysicists are very skeptical and conservative by nature," observes Klingbeil, an accountant by training. "The employees questioned how a new company could be profitable when the Calgary office had effectively been losing money over time. There was a real skepticism about the revenue that was out there."

Management held a meeting with all the employees to discuss possible revenue. Klingbeil told them, "In any business, a lot of the time you don't know where the revenue is going to come from or when it's going to come. You just know it's out there based on past performance." Management argued that since they already had a handle on where about 70 percent of the revenue they needed to break even would come from, they could be comfortable that the other 30 percent would be unearthed.

To address the distrust of management, Klingbeil and his team pledged to run an open-book company. That would mean all information, even financial statistics and payroll, would be available to everyone. Included in that was the variable compensation scheme: everyone would know exactly what share of the profit pie everybody else was scheduled to receive.

The final major issue to settle was the nature of shareholding. Should every employee be required to be a shareholder? Should shares be available only to employees? Would shares be given away or be paid for? They ultimately agreed that shares would be bought and shareholding would be distinct from being an employee. Some employees could choose not to buy shares.

As well, shareholders would not have day-to-day control of the company. Instead, management would continue to manage. Shareholders would elect representatives to the board of directors, which could hire and fire the president and give general policy directions. But the rest of the management team was chosen by—and reported to—the president. In that way, employee shareholders would have general control of the company, but the role of being a shareholder would not be so extensive as to interfere with the employee's daily work. It also meant shareholding employees wouldn't be wandering off to special meetings every few days to make decisions while their non-shareholding colleagues stayed at their desks, grousing.

As those parameters were being developed, management began to negotiate with Landmark. Again the negotiations were quick, since both sides shared a common objective. Landmark wanted the Calgary office spun off into a viable organization since that operation would be selling Landmark technology; the employees also wanted to ensure their new organization would be viable.

Landmark agreed to give the new company three years to pay off in monthly instalments the costs of their current office furniture and computer equipment. It also furnished a working capital loan, because the new company had no track record and wouldn't have much chance of getting assistance from a bank. As well, Landmark gave the company access to its technology for a three-year period at a cost of $750,000. Access to this technology was critical if the new company wanted to continue servicing existing customers and eventually develop its own technology.

In return, Landmark demanded it be relieved of any severance claims for the employees being set adrift. That became even more controversial when Landmark gave three employees a significant lump sum payment in recognition of their service to Landmark but argued it was not severance. In retrospect, some employees were probably not clear on the value of what was being given up. Landmark, of course, was: severance would be a substantial sum even compared to the financial assistance it was offering the new company.

The final edginess was over the size of the employee investment. Landmark wanted to know that the employees would contribute enough to fund the new enterprise, since otherwise it was bearing much of the financial risk. But management couldn't tell exactly who would be investing, or how much, since employees were uncertain or playing it close to the vest. "We didn't know exactly what some people were thinking. They would tell you one thing and later you would hear rumours that they were not really going to invest that much money. They were just playing along because they were scared that otherwise they would not have a job," recalls Tom French.

But Landmark kept pressing and management was caught in the middle, thinking it could raise the agreed amount but not sure. In the end, 18 of the 21 employees invested, contributing a total of $250,000. It was enough—but only for the time being, as it turned out.

The New Company Hits Rocky Times

On March 31, 1994, the deal took effect and those 18 employees were owners of Integra, with Klingbeil as president. And the distrust that existed soon magnified. It was fuelled when management took the bulk of the spots on the new board. But it also flowed from the nature of being shareholders. Everyone had an opinion on everything. And nearly everybody was now chintzy about spending, since it was coming out of their pockets twice—once reducing the amount up for grabs in the variable compensation scheme and then a second time reducing the potential dividends they might receive.

French had worked previously for an employee-owned company in the United States, CH2M Hill Inc., which handed shares out as performance bonuses rather than requiring them to be bought. "There was a different mentality here," he says of Integra. "People put up hard cash to get the shares and expected more in return. They expected to be able to put their two cents in. We were schizoid. If there was a major purchase, there was a lot of second-guessing going on." When they decided to hold an out-of-town Christmas party with the company picking up the hotel tab for everyone, complaints were rampant.

And that was in the good times. It only worsened when they hit a financial crisis in late 1995. In retrospect, they had probably become somewhat cocky and expanded too quickly—and were now paying the price, as expenses soared and revenues didn't. Nine new employees had been added, bringing the total to 30. Over $300,000 had been invested in new computer work stations, providing not just greater processing power but opening the door—with the recent addition of a controversial supercomputer—to returning to research and development.

The first signals came in June, as they lost money. For the next seven months, loss followed loss. But although the financial reports were shared and discussed at monthly all-hands meetings, a general paralysis gripped the company. One employee suggested, "When mistakes were made, people were not held accountable. Nobody ever got reprimanded because it was always a collective responsibility." In this case, collectively or individually, nobody was ringing the alarm bells.

When the wake-up bells came, the company responded with a cash call, asking employees to buy more shares, provide a loan, or guarantee a loan with the bank. But response was tepid. The key managers bought more shares, changing the ownership profile from one that was reasonably equal—with nobody holding more than 7 percent of shares—to one in which the top three managers now controlled 48 percent of the company. That would only intensify the divide between the two groups, however, and the second-guessing. French feels that he, Klingbeil, and Downton began increasingly to view Integra as a normal small company that they effectively owned and were managing with a high degree of employee input, while the staff, of course, still viewed it as employee-owned.

In January 1996, management announced that some employees would have to be laid off. Although financial information had been shared with everybody, many employees were still shocked to learn how significant the financial problems actually were. It was also difficult for some employees to accept that even though they were employee owners they were still vulnerable to having their employment terminated. By mid-February the staff had been reduced by 9 employees to 21. Teams were dissembled, and management began to run the company in a more top-down fashion.

The financial situation improved and Integra became profitable on a monthly basis. The R&D effort continued and began to produce some new products that could be offered to customers. By the end of the year, the company even began hiring again, adding about one person per quarter.

Struggling with Board Issues

The company was selling itself as an employee-owned company, finding receptivity amongst clients. They wanted a service provider that they could trust and felt more comfortable with employee owners. But Integra found that it had to apply the same formula to itself, Klingbeil recalls. "We basically developed a little bit of a mantra that for the customer to trust us we had to trust each other," he says.

To show trust, and tired of the innuendo, key management withdrew from their board positions, leaving it to other staff, with Klingbeil attending in his role as an officer. "We figured that we're managing the place; we don't need to be on the board," he says. "My perception was that managers had more trust in the employees than the employees had in the managers."

At the same time, he feels the board's effectiveness diminished and they floundered. The controller, who served as corporate secretary and had been ensuring the meetings ran professionally, was no longer attending. The group lacked the financial and strategic skills that a board would normally have. And the turnover was high, with many people staying only for their one-year term, so the board failed to develop a methodology and system of reports.

Members would come on the board feeling timid and would go along with the flow, says Downton. They wouldn't push a point. Then just as they were gathering confidence and knowledge, prepared to play a stronger role, their term would end and they would leave. "There was a perception that they were ineffective and not that powerful. They ended up being a sounding board for the president to work through ideas," he says.

French got so fed up he stopped even attending as an officer. He recalls working as a senior executive with the Petroleum Industry Training Service, where board members would deal with issues about the future of the industry and the organization over the next few years. But he feels Integra's board acted not as strategists but as police officers, double-checking what management did. "Our board meetings got down to where did this $62 get spent and why?" he says. To his mind, the board members simply didn't have the business skills— they were geologists after all, catapulted into the positions—to handle the job. "Mark wasn't bothered. But I was. I'd wonder, what are they spending three hours doing?"

Jan Dewar, a senior processing geophysicist who sat on the first and last board, agrees that the members were in over their heads and to some extent merely fulfilling the legal obligation to have a board. Indeed, she didn't see management's abdication of its board positions as positive. "I resented that they wouldn't look after their own interests and were forcing peons like me to do the work," she says.

She went back on the board in the final year because nobody else would serve. No remuneration was paid for board meetings and the company couldn't afford liability insurance, so many people were scared of sitting on the board. "I did it because somebody had to. I didn't enjoy it," she says.

Tinline is more positive, although he does agree the board was better in its first year—when managers were still members—because it set policy. But he feels that some of the issues that weren't settled by the board were very difficult matters, like how to diversify. "It was an advisory group, which a board should be. It should have control of the main manager on financial responsibilities, which it did," he says.

Leong always felt uncomfortable in his board role: "Although I was chairman and that sounded impressive, the task didn't fit the role." But he did feel the group was effective as a sounding board, helping to build buy-in. Dewar challenges that notion, however, since members were limited in what they could tell others about the board activities. She was initially warned to be clear when she spoke on issues outside meetings about whether she was talking for herself or the board. Eventually, she simply stopped talking to others about board issues since it was less complicated.

They talked of recruiting outsiders with better board skills. It was an obvious solution to the skill deficiency. But who would come onto a board that didn't pay and didn't even offer liability insurance? To protect themselves, the board members would have major decisions discussed at an all-hands meeting the week after each board meeting, checking that others were onside. Nigel Kellett, the chairman the last year and a half, feels that they should have brought in somebody who could train the board members and improve their skills. But still, he feels the board was better than people give it credit for being: "Some people say the board was just a front man for Mark. But there were issues we disagreed with him on and he followed us."

The open-book policy met with some success. As always with this program—which is used effectively in many non-employee-owned situations as well—the impacts of the financial statements and reports are limited by the extent to which employees understand the information. Klingbeil found in the early years that "scientists tend to see things differently than accountants. They tend to view things more graphically. It was a surprise for both myself and the controller how meaningless the information being given really was because the employees didn't understand what it meant in practical terms."

Bailing Out

In mid-'97 the oil industry started to crumble around Integra again, and some of its competitors hit serious trouble. Integra was actually faring

Effective Boards in an Employee Ownership Company: Issues and Suggestions

Issue	Suggestions
Employee Representation	• 0–1 is probably too few
	• 2 can work, depending on the total size of the board
	• 3 can work well, because employee reps have support from each other and can give effective input from various points of view.
	• a majority of the board—may not be optimal especially in a unionized company where relations with management are poor or where reps do not have sufficient business acumen.
	Don't leave out salaried employee reps in a unionized company. Be sure to seek outside directors as well as a balance of skills.
Training	Employee reps need training in the role and skills required for the job of board member. A good training program can mean the difference between a weak, conflict-prone, or demoralized board rep and an effective one.
Liability	In cases where directors may be liable for costs related to business failure, liability insurance is a must to encourage employee reps to serve.
Duties	Directors must act as the agent of the owners; set policy and goals to increase shareholder value; delegate operations to management and evaluate and supervise management's results; hire (and dismiss) the CEO; and ensure the terms of the employee ownership agreement are fulfilled. In addition, members must abide by the decisions of the board and respect the confidentiality of certain key information.

well. Some of the technology it had developed was highly useful for finding natural gas, and when oil prices went down, natural gas prices weren't affected. But fear grew that if Integra wasn't affected by the downturn that year it certainly would be the next year.

The company was productive. The pay-for-performance scheme was working well. But the company had been unable to raise any more capital, a problem that confronts smaller employee-owned ventures. New employees weren't interested in buying shares—at $400 apiece they were expensive—and old employees didn't want to add. Some employees who left had to be paid out, which depleted funds. The company wanted to expand—the next logical step was to open a seismic processing office in Houston and also try to sell specialty services there—but it lacked the $500,000 that venture was estimated to require over the near term.

The company was also running into a problem that Klingbeil terms "the elevator ride of value." At Integra's worst moment, February 1996, the company was worth virtually nothing if it had to be sold. Everyone would have lost his or her investment. Now, after two and a half years of profitability, it was probably worth 10 to 20 times earnings, a significant value per share. However, if they hit another recession, with no earnings, the company's value would drop or even disappear again.

Employee capital should theoretically be patient capital. Recessions may come and go but employees should be in for the long haul. In the oil industry, however—and in this particular slice of that industry—no guarantee existed that Integra would recover from a slide. Some people were patient and prepared to see the company grow over time, but at the same time they were also frightened about losing everything. Others were impatient, preferring to capitalize on their gains soon.

The third financial irritant was a $300,000 lump sum payment due to Landmark to cover the working capital loan. Paying in one burst would be a struggle, so Integra asked Landmark to give it some time. In the course of discussions, however, Landmark asked for some concessions in the technology licensing agreement that were unacceptable to Integra, since they would push the cost too high. By securing some early payment on receivables, Integra cleared the debt. But that meant, in turn, it had to slow down payments to employees on variable pay, since normally those flowed in harmony with receipts.

With those various issues floating around, Integra was approached by the Scott Pickford Group, a large U.K.-based geosciences consultancy that in turn was a wholly owned subsidiary of Core Laboratories, an international company with over 60 years of experience in the petroleum industry. Scott Pickford had a Houston operation and now wanted to push into Calgary to build up some seismic processing capacity. It was interested in either teaming up with Integra or buying the company out. For Integra, it boiled down to whether they wanted to fight another competitor—in what they expected to be a shaky period—or reduce the risk by joining forces.

Managers asked the staff—not just the shareholders—whether they would be willing to sell. And the answer came back quickly: What's the price? In the end, it was awfully good. The 15 remaining Integra shareholders traded their shares for Core Laboratories shares in a ratio that at that point was worth 10 times their original investment. "My understanding is that in venture capital if you are doing four or five times the original investment in five years that's a home run. So we were doing 10 times in five years," says Klingbeil. "It was a vindication—that we could turn this into a viable company."

A lock-up provision prevented them from converting those shares for a year, however. By then, the share price had dipped somewhat, reducing the return to about eight times the original investment—still a home run. Most of the shareholders kept their new shares rather than cashing in. "Not as many sold as I expected to. I don't know whether it's faith in the company, the industry, or the U.S. stock market," Klingbeil noted.

After the Sale

Not everyone relished selling off Integra—although nobody was talking about holding onto the firm in the long term. The dissent came from those who felt it would be wiser to hold on for a few more years because the value of their investment would multiply further. "My instinct was to hold on," says Tinline. "If we hung on for two or three years we probably would have got more money. But that's hindsight. You don't know."

However, those inclined to wait gave their approval to the deal when they realized how much support it had. There was little talk about the other values that were being sacrificed as they once again returned to being part of a large company. "People saw the only way to make money was a one-time sale of the company and lost sight of having control of their own jobs or the feeling of ownership," says Dewar.

French left, eager for change and not willing to work for a large corporation—particularly one traded on the U.S. stock exchange, given the quarterly bottom line pressures those companies face. Most who stayed felt an immediate change. Kellett noted that salaries were now higher, since the variable compensation scheme was brought closer to the less aggressive pay scheme of the parent. "I see it slowing down. It's more stable. People do the 8:00 to 4:00. People before would come in at 10:00 and work to midnight," he said. Ciprian Mihai, seismic processing manager, agreed: "The entrepreneurial spirit has disappeared. People don't count as much as in the past. We're part of a large company. It's a $500 million company and our effort counts for less than 1 percent—.08 percent, to be precise."

Klingbeil initially remained as president and general manager of the newly named Integra Scott Pickford, maintaining the open-book style for their own operations. He found that the parent left the Calgary group to manage its own affairs, with him reporting to Scott Pickford's managing director in the United Kingdom. "Instead of reporting to a five-person employee board I report to one guy, who works for a multinational company," he said with a laugh. "But it really doesn't change it. Our concern the three years prior to selling out was revenue and growth. And gee, that's exactly what Scott Pickford is concerned about: revenue and growth. So it's almost like business is business and the goal under either model is the same."

But that desire for revenue and growth led to a Calgary competitor being bought in mid-1999 and Integra being forcibly merged into the new operation. Klingbeil, who was to play a lesser role in the combined outfit, departed in May 2000, after overseeing his unit's move into the competitor's quarters and the integration of compensation plans. A culture clash arose fairly quickly between the two organizations. "People from the Integra side are unhappy with how they see the company managed," Klingbeil noted seven months after leaving. "There's a high expectation of openness. They have come to expect communication about what is going on and how they fit. Now, like 90 percent of the companies out there, they aren't getting it, and there is disappointment."

When a couple of ex-Integra employees were laid off, many of the old team gathered for a secret going-away lunch. Klingbeil was impressed by how calm the laid-off employees were, confident that with the skills they had picked up from employee ownership, they could go off and run their own businesses. "They weren't the victims that you usually see in other companies in that situation," he notes. Indeed, others were also musing about leaving the fold and starting their own ventures.

"I'm still a strong, strong believer in employee ownership," Klingbeil adds, noting that at another lunch with Jonathan Downton they had duelled over the matter, with his ex-colleague preferring that only key people have ownership. "I still believe that broad-based employee ownership is the way to go. It makes the business much more sensitive to the marketplace and what needs to happen. You are able to react and streamline costs easier than non-employee-owned companies in up and down markets. It's much more flexible."

But that flexibility has been lost. They all had something special. Something different. It had its limitations. But now, it's gone. "It probably took until we sold the company to clarify what we were doing it for," says Dewar. "But I don't hear people say, 'I wish we still owned it.' They curse that they have to do things that they don't want. But they don't talk of going back."

At the same time, the model worked. They kept together as a team. They grew their new company. Then, given their small size and the nature of the industry they were in, they joined up with a company that offered them greater resources, even if—as they expected—the new arrangements would include some bumpy times. And, yes, they all made some money—a home run, in fact.

Canadian Pacific Express and Transport

&

A Bumpy and Impassable Road

"The operation was successful but the patient died."
—Brent Neill, Vice President of Human Resources

Perrin Beatty was snaking through Toronto traffic in fall of 1994, on his way to Highway 401 and the two-hour drive to the University of Western Ontario where he was teaching a course, when his cell phone rang with an opportunity. KPMG consultant John Palmer was helping to put together a new board for Canadian Pacific Express and Transport (CPET) following the largest 100 percent employee buyout in Canadian history, and Beatty was first on the list of prospective board members.

Beatty was flattered, but initially concerned about whether he would be acceptable to the union, given his background as a longtime Progressive Conservative MP and cabinet minister during the Mulroney years. Palmer reassured him that the union was positive towards his appointment but warned Beatty that it would be a difficult challenge, given deregulation in trucking, the recession, the legacy of mistrust between union and management at the company, and the division within union ranks on the takeover.

By now, Beatty was on the entrance ramp of the 401; he found himself merging into traffic behind a CPET truck. On the back was a huge sign indicating the driver's view about the buyout: Vote No. "It was an indication to me that the road would not be without its bumps," he recalls. As it turned out, Beatty made a quick exit a few months later, when he was tapped to head the CBC. But the road the company followed over the next two years proved to be exceedingly bumpy and, in the end, impassable.

According to Tim Armstrong, a former Ontario deputy minister of both labour and economic development who joined Beatty on the board, "one of the difficulties with these experiments in employee ownership is that you are at a disadvantage, because you are dealing with a company that some sophisticated owner has decided has no long-term future. So people are pinning their hopes on a failing enterprise. You can control some factors, but others—the state of the economy, competition—are out of your control." What remains interesting about CPET, is not its ultimate closure, which was probably preordained, but how despite so many obstacles, it made such progress that many believe it came within six months of achieving success.

The History

The company—the oldest freight transport operation in Canada—traces back to 1873 when the Dominion Express Company of Winnipeg was founded as a courier and stagecoach service. Canadian Pacific Ltd. bought it in the late 1890s but didn't change the name until 1920, when it became CP Express. In the business of parcel pick-up and delivery, with the focus on light delivery service from CP rail stations to customers within the same city, CP Express trucks didn't take to the highways until the late 1960s.

By contrast, CP Transport—a family-owned business bought after World War II—delivered heavy industrial equipment and dangerous goods from city to city. By the 1970s, however, the lines of business had blurred so much that the two companies were competing head on for much the same business, even though they operated separately within the CP Trucks division.

In 1982, when the U.S. deregulated trucking, the chairman of CP Ltd. predicted that Canada would follow. That had big implications for the trucking division, which included companies such as CP Moving, CP Bulk Systems, CANPAR, Highland Transport, and CP Express Air. In preparation for deregulation, CP Express and CP Transport were merged into one company. Before the merger, a different union had represented each slice: the Transportation-Communications Workers (TCU) at CP Express and the Teamsters at CP Trucking. The TCU won the vote to choose a union for the new entity, but bitterness remained among some Teamster supporters.

By the time the federal and provincial governments completed the deregulation process in 1989, U.S. companies had a seven-year head start in adjusting to the new environment. Meanwhile, CP had started to divest itself of some of its trucking companies. That effort sped up after deregulation. From 1989 to 1993, trucking's small contribution to revenues steadily dwindled, with the sell-off and the recession, while by contrast total share value doubled for the company from almost $15 to $30. Trucking was no longer vital to CP.

In 1994, after Highland Transport and CANPAR were sold, only a slimmed-down CPET remained in the CP stable, operating out of 45 terminals in Canada and four in the United States. It too had been for sale over the previous five years but buyers were scarce: high termination payments would be owed to employees in the event of a closure. For the same reason, CP was reluctant to shut the company down. But it was also fussy over a buyer. The federal government had recently been embarrassed by the scandal surrounding its sale of CN's Route Canada freight transportation company, which was quickly stripped of assets by the purchaser and shut down. CP wanted no part of a deal that could lead to a similar situation. It wanted to get CPET off its hands—but it also wanted CPET to succeed at least long enough after the sale so that no recriminations could flow to CP.

Beyond public embarrassment, another practical reason existed for that caution: CP dealt with the TCU in its negotiations for rail and marine workers. Both management and union, with over a century of experience, had raised adversarial relations to a fine art. The company didn't want to enter negotiations with TCU after having just put 2,000 TCU drivers out of work.

A management buyout was considered in 1992, but that failed. When it sank, most of the trucking firm's executive team departed. In April 1993, Keith Robson, a turnaround specialist, was brought in to seek a solution. A graduate of the University of Aston in Birmingham, England, Robson started his career with Chrysler in the United Kingdom and then joined Perkins Engines, a Massey-Ferguson Ltd. subsidiary, before moving into the turnaround game.

Towards Employee Ownership

Within a month, Robson concluded that the company could be saved with a combination of cost cutting, better marketing, improved technology—and an employee buyout. "Selling wasn't an option," he recalls. "So what other option was there?" His hope was that the company would emulate National Freightways, whose shares multiplied from £1 to £125 in value in the ten years following a buyout. He was fascinated by one of its subsidiaries, Excel, a logistics company, which went beyond simply handling freight to becoming a consultant on transportation for customers, overseeing warehousing, distribution, and inventory in a one-stop-shopping arrangement. "The buyout was a means to keep the company alive. The strategy was to go beyond the freight company to broader management services. We had been through a period of just-in-time management in Canada, and that could benefit a logistics company," he says.

Robson hired a new vice-president finance to analyze operations in order to remove redundancies and strengthen the company's capacity. KPMG was brought in to develop a buyout proposal to present to the union. In September, he gave the proposal to Jack Boyce, president of the union, and Dennis Dunster, the newly elected divisional vice-president, who was to end up carrying the ball for the union side. They were positive—aware that the workforce represented about 20 percent of their total membership, so a shutdown would be disastrous. But when Robson later went to CP itself, the reception was lukewarm, since officials didn't believe management buyouts worked and placed his proposal in the same category.

Discussions continued, with brinkmanship galore. The first skirmishes arose when CPET suggested to the union that they use a single law firm and investment banker for the process—the same one the company had already engaged. Instead, TCU brought on its own team: Gowling, Strathy & Henderson, the legal that acted for the union in the Spruce Falls, St. Mary's, and Algoma buyouts in Ontario, and U.S. investment bankers Keilin and Bloom, which had overseen many union-led buyouts.

The company drew a line in the sand, threatening to walk away from the buyout unless the TCU accepted its financial advisors rather than Keilin and Bloom. But the union refused. The company conceded. As for legal advice, the two parties agreed to split the legal duties between their individual firms in order to present a united front to parent CP. The union's firm dealt with labour relations and corporate governance, while the company's legal advisors oversaw matters involving the purchase of the business. Since the union lacked the financial resources to pay its advisors, that ended up being covered by CP in the buyout deal.

The next battle was over how to split the power and the pie between union and non-union employees. Since the unionized employees had no capital to purchase the shares, the union argued that the wages and benefits members would forego in restructuring—ultimately estimated at $15 million—should serve as payment in kind for ownership in the company. At this stage, CPET management balked, but officials at the parent company were unwilling to let the deal die, fearful of a protracted court case over job security payments accompanied by negative public and labour relations. So they accepted the payment-in-kind principle.

The third problem came, however, in convincing the parent company to negotiate directly with the union. It preferred to deal with Robson, who happened to be its employee. That dispute dragged on until March 1994, when the union declared the deal dead unless it was brought directly into the negotiations. CPET executives supported the union. The parent company eventually backed down, although the union felt CP still kept trying end runs throughout the negotiations.

In the background were the years of mistrust between the company and the union. For example, over 750 grievances clogged the system at the time the buyout was suggested, partly because union members used the grievance procedure to aggravate management and partly because the company stonewalled grievance processing, forcing many to arbitration. But at this point (it would change later) Robson and most of the union officials had no shared history and were willing to give each other the benefit of the doubt. When evaluations of the business from both the company and union investment bankers fell within $500,000 of each other, that added to trust, indicating they were being honest with each other.

The collective agreement, negotiated two years earlier and with one year left to run, had to be set aside to provide flexibility for each side to create a new, viable business. The 6 percent wage rollback included in that agreement had in management's opinion not actually provided any financial relief to the company. And, indeed, Robson is not a fan of such measures, arguing that companies never manage to gain the anticipated savings: "People have a remarkable ability to spread the hours to compensate. They get it back in overtime."

Instead, the negotiators devised a new variable rate compensation system, which fit more with Robson's proclivities. It reduced the basic rate to 85 percent of its former level but drivers could earn that back—and more—by enhancing productivity. Aimed primarily at the drivers who handled pickup and delivery within a city, it featured a payment per kilometre, along with extra money as the weight of each delivery increased. The full rate, however, would be paid in situations when the incentive didn't fit, such as customers' requiring extended pickup or delivery time, the time drivers spent waiting for repairs, and training. The two rates varied by region, and the new system would be open to testing and refinement after implementation. A committee of company executives and union executives would meet every six months to review the program.

The deal would not be easy for union officials to sell to their members. In the past, CP had used the threat of closure as a negotiating ploy to gain union concessions. Many employees had worked with the company for so long that they figured they had a civil service-like sinecure and CP would never shut down their operation. Indeed, well after the buyout some employees remained unconvinced that the notice of closure issued to the union was genuine.

Augmenting this was the healthy job security agreement the union had previously negotiated. To many members, the payout on termination was an attractive alternative to the cuts and increased productivity pressures that they were being asked to endorse if they kept the company going. As if that weren't bad enough, the union had agreed to the parent company's request to keep negotiations secret until investigation of the buyout was complete—but news leaked out. Although the national union immediately contacted its 24 local chairmen across the country, officials realized their credibility was damaged by appearing to operate behind the member's backs.

Ontario securities legislation, based on the Algoma buyout, required that the company produce near-prospectus-level disclosure for the private issuance of shares to employees in the deal. And since employees extended across the country, the company had to secure exemption from each provincial securities commission in order to issue its Class B shares, aimed primarily at managers but available to all employees.

The union was insistent that management take a tangible and substantial stake in their joint future by buying shares in the company. Initially, the managers and salaried staff could not raise the required $2 million in shares. It looked as if the deal might collapse. But then some managers, to meet the minimum target, borrowed by mortgaging personal assets such as their homes.

Dividing the Shares

Various classes of shares were issued in the CPET deal, to reflect and balance the different parties' interests:

- 1,333,333 Class A common shares designated for employees, in compensation for the salary and benefit cuts, but held in the Unionized Employees Co-op. These were to be distributed to employees in six portions over the life of the next collective agreement, allocated according to the percentage of total payroll that each individual earned. The first one-sixth would come when the agreement was concluded and the remainder in similar tranches at the end of each year.

- 1 million Class B shares, each worth $2, primarily for managers and non-unionized employees, held in the Salaried Employees Co-op. Each subscriber had to buy a minimum of 50 shares. Although union members technically could have bought these shares, its executive discouraged them from doing so.

- 1 million Class C shares for the managers and non-unionized employees, also held in their co-op.

- about 9 million non-participating, restricted voting shares—Class S for non-unionized staff and Class U for unionized staff—equalized according to their proportion of the work force.

Different corporate governance rights were attached to each of the five levels of shares. Certain fundamental matters, for example, required ratification by all classes of shares. On the other hand, Class B, C, and S shareholders—essentially the non-union group—had the right to elect management directors. While the share structure was complicated, unionized employees owned about 66.6 percent of the company, non-bargaining unit employees owned approximately 25 percent, and the remaining 8.4 percent was owned by those who chose to buy extra shares through a purchase plan.

To replace the lost benefits, a profit-sharing plan was instituted. Employees would divide up 20 percent of pre-tax income, after interest, depreciation, special charges, and extraordinary items. The payment, based on an individual's earnings as a percentage of payroll, would be issued within 75 days of the fiscal year-end. A Negotiations Protocol, signed by both parties as a prelude to developing a new collective agreement, also allowed for negotiations over wages and contract benefits for the third and fourth years of its term, with a minimum increase stipulated of 3 percent of wages.

The protocol called for redesigning the workplace to make it less authoritarian, safer, and fairer. The parties agreed to establish a work design program, allowing workers control of day-to-day operations. The program also sought to improve productivity, through better equipment, less waste and maximizing efficiency. They also would institute an Employee Participation Program, encouraging workers to solve operating problems themselves, and a commitment was given to upgrading employee skills.

The parties also agreed to meet and discuss all outstanding grievances, other than those related to job security and dismissal. Grievances not resolved were to be automatically submitted to arbitration, with a quick decision expected so the new company could move on.

But first, employees had to be persuaded to approve the proposal. And as Perrin Beatty suspected that day he found himself behind a CPET truck, it wasn't an easy task. When the votes were counted, the deal was agreed to by only 54.6 percent of the roughly 50 percent of eligible members who voted. It might have fared somewhat better but a Canada Post glitch prevented votes from the West, believed to be favourable, from being counted. In Montreal, a key facility, 65 percent of the membership participated, voting overwhelmingly negative. The local was not only skeptical of the deal but also of the union leadership's ability to represent its membership.

Building a New Company

Now a new company had to be built. The new board of directors was recruited, with three representatives from the union, three from management, and five independent directors. The union named president Jack Boyce, who had first started working for CP Express in 1957; Leo Gerard, then secretary treasurer of the United Steelworkers of America, who had taken part in the Algoma buyout; and Brian Lind, a local chairman and driver. The management directors were Robson; Bruce Morrison, the vice-president of finance; and Brent

Neill, vice-president of human resources. Neill was the only one with a long employment history at CPET, which he had joined in 1969.

With that in mind—and already concerned about management's knowledge of the industry—union vice-president Dunster recommended as an independent director George Lloyd, who had spent 39 years with CP in trucking before the company sold CP Bulk Systems, which he headed, to Trimac Ltd. That nomination from the union surprised others because Lloyd not only had a management perspective but also negotiated contracts across the table from the TCU. Since Lloyd was also on Brent Neill's list of possibilities, the company readily agreed to his appointment. Rounding out the board were Beatty, Armstrong, Real Sureau, and William Dimma, who became chair, a post he held over the years with a number of leading companies.

A retreat was arranged to develop a mission statement. Beatty remembers trying to keep the union from being isolated at the conclave. Already he sensed a mutual suspicion—and at times intransigence—between union and management, as their different visions of the company clashed. Robson wanted to invest in technology and develop the broader contract logistics mandate, while the union wanted to play to its traditional strength.

This was not an abstract debate. Robson had persuaded CP before the buyout to invest in technology and wanted to continue to bring in computers and other technology to make his vision work. The union viewed that as unnecessary overhead, in a cash-strapped venture. "They didn't understand that we had to develop the capacity to help customers manage their own shipments and also learn more about their own business through the technology so that we could become more efficient," Robson says.

Lloyd, as he started to re-familiarize himself with the company, was shocked at how much it had deteriorated. He felt management lacked depth and experience in trucking. "Keith Robson had no knowledge of the business. He was trying to learn. But it's a fast-paced business," he says.

He felt the company's natural market was in the middle, between couriers and heavier transport companies. But it was dabbling in too many other segments, rather than playing the card it had been dealt. Worse, it didn't understand pricing in those other areas and therefore didn't really know whether it was making money on specific shipments. "They were cutting their own throats," Lloyd says.

Boards of Directors under Employee Ownership: Pitfalls and Remedies

Pitfall	Possible Remedy
Employee directors lack the confidence, skills, and experience to contribute effectively	• Training • Ensure terms of employee directors are long enough to allow them to learn • Appoint employee directors on sub-committees where their front-line experience can be very valuable
Board meetings turn into union-management confrontations	• Set up the composition of the board so that union reps are not in the majority. A balance of union, internal, and external directors helps • Keep the union fully informed and treat it as a partner. Don't "go around" the union to communicate with employees • Consider a team-building intervention to build the cohesiveness of the board and to establish superordinate goals
Employee directors are focused on narrow or parochial concerns such as questioning minor budgetary items	• Give the board an orientation, preferably led by an outside expert, about the role and responsibilities of a board of directors • Emphasize the policy role of the board constantly. Structure the meeting agendas so that operational items are not dealt with at the board level

Board meetings became like Parliament, with management under siege. Instead of developing strategy, as Robson had hoped, the sessions became a forum for debate and negotiations between union and management. Robson felt that management had too easily agreed to the independent directors while the union had been pickier, so those directors were more likely to side with the union. And Dunster attended meetings as an observer, often with a representative of Keilin and Bloom. "They wouldn't observe, however, but would be speaking," says Robson. "So you would end up with five or six people speaking for the union and one from management—me. Very quickly the meetings would disintegrate into management-bashing," he says.

He feels it was a mistake not to give shares directly to employees—as in the National Freight buyout—rather than leaving the block of shares in the hands of the union initially. He felt that he fared better in selling his vision when he met employees on visits to the various terminals or joined them for trucking runs rather than when he sat with union leaders in the boardroom. "It was pretty clear to me that a lot of unionized employees appreciated what we were trying to do. But the more I talked to the employees the more the unions got concerned. Some employees began to wonder: if we have employee ownership, why do we need a union?" he says.

But Armstrong felt that Robson created some of his own problems, by leaving the union out of the loop and then dumping measures out at board meetings. "He would make decisions and announce them to the surprise and chagrin of Dunster and the union. He didn't do it all of the time but he did it sufficiently to cause resentment," says Armstrong. "Though Keith was architect of the employee buyout, I don't think he ever quite understood the role of the union. I think he viewed the union as an environmental interference. He would have preferred to deal directly with the employees."

The union was between a rock and a hard place. Its members weren't enthusiastic about that buyout. Given the history of poor labour relations, those members didn't believe much that the company said. But as Dunster notes, "they didn't believe the union either." And then, as soon as the ink was dry on the buyout, union leadership felt the CEO was pushing it off to the side. "From a union standpoint, we felt management was giving us lip service at best and better lip service when we were in front of the board," says Dunster. "It was not like they were pissing on the union, but by and large they excluded us from the important aspects. It was never the union intent to be running the company, nor would we have ever got off the ground if we pursued that avenue. But we certainly wanted to have at least equal knowledge of what was going on in the company. We never got that, initially."

A labour-management committee, modelled on the Algoma system, was established. The union and management met on grievances and cleaned up many of them. "Under the old system it was an adversarial approach and neither side would admit they were wrong," says Neill of the backlog. "For the union, it's easier to fight than close a file as the union members would get mad at them. So they wouldn't close a file. The company figured if the union wasn't closing a file there was no benefit to us to admit we're wrong and pay grievances, as it's a one-way street: all the union wants to do is take, take, take. So basically the change was to decide it's now our joint problem—the owner's problem."

In sorting through grievances, the committee tried to look at root causes and put them into categories, so they could learn what was causing the disputes. Was it by area, department, or routes? It confirmed what management suspected: most of the grievances were from the linehaul drivers, who operated the big rigs on the highway. They accounted for 20 percent of the company but 80 percent of these headaches. So management and union jointly held meetings with the linehaul drivers to find solutions.

But it was an edgy process of transformation that wasn't helped when, to the union's mind, the company violated key elements of the new collective agreement right out of the gate. Neill notes that even under employee ownership, management and union have different responsibilities. Management must act in the best interest of the company and its shareholders, who even if they are employees have different interests as shareholders from those they have as employees. The union's legal obligation is to protect the rights of its members. "We were able to get a lot closer but divergent needs and responsibilities meant a separation between the two of us. And that was healthy," Neill says.

The variable rate plan also imploded. It was great in theory but too often proving ludicrous in practice. "We had to smarten management up," says Dunster. "I would be in meetings where a manager would come in and say a fellow made $450 in Toronto yesterday. He was so excited about it—the variable rate in action. But the guy didn't do $450 worth of work."

The problem was that delivery runs differed dramatically; what worked in downtown Toronto might not work in Red Deer. A driver in Toronto might only have to cover a five-square-mile area to move hundreds of pounds of freight, while somebody in Red Deer was driving 300 miles a day to move 20 percent less freight. "Some people were getting rich on the variable rate program and some were starving to death," notes Neill.

The program was tweaked. An employee was assigned full time to try to develop a better formula. But it was causing a severe morale problem and in the end was dumped. "If it had been a new company or a smaller company it might have been possible to successfully implement it. But at CPET there was too much history—and the geographical differences even within a city were too great," says Neill. Robson still remains convinced the program could have been saved and that some vital productivity gains were being achieved. He feels the real problem was that the union only gave the program lip service: fundamentally, if one employee makes more than another employee the union doesn't consider that fair.

Overall, some progress was achieved. A few pilot projects on changing the workplace environment were developed. The company tried to adapt the Algoma model, which was based on one site, to a trucking operation with locations scattered across Canada and in the United States. "The difficulty was that while these co-operative endeavours were being tried in the field, the same spirit didn't apply to the macro items at the centre," says Armstrong. "It was dysfunctional. You had this talk of co-operation in the pilot projects but at the centre there was someone who seemed to only pay lip service to them there."

As planned, the company had taken on a new name: Interlink. But the trucks still said CP Express and Transport. So did the cheques. That infuriated Lloyd, who went to Robson to complain. "To make the employees feel like owners you have to deal with the smallest things. When the paycheque and the truck door that the driver opens 100 times a day still say CP, he doesn't feel anything has changed," Lloyd says.

Trouble Strikes Again

As if those tensions weren't bad enough, the company hit a giant pot-
hole: a mini-recession in the trucking industry. The company had
been undercapitalized going in, with the deal only providing in cash
a $5 million loan from the parent and the $2 million from shares.
Meanwhile, the deal had taken a year to negotiate and professional
fees had soaked up $8 million, rather than the $4 million anticipated,
a significant drain on cash flow. Robson didn't accept that the company was in a downturn, however, and continued to make the investments he felt were necessary for success. "We didn't turn off the tap
and conserve cash. Month after month the results continued to dete-
riorate until we were in the fall and we found ourselves with a significant problem," recalls Neill.

But even then, the full extent of the problem wasn't picked up
because the company didn't have a proper handle on its finances.
Projections showed, inaccurately, that the cash flow shortage difficulties could be managed. Lloyd remembers attending an audit committee meeting in January 1996, reviewing the first full year of
operations. After half a day, the outside auditor asked the recently
recruited chief financial officer about the current quarter. "He said, 'I
don't think we'll make the next payroll.' In his defence, he didn't
know trucking and was new. There had been no signals to the board.
The outside auditors didn't know. I've never seen auditors so upset in
my life," says Lloyd.

While still trying to run his own trucking company, Lloyd made
eight trips from Vancouver to Toronto in the next three weeks, as the
company scrambled to recover. If the company went under, board
members would be liable for some debts, and Dimma, who happened
to be testifying before a Senate Committee on board governance, mentioned the Interlink plight, without naming the company, in arguing
against such liability. But reporters made the connection, Dunster
recalls bitterly, and as it became public, customers became wary of
using Interlink.

At an evening board meeting, a legal expert gave the directors a
grim estimate. Their liability for back wages and unpaid vacation in
the event of bankruptcy was $15 to $17 million. That amounted to
about $1.5 million apiece. A silence hung over the room as that sank
in. The first to speak, Dimma recalls, was Gerard: "You know, there
are only two things in life I value—my wife and my pickup truck—and
there is one thing I don't want to lose: my pickup truck." With that

black humour, the board members came to quick consensus. They resigned around midnight, leaving the company without any directors. "You want to stay and fight. But who can take the financial risk?" asks Dimma.

The Turnaround Effort

Robson had also left, and the board's last major act before resigning was to bring in another turnaround specialist, Bill Aziz, to try to rescue the company yet again. Finally, management and the union, with their backs against the wall, came together and truly started to work as a team. "The ship was sinking. Management realized everybody had to work together or it would go down," Dunster says.

The first step was to persuade CP to provide a cash infusion. CP was on the hook for a large portion of the job security agreement reached in the 1994 negotiations. The union joined Aziz in those negotiations and they obtained $10.5 million—$8 million in cash and $2.5 million in a write-off of outstanding debt.

Aziz worked through the spring and summer developing a reorganization plan that the lenders—notably GE Capital—would accept. That included massive changes in management. Negotiations continued with CP for more assistance, but CP was demanding that Aziz prove this wouldn't just be throwing good money after bad. The number $42 million was tossed around, and in the end CP management balked, turning down the request on a Friday afternoon.

Their bid appeared over, but with a board meeting scheduled for the following Monday, and with the quiet assistance of a CP negotiator, Aziz and Dunster began to lobby board members at their homes. The board approved their appeal, overruling management and agreeing to provide $36 million more but to sever any future ties. "That was a great relief. We would have been bankrupt at the end of the week if they had not come through," says Dunster.

Dunster and Neill began to work on getting the reduction in compensation needed to make the restructuring fly. In the old days when restructuring was required, the company would call the union in and advise it of the amount required and how many jobs were being cut. The union would challenge the numbers and the specific steps, fighting every step of the way. This time, union and management worked together. They jointly asked the financial advisors to figure out what was needed and accepted the 10 percent cut in compensation that was recommended. They then scoured the possibilities, together, putting together a program that they thought was saleable. "It's easier with the union there," says Neill. "I've got a partner. I have my partner working with me. I don't have to fight with him to sell it. I don't have to make my demands and pound the table and try to force it down his throat."

He points out that it's particularly helpful to hear the union leaders on the various possibilities before those are cast in stone. "The union executives know their members very, very well. A lot of companies refuse to accept that. They'll say, 'I know my company's employees better. You're just the union.' But in my mind that's incorrect. Unions know what will sell and what won't," he says.

And sell it they did. A vote was held and union members ratified the plan, with 75 percent in favour. Wages were rolled back 10 percent, and employee ownership rose to 92 percent while the salaried share was compressed to 8 percent. By then, the we-they had been obliterated, as Neill and Dunster worked together. They would give speeches together. When the ballots were counted in the top floor of a Toronto hotel, Neill was invited to be present. It was the first time in the union's history that an outsider who wasn't a union lawyer or a scrutineer was allowed in. "We were in it together. And that's how we operated from then on. It was a total partnership," he says.

Whenever a problem occurred—be it an employee-management dispute or a financial reversal—Neill and Dunster were on the phone together, consulting and working out a joint plan. Dunster would joke that dealing with the company in the past had been like being invited to dinner at the big house but only getting to eat in the kitchen. Now he was in the dining room. It was a positive change, but in the end wasn't enough. "The operation was successful but the patient died," Neill notes.

Searching for a Buyer

Aziz had left after his task was completed, but the CFO he had recruited, Paul Henry, took the helm. Everyone was excited at being given a new lease on life. Morale improved. But instead of business building, it was dropping off. The information about Interlink's financial woes was on the street. No customer wants its freight stuck in a transportation pipeline with a company that goes under.

Clearly, if the company were to be successful, it would need to find either a partner to merge with or a purchaser. A couple of parties were interested; negotiations transpired through the winter months. Then Interlink suffered another unexpected blow on Easter weekend when its U.S. partner, Viking Transportation Co., closed its operations east of the Mississippi. The two had traded shipments at the Buffalo terminal, with Viking taking loads south and Interlink bringing goods north. On Friday, they were partners. On Monday, Interlink was stranded, losing the northbound shipments, which were four times what Interlink had been taking south. The company scrambled to find other partners but couldn't get preferred rates, having to pay premium prices for its goods that needed to be delivered in that part of the United States. The blow to the bottom line was about $400,000 a month.

Interlink was now failing to meet some of its revenue targets in the loan covenants, but GE Capital gave it some room, knowing there was still a chance for a sale. They searched for a deal, but Dunster notes that "the other companies didn't have to buy us to get our business. They just had to let us sink." The final effort came as the union tried to use its leverage with the Quebec Solidarity Fund, which was a major shareholder of Kingsway Cubano, to get that company to take Interlink over. Although the projected deal would mean further cuts, half the jobs might be saved. "It went right to the final 48 hours," recalls Dunster.

Interlink had given itself a deadline, determined that it would go out by its own accord rather than have somebody external pull the plug. On July 4, 1997, officials appeared before a judge; Interlink was put into bankruptcy on July 6, with a court-ordered receiver taking charge. The company had $51 million in assets and only $27 million in liabilities, but it was losing money—and there was no sign that could be turned around. Sensing the outcome, and knowing trucking windups can be ugly, a forbearance agreement had been negotiated with the lender allowing the payment of $7 million to cover outstanding wages and vacation pay. "The union, on behalf of its members, agreed to this," Dunster says. "When the company went bankrupt we encouraged our members to do the right thing. It worked. There was no significant equipment loss or damage in the windup. It was a good work force, and I think the way they handled the breakup of the company indicates the calibre of the people."

That work force had been the owners as well as the employees; but ironically throughout the crises in their company they had to be kept in the dark. To tell workers the extent of the problem would have been to risk it getting out to the media, adding to the tailspin. "We were walking around with this dreaded secret. We had to hold it very close," recalls Neill. "The union represented their members. In the old days, they would have been outside the boardroom, blissfully unaware of the problems. In this situation, an employee-owned company, they were in the boardroom but couldn't publicize it." But he stresses that the same secrecy pervades public companies, where shareholders—the owners—must await financial statements for full details on their investments.

The Assessment

The union impressed Lloyd. "It did a tremendous job. They stepped up to the plate. There were a whole lot of philosophical barriers for them to overcome, and they did it. Dennis Dunster and Jack Boyce worked their hearts out to make the company work. If management had not been so weak and the marketplace had been better, they might have survived."

Dimma was less impressed, noting that in the early days the union was resistant to vital changes like shutting down terminals, slowing down some possibilities and blocking others. "I am totally opposed and think it's unworkable in a capitalist system to have a union and management on the board with the union having a majority share, as they can't reconcile their role. I'm convinced that part of the failure was the inability to reconcile the objectives and needs of a trade union with the objectives and needs of a profit-making institution. We tried very hard and talked. We had a lot of consultation. But we never reconciled that irreconcilable dilemma."

Dimma, who has served on 50 profit-making boards and 37 not-for-profit boards, feels there is a better chance if the union has a minority share. But even then, he dislikes representation by constituency, since that inevitably prevents those directors from representing the whole company. He does see some value in employees' serving on the board—but prefers individual workers, rather than union leaders. When he chaired the board of Polysar Ltd., a retired leader from the union local sat on the board. That provided insight on worker interests, but, Dimma notes, "because he was retired some of the fire was gone. He could stand back from the fray and provide a balanced view."

Robson remains a supporter of employee ownership, arguing that with bonus and incentive plans worked into the scheme it can give a company greater flexibility. In good times, employees see their pocketbook improve with the company's good fortunes, through dividends, a rise in the value of their shares, and bonuses. In bad times, those retract, but if the wages have been set at a reasonable level, it can preclude the need for layoffs since the total compensation to employees has already been trimmed automatically.

Dunster had been a dispatcher at the CPET terminal in Ottawa before running for the union executive. A month later, unprepared, he got caught up in the buyout, which was not only to take him into the figurative corporate dining room of CPET-Interlink but also into the well-furnished offices of Bay Street and corporate Canada as he fought to keep the company afloat. He bought shares in the company—the first time he owned any shares. "Algoma does this and the price of steel goes through the roof. We do it and the bottom falls out of the trucking industry," he says. "If we could have survived six more months, we could have made it."

It took him a long time to get over his disappointment, but now he's philosophical about the venture. "From the union standpoint and the employees' standpoint, that was not the end we were looking for. But the company was bankrupt in 1993. It could have gone bankrupt then. We kept it going for four years. We had 250 people retire with full pensions in that time. There was over $300 million in wages earned. We probably could have made it if we had hung on, because the industry had a turnaround a bit later. But the cards didn't fall right."

The CPET story can be read in many ways. There was plenty of discord. There was also, when times got bad, a total turnaround, as management and union worked in harmony. Was it a failure? A success? It was all that, and more.

SFG Technologies

&

Timing the Cycle

"Bruce has been careful to not oversell employee ownership. It comes with no guarantees—as has been borne out. We saw it go from improving year to year to being worth nothing."

—Simon Drake, vice-president
research and development

After 12 years of owning shares in software manufacturer SFG Technologies, Simon Drake found himself in the late '90s back where he started: with some ownership stake in the company that wasn't worth anything but might be in the future. He had seen others cash in, selling shares back when they left, but after bad times for the company his own shares dissolved into nothing while the market for his more recent share options was frozen. "If this doesn't work out I'll consider myself bamboozled by the whole process—the biggest sucker ever born," he noted.

SFG originally stood for Solutions for Government. That was eventually changed to Solutions for Growth, as the company expanded its horizons. And after some rough times, the Vancouver-based company started growing again in the late 1990s, selling its newly developed software installation for utilities across North America, providing a new, potentially booming market after years of simply serving local governments.

The company was founded in 1980 by Bruce Elliott, a New Zealand expatriate who came to Canada in 1975 with his wife for a year, loved it, and never returned home. He worked for Hudson's Bay Mining and Smelting Company and then Cominco, where he was in charge of financial systems for worldwide operations, before moving on to consulting in 1980.

SFG evolved out of a contract to install a computer system for the municipality of West Vancouver in 1983. Elliott hired Drake, a systems analyst with B.C. Hydro, to help him. The original intention had been simply to install a Wang system already being used in Surrey that they bought the rights to. In the end, that wasn't possible because that system was custom-coded. Virtually every line of code had to be rewritten.

Now, though, they had a product of their own, and Elliott spotted a market opportunity. He hired software developers and coders to produce, sell, and install computer applications that could be run on the many Wang systems—primarily word processors—being used in municipal governments. The company grew steadily, from the initial two employees to about 30 in 1990 and about 110 at the end of 1999.

Elliott introduced employee ownership in 1988 because it fit the flat, empowered, team-oriented organization that he wanted to nurture. He also felt that the company would create a lot of wealth and believed it was reasonable to share that bounty. But other entrepreneurs he talked to about the idea thought he was nuts, since they figured employee ownership would simply inspire employees to interfere in management. "It wasn't popular back then," he recalls. "But it's what I wanted to do."

The shares, however, did not come with any voting rights. He viewed that as too complicated, since in some cases it might involve getting shareholder approval from too many people for actions that a private company should be able to take simply. And he also wanted the lines of authority clear: "I don't want employees on the board of directors. The board of directors are my boss. It's dysfunctional to have people both your boss and reporting to you."

The Yin and Yang of Employee Ownership

On the one hand	On the other hand
"Shares shouldn't come with voting rights, since that might involve getting shareholder approval from too many people for actions that a private company should be able to take simply."—*Bruce Elliott, SFG*	"Employee ownership engenders optimism because employees know they can gain financially from the sale of their shares. As such, it is more fitting for a technology company than a manufacturing company because it's a fast-growth and high-wealth plan."—*Bruce Elliott, SFG*
"I don't want employees on the board of directors. The board of directors are my boss. It's dysfuntional to have people both your boss and reporting to you."—*Bruce Elliott, SFG*	"Employee Ownership fits a flat, team-oriented organization. If the company creates a lot of wealth, it is reasonable to share the bounty."—*Bruce Elliott, SFG*
"Employee ownership should be viewed as a short-term solution."—*Peter Tanaka, senior government official and later board member of Provincial Papers*	"Employee ownership is helpful for attracting talent, but primarily it is morally right to share the wealth created by everybody in the firm with everybody."—*Dan Gelbart, Creo*
"The first thing I learned is that everybody goes into employee ownership with an altruistic attitude. I learned that was a recipe for disaster in that it all sounds good— fuzzy and warm—but this is a business."—*Chris Worthy, PRT*	"We believe in employee ownership."—*Charlie Johnson, PRT* "You get buy-in. I really believe you have a special commitment from employees."— *Ev Van Eerden, PRT* *cont'd*

"Employee ownership in a manufacturing facility is an oxymoron, because when an employee owner enters the mill to do the daily job, he or she must necessarily assume the role of employee. The ownership role, on the other hand, must wait for monthly performance results. That tension and lack of clarity in roles negatively affects morale."—Ian *Ross, CEO, Provincial Papers*

"You have to put on two hats. It's very hard to be a member of a union and an owner. It's almost contradictory. One hat wants shareholder value to go up and the other wants security."—*Bill Joblin, union officer, Provincial Papers*

"Employee ownership kept people at the company, and they worked harder to make their company and their investment successful. "It's different when you have a major chunk of money on the line. You'll do what it takes to keep the company growing."—*Henry Leong, Integra Geoservices*

"I still believe that broad-based employee ownership is the way to go. It makes the business much more sensitive to the marketplace and what needs to happen. You are able to react and streamline costs easier than non-employee-owned companies in up and down markets. It's much more flexible."—*Mark Klingbeil, Integra Geoservices*

"I wouldn't do it again, but I'm also a lot older. When you are in your early thirties, giving up everything is fantastic. When you're in your mid-forties, no. But I'm happy I did it. Heavenly days! We built a technology that is world-class.

"Employee ownership, with bonus and incentive plans, can give a company greater flexibility. In good times, employees see their pocketbook improve with the company's good fortunes, through dividends, a rise in the value of

cont'd

We have 50 people employed. We have kept this level of people employed—not including the dry gas seal people—for many years. We built something, made it grow, and I learned a tremendous amount about managing organizations."—*Kim Sturgess, Revolve Technologies*

their shares, and bonuses. In bad times, if the wages have been set at a reasonable level, it can preclude the need for layoffs since the total compensation to employees has already been trimmed automatically."
—*Keith Robson, CPET*

"Employee ownership can be counterproductive when times are rough. When employees leave, the company's cash position can be aggravated by the need to buy back shares. And the chance to cash in before the share value decreases can also be an incentive to leave. "When things are going down, there's a gain if you leave or you can be a martyr and go down with the ship. Employee ownership was structured for success, not for bad times."—*Simon Drake, SFG*

"Employee ownership is more fitting for a technology company than a manufacturing company because it's a fast-growth and high wealth-building industry, with lots of employee mobility. In a more stable industry, for a privately owned company, employee ownership might not be as valuable because no exit strategy might exist for everyone to cash in shares."—*Bruce Elliott, SFG*

cont'd

"Employee ownership at any level is very exhilarating. To be a small group in a David and Goliath struggle is exciting. But when you can't make the mortgage, or your kids can't go to hockey school because you don't have the cash, or the dividends aren't forthcoming, the romance comes off and it's a very difficult experience,"—*Ron Waldman, Great Western Brewery*	"I think that any employee ownership that doesn't have an exit strategy is a very frustrating experience for the employees. They have no option but to ride with you. An exit strategy must be part of the equation— and they have to have a time horizon for that to occur."—*Ron Waldman, Great Western Brewery*
"I find it makes a little bit of a difference in how I view the company. You want the company as a whole to do well, rather than just your department. It changes your focus. If you can help other people to do well, that helps the company to do well and improves the bottom line."—*Nigel Richardson, SFG*	"You get a 10 to 15 percent edge with employee ownership. It can be zero if I don't get them involved. But if I can get them involved and motivated, and they believe, I've got a 10 or 15 percent edge. Absolutely." —*Frank Dottori, Spruce Falls*

During the company's first two decades, there were ups and downs, as the company struggled to maintain technological currency in a very demanding field. In the mid-'90s, revenues dipped as vendors of enterprise resource planning software like PeopleSoft, Oracle, and SAP entered the field and started picking up the larger municipalities as clients, leaving SFG with just six large customers and not much hope for expanding beyond small municipalities.

New Opportunities and Big Problems

That might still have served as a viable market but a new and exciting opportunity captured SFG's attention: deregulation of utilities. While regulated, the utilities simply focused on billing and let their captive clientele suffer any consequences from inadequate software—billing errors, for example, or inability to handle customer moves easily. Now, in a competitive market, they would need software to allow them to become more customer-focused, developing long-lasting relationships and scouting opportunities for increasing their revenues. As deregulation moved from state to state in the United States, it became clear that existing utility software would become obsolete; every utility would need new computer applications within a decade. If SFG could develop an appropriate product—and hold on for dear life during the development period—it could re-emerge stronger than ever.

As if that weren't enough of a challenge, the company was also enduring a management crisis that had started a few years earlier. Elliott could be a very demanding manager, with what some called an "it's my way or the highway" style that by the mid-'90s had worn thin on some employees. He also had wanted to strengthen SFG's appeal to the American market so he had hired a new general manager from the United States to grow the company. The general manager in turn hired his own cadre of vice-presidents and moved the head office to his hometown, Atlanta, controlling everything but software development from there.

The result was a disaster. The culture clash started with clothes: the old SFG gang were a casual bunch, while the Atlanta crew were spiffy suit-and-tie sorts. Their management approach was out of the 1950s, as far as the Canadians were concerned. And their motivational program, Uplift, produced guffaws with its American eagle awards to celebrate success by a bunch of Canadians.

People began leaving both because of the culture clash and the tailspin. "It was a miserable environment to work in," noted Drake. He remembers struggling with the fact that he had wanted somebody to come in and change the company—but now the actual change he was witnessing seemed wrong-headed. He was also growing to realize, as were others, that while their major market may be the United States, this was a Canadian company, with a low-key, understated manner that its new managers didn't appreciate.

As it turned out, neither did many clients when they were canvassed. And so several of the long-time senior staff invited Elliott out to lunch and warned that if the new managers weren't booted out, they would leave. "It was a pretty tough time," Drake recalls. With that warning, Elliott assumed control again as president and CEO. But he was losing control in other ways, as sales waned, and outside capital was needed to stay alive.

Elliott was caught in a vise. He was fundamentally against taking the company public, fearing the consequences of the stock market's quarter-to-quarter mentality. He was following a high-revenue, low-profit growth strategy but felt that it would have to be abandoned for a high-profit strategy if public shareholders were introduced. As well, his market for selling had been seasonal under government, since decisions were made only after budgets were determined each spring. The company then had to endure a cash flow lag between the purchase decision and the post-installation payments. It wasn't a financial situation suited to today's stock markets.

He had turned to venture capitalists earlier in the company's growth and by the mid-'90s had seen his share diluted to 55 percent with 7 percent owned by employees, 20 percent by Ventures West and 18 percent by the B.C. government (through its Discover Foundation). Now he would have to accept further dilution, to stay alive. Venture capitalists took over 70 percent of the firm, with Elliott retaining just 20 percent. "Bruce came very near to losing the whole company," recalls Drake. "He dodged the bullet."

Building Again

But employees were also hit hard as their shares were basically cancelled in the new arrangement. It was time to start again, Elliott realized, and capitalize on employee ownership's ability to bind people to the company if he was to get to market with his new product in time. He decided to beef up the employee share of the company, this time to 10 percent.

In the past, employees had been able to get shares through options offered as incentives. As well, in the late 1980s, during a rough period, some employees took a 10 percent pay cut but received shares as a substitute for the loss in wages. An employee share ownership plan also allowed employees to direct 15 percent of their salary to purchasing shares through a payroll deduction. But hardly anybody was enrolled in the plan, because management, wary about the risk associated with stock, wasn't drumming up enthusiasm.

This time, SFG chose to boost stock options significantly. That way, everyone would have some ownership stake in the company. "We had to really focus our employees. We made sure everybody had some level of ownership, and I think that has made a huge difference," Elliott said. Those who were uncertain about the future or still in a funk over the Atlanta episode were encouraged to leave so the company could consolidate and build again. Elliott started to meet with customers and to improve customer management.

In 1998, SFG finished the new product and installed it at its first utility, Berkshire Gas in Massachusetts. At that point, the company had cut its entire sales and marketing group in the struggle to stay afloat; it was fixated on developing and installing the new product in order to prove effectiveness. In 1999, the company started to rebuild its sales staff and gain additional sales, pulling in about $13 million in revenues and a profit of about $2 million. The company managed to gain enough operational sites in that period for potential clients to easily visit and ensure SFG's solution was right for their needs, a critical aspect of marketing such systems.

Share options came in handy at one of those early installations, at Winnipeg Hydro. The staff had dwindled, and Drake couldn't hire and train in time to complete the installation. He told his team they would simply have to get it done by themselves, whatever the stresses and overtime involved. Share options were assigned arbitrarily, with senior people on the development team getting more than junior people but with everyone standing to gain something by meeting the deadline.

"For me, the options were a motivator, and I think that was true for other people," he says. But then, a little more cautiously, he adds that people are different on what motivates them. "It was a 'circle the wagons' situation—a 'we'll show them we can do it' situation. That was probably more of a motivator than options, frankly."

Nigel Richardson, director of support, joined the company in 1975 but with a wife and three young children only bought his first shares in the mid-'90s. He supports employee ownership because it fosters greater co-operation: "I find it makes a little bit of a difference in how I view the company. You want the company as a whole to do well, rather than just your department. It changes your focus. If you can help other people to do well, that helps the company to do well and improves the bottom line. Employee ownership has been good for SFG."

Elliott made it clear after his near-death experience that he intended to strengthen the company and then sell it to a strategic buyer before anything might happen that further trimmed his share. Richardson took him at his word, continuing to buy shares and accumulating options that he had ten years to exercise. "If the company goes public and the share price goes up, we'll make good money," he noted in the summer of 1999. Indeed, he pointed out that at the monthly staff meetings it was not unusual to have somebody ask questions about ownership or going public.

That's exactly what Elliott wanted. With the sale of the company on the horizon, options were making staff feel good rather than apprehensive about the prospect. Employee ownership engenders such optimism since the employees know they can gain financially from the sale. But Elliott also noted that it's more fitting for a technology company than, say, a manufacturing company because it's a fast-growth and high wealth-building industry, with lots of employee mobility. In a more stable industry, for a privately owned company, employee ownership might not be as valuable because no exit strategy might exist for everyone to cash in shares.

Throughout the years, SFG employees who left had been able to sell their shares back to the company. That meant when the company hit the skids, those employees who left fared better than those who stayed and lost the value of their shares. But Drake, who suffered that fate, stressed that Elliott was clear from the start about the risk: "Bruce has been careful to not oversell employee ownership. It comes with no guarantees—as has been borne out. We saw it go from improving year to year to being worth nothing."

Drake pointed out that employee ownership can be counterproductive when times are rough. As employees left, the company's cash position was aggravated by the need to buy back shares. And, of course, the chance to cash in before the share value decreased was an incentive to leave. "When things are going down, there's a gain if you leave or you can be a martyr and go down with the ship," he observed. "Employee ownership was structured for success, not for bad times."

The Exit

As it turned out, Drake and the others who hung on were to experience success as well as bad times. In late December 1999, Elliott found his strategic buyer, Cayenta, a San Diego-based systems integrator with 400 employees that had already bought three other software companies. It, in turn, was owned by Titan Corp., a fast-growing space satellite, telecommunications, and software company. SFG became an operating division, with Elliott originally senior vice-president and general manager of the division before he was asked to spend a year as chief operating officer of Cayenta itself. The Vancouver office remained but he moved to Washington State, along with some senior employees, because of the favourable tax situation on their options and salary.

Shares that had been selling for 20 cents apiece to employees a few months earlier—and that could be picked up for 5 cents under options—were valued at 50 cents in the Cayenta deal. Long-term, senior employees like Drake, who was then vice-president of research and development and became chief technology officer for three product companies within the Cayenta umbrella, found the value of their shares worth as much as $400,000, Elliott notes, while relatively new junior employees got a few thousand dollars. The median was about $20,000. "We turned it around. We recapitalized it and have really done well," he says happily.

And he expects them all to continue doing well. Everyone was granted options in Cayenta, which itself was planning on going public. "They have a similar approach—they believe every employee should have an ownership stake. Often it doesn't go through the company to everybody. Here it does," he says.

SFG could also now target larger utilities, because Cayenta and Titan had the vital access to directors of those utilities that SFG lacked and provided the assurance, by their size, that the system developers would be around for the long haul. In the first year after being bought, with the Y2K fear gone and utilities focusing on buying new systems, sales grew 30 percent; Elliott expected them to jump a further 70 percent in the second year. "This takes us to the next level," he said. "It provides the capital for expansion that venture capitalists could not have provided."

Companies have life cycles. SFG, as it entered a new stage in the life cycle, was a reminder that employee ownership is very much tied to those cycles as well as to the vagaries of the market. Shares don't just go up in value. They can be cyclical. Employee ownership has to be structured for the good times and bad, or it can become a sore point rather than a stimulus.

Great Western Brewery

&⁣&

David and Goliath

"It was scary—a big step. There were 16 guys for whom the biggest investment we ever made was in Canada Savings Bonds. We weren't business people, used to investing. But we had a lot of experience in brewing and we thought we could do it."

—Don Ebelher, operations manager

If you had to write a Hollywood script about employee ownership, it would resemble the inaugural years of Great Western Brewery in Saskatoon. It would tell of a small brewery in an isolated part of the country, without a huge market, that gets bought by a few gutsy employees after a giant corporation shuts it down. To their amazement, the citizenry rallies to their side, and they can't brew the beer as fast as everyone is buying it. The title is a natural: *The Little Brewery That Could.*

Hollywood would stop there. But for the owner employees of Great Western Brewery, reality didn't end there. The Little Brewery That Could became the Little Brewery That Couldn't, as production and quality failures—and the fickle attention span of beer drinkers—deflated their fantasy. They had to regroup under the new leadership, ironically, of a Coca-Cola bottler, trying to rebuild a brewery with sufficient long-term viability to attract a buyer that would provide a much-needed exit strategy.

"Employee ownership at any level is very exhilarating. To be a small group in a David and Goliath struggle is exciting. But when you can't make the mortgage, or your kids can't go to hockey school because you don't have the cash, or the dividends aren't forthcoming, the romance comes off and it's a very difficult experience," says Ron Waldman, president of Great Western Brewery.

The brewery traces back to the 1920s, when the 2½-city-block facility was built. Since provinces control liquor and beer distribution, beer brewed beyond Saskatchewan's borders was traditionally kept out, ensuring the brewery a reasonable market. But in the late '80s, it was clear that would change, as interprovincial and Canada–U.S. barriers to trade started to evaporate. Canadian breweries were grossly inefficient compared to their American competitors, which could count on breathtakingly large production runs since they served huge markets. The Canadian industry became preoccupied with consolidation and economies of scale, although, as is often common in business, a successful counter-trend emerged, in the form of premium-oriented microbreweries.

When Molson and Carling-O'Keefe Breweries announced a merger in July 1989, restructuring of their now-joint operations across the country was inevitable. The casualty, it soon became known, was Carling-O'Keefe's Saskatoon brewery, which was to be shut down with production consolidated in Regina. Employees were left with a stark choice: they could leave town, joining their long-time rival Molson at the Regina brewery, or they could accept severance payments and try to find gainful employment in a province where an estimated 1,000 people were leaving every month in large measure because of the lack of jobs.

Even before the announcement, there had been unease at the brewery. At one point, Greg Kitz, the vice-president of the union, who had joined the company in May 1975, took to wandering about the plant on his spare time during the night shift, photographing all the machinery and recording their power ratings and capacity. In effect, he was taking an inventory of the plant—but unsure of the reason. "It was a feeling I wanted to take stock of things. I didn't know why," he says.

Employees Fight Back

Now, after the closure announcement, he approached the union to pay for a brochure displaying that inventory, which would be mailed to American breweries, inviting them to buy the plant. The local union president opposed him, but the treasurer agreed. With a bit of cash, he went to work on his early-model Apple computer and sent out 100 copies of the 16-page announcement across the United States. Since the invitation was to approach the owners of the plant rather than the union, he was never to learn how successful he was. However, he heard reports one company did express interest but was rebuffed because it wanted to purchase a Montreal plant as well.

Few employees were prepared to leave Saskatoon. "We just wanted to stay home. Our roots are here," one of the employees, John O'Connor, recalled. Even those who contemplated moving were wary, fearing the Regina brewery itself would be shut down in the near future when the provincial government passed legislation allowing companies to brew beer in one province and sell in another. The whole province could easily be served from Edmonton or some other, bigger centre.

Kitz too was caught in the dilemma. He was inclined to consider moving to Regina, but his wife, Brenda, told him that he would be going without her. Then one day as they were at a gas station, waiting for the car to be filled up and brooding about the situation, she said, "Why don't you buy the plant yourself?"

But buying the plant, the employees were warned, would be a foolish gamble. Saskatchewan was the country's smallest beer market. A tiny, independent brewery clearly could not succeed battling for those beer drinkers against well-financed, heavy advertisers like Labatt and Molson. The only possible chance might come, analysts suggested, from dropping prices and producing a low-quality alternative, which was anathema to the employees, who were proud of their beer-making expertise.

As well, Molson wasn't particularly interested in selling off the facility, either fearful that it would be accused of peddling a white elephant to starry-eyed ex-employees or wanting to keep competition limited. And officials from the United Food and Commercial Workers were equally leery, to the point where they pointedly warned members to guard that no union funds should be used in the endeavour.

But employees started to rally to the cause. Brenda and Greg Kitz began to send letters to political figures—locally, provincially, and federally—seeking assistance and warning about the dangers if the brewing industry became concentrated further. Included in the recipients were Calvin Goldman, head of the federal competition bureau, and Bernard Valcourt, minister of corporate affairs. Whether those letters had any impact is unknown. But suddenly, Carling-O'Keefe switched positions. After several weeks of the brewer's insisting it would not sell the plant, a corporate official called Greg Kitz and suggested they get together to talk. "It came out of the blue—a real shock," he says.

Since the union insisted on not being involved, an employees' association was formed to investigate a buyout. Brenda Kitz, a secretary at a law firm, got her boss, Gerald Muzyka, to file the incorporation papers for free. Then one evening, on the spur of the moment, the couple wandered over to Peter McCann, who lived two blocks away, to see if he would help. McCann, who had been plant manager a few years earlier, had transferred to Calgary before quitting Carling-O'Keefe to become president of Prairie Malt.

As it turned out, he had just finished his mandate there and agreed to conduct a feasibility study—for free. With lots of government contacts, McCann quickly rounded up some cash for the study. He also recruited Muzyka and accountant Lorne Broten to assist him—also working for free. Employee Don Ebelher recalls that he was quite dubious that an employee-owned brewery could be successful—he expected he would use his mechanic's ticket to find work with some other company in the city—but to his surprise, the study did suggest it was a viable opportunity.

With McCann willing to serve as president and veteran Gib Henderson recruited as the all-important brewmaster, the Saskatchewan Economic Development Corporation agreed to put up 75 percent of the estimated $3 million required to purchase the plant and start up the new company. The 29 employees agreed to take a 15 percent wage cut so the operation would be more economic. And 16 employees invested from $50,000 to $100,000 apiece in their new company, supplying the other 25 percent of financing in return for 100 percent ownership. A chartered bank agreed to provide an operating loan.

It was a brave move by the employees. As well as plunking severance money into the company, many canvassed relatives and friends for loans. Ownership was formally restricted to employees, so Brenda Kitz arranged for legal trust agreements to be signed formalizing such arrangements. A private member's bill was also passed in the legislature that reimbursed employees for 25 percent of their investment in a company in a buyout situation. Brenda Kitz, who had originated the idea, was positive throughout: "I'm always a pessimist but about this I had a good feeling all along. I don't know why."

The strategy was the reverse of what the analysts had recommended. The employees would brew quality beer. And with proper marketing, McCann felt, the people of Saskatchewan would help them to succeed. But it was far from a sure thing—as even Brenda Kitz recognized. "It was like going to Vegas and gambling," she admits.

Ebelher recalls: "It was scary—a big step. There were 16 guys for whom the biggest investment we ever made was in Canada Savings Bonds. We weren't business people, used to investing. But we had a lot of experience in brewing and we thought we could do it. We had a good core of people and an excellent brewmaster, so we just needed faith in the people buying the product."

The Roughrider of Suds: A New Company Begins

The people came through in spades. The deal with Molson was announced in mid-January 1990. The employees worked without pay throughout January, and two months later the company introduced two new premium beers—Great Western Lager and Great Western Light. The launch was scheduled for March 26 but in preparation the beer was delivered to liquor stores a few days early. It sold out on the weekend before the beer was even supposed to be officially available—420,000 beers bought (and perhaps much of it consumed) on that merry weekend.

The brewery immediately scheduled extra shipments and increased production to keep up with soaring public demand. But again by the end of the week, stocks were depleted. That became the pattern for the next few weeks: as soon as the shipments went out the door, eager consumers would buy them all up. At one point, the brewery even ran out of bottles; when its supplier, Molson, refused to provide any extra, Great Western had to seek emergency assistance from Consumers Glass in Ontario. The company had based its business plan on trying to win a 5 percent share of the market. It was now pulling in 20 percent.

Saskatchewan Business magazine captured the mood when it rhapsodized about the beer: "It is the Saskatchewan Roughrider of suds, the product our sympathy for the underdog compels us to support. In a province treated shabbily by Mother Nature, dismissed by the 1,000 or so who leave every month, ignored by the national media and given the status of a corporate outpost by the corporate big boys in Toronto, Great Western provides foamy evidence of our ability and pride."

How to Sell Employee Ownership to your Customers and Clients

1. Appeal to local pride.

   If your employee-owned company was formed by buying operations from a large, impersonal or distant owner, you may be able to make an emotional appeal to customers based on regional identity. This can be especially powerful if the product itself has emotional appeal, as was the case with Great Western Brewery.

2. Get your front-line employees to work better with customers.

   Customers might be better served by direct contact with the employee owners who are responsible for the product or service. Some self-directed groups at Algoma, for example, worked directly with customers and became "a model of co-operation."

3. Give empowered employees latitude to make decisions affecting clients.

   For example, at Creo, employees can spend money to satisfy customers without getting permission, as long as they know it makes economic sense. As Project Manager Colin Evans puts it: "Let's say a problem comes up in North Carolina and the client needs me tomorrow. It costs $2,000. I can just make the decision. I don't have to ask anyone."

4. Sell clients on the basis of employee ownership itself.

   You may find customers will assume that employee owners can give them superior service or products because they have a stake in the company's success. This was the case at Integra Geoservices, where the firm sold itself as employee-owned. They found many clients wanted a service provider that they could trust and felt more comfortable with employee owners.

5. Use a connection.

   If your employee-owned company is a spinoff from a larger one, you may be able to negotiate not only a good separation agreement but also favourable contracts to sell your products or services to the former parent over a long time period. That was the case at Revolve, as former parent NOVA became Revolve's first customer, continuing all the research and development programs that the group had been carrying out for it. An agreement that NOVA held with Pacific Wietz to market a dry gas seal worldwide was also assigned to Revolve, providing significant cash flow.

Employees were working 16-hour days—including Sundays—to keep up with demand, the atmosphere reminding people of a WWII munitions factory. "You are on a high everyday," recalls Ebelher. "It was nice problem to have: not being able to fill all the orders." When they decided to build a canning line—the first in the province—the employees jury-rigged it themselves from parts picked up from all over the continent. "It was all used equipment and it took a lot of work and effort," McCann said. "But it's working."

That seemed to describe the patchwork nature of the company, which was to be named Entrepreneur of the Year that fall by *Saskatchewan Business*. It was a lean operation—management had been thinned and a team-based approach adopted. But McCann was wary, realizing the craze wouldn't last and sales would drop as curiosity wore off. And he also knew his competitors—Molson and Labatt—wouldn't sit back. Indeed, Judy Lynn Heartwell of Labatt was quoted in *Saskatchewan Business*: "Do we view them as a long-term threat? The beer industry in Saskatchewan, as in every province, is flat. You get your customers from your competitors. I don't think Great Western brought many beer drinkers into the market. Yes, there is an impact on Labatt's."

This was not Hollywood. As those national competitors issued new brands—notably ice beer—Great Western's market share slid. The national companies also had cut back their advertising in the province for the first two years, presumably not wanting to be accused of anti-competitive behaviour, but then pumped it back up to normal. Great Western responded in 1994 with GW Ice Draft, putting a new twist on the product by packaging it in a 2 litre recyclable plastic bottle. But it was still a late entrant to that new market segment. As Great Western issued new beers, it seemed to be losing its focus and its special appeal. People were simply turning their interest elsewhere. Market share slid to 8 percent and the trend line was clearly plunging downwards rather than heading up.

The brewery compensated somewhat for its reversal in fortunes by expanding into nearby provinces, picking up about 1.5 percent of the total Western Canadian market. It also began to produce a non-alcoholic beer for Western Canada under the President's Choice label, stealing that business from the generic king, Cott Inc. And as planned, it worked to bond with the Saskatchewan public as a community brewer, sponsoring more than 2,000 events a year and serving as the exclusive supplier to those other Roughriders, of football fame. But despite such efforts, by the end of 1993—three years after it opened— the brewery was running at less than 50 percent capacity.

The ownership structure had been working reasonably well. Naturally, there had been unsettling moments at first, as everyone acclimatized to the situation. The 16 shareholders would meet once a week to check how they were doing. And they had a difficult balancing act on the shop floor, trying to preserve their equality with long-time colleagues who hadn't invested and acceding to the day-to-day authority of managers, while still feeling within themselves that special responsibility and concern—and fear—that flows from being an owner. But if it was a balancing act, they also knew which way they had to lean: the managers had to be in charge on a daily basis. That had been a basic organizing principle from the outset.

Another instinct had been to get outside help. As well as employees, the board of directors included Jim Yuell, president of Prairie Industries Chemical, and Maurice Werezak, president of the United Food and Chemical Workers local at Mitchell Foods. "Jim and Maurice—one a self-made businessman and the other a union leader— got along famously," says Greg Kitz, who was the first board chair.

The union disbanded its local at the plant just before the buyout. But the employees wanted a union; they formed a new local, allying again with the same international union, since it understood the industry. A key motivation was to be able to indicate on the bottle that the beer was union-made—an important issue with many buyers in Saskatchewan. They tried to arrange it so that most of the new executive was not composed of owners, but one of the oddities that drew lots of media attention was that John O'Connor was not only a new owner of the brewery but also president of the union local. He attended the weekly owners' sessions while also chairing union meetings— and carried business cards with both the company and union logos.

As it turns out, the union has been good for everyone. When times grew rough, and pay cuts were required, the employees felt more secure with a union negotiating on their behalf—even if it was with the management some of them oversaw. And Greg Kitz believes having some owners in the union makes everybody feel more comfortable, because they know negotiations will be more honest. "The union's attitude is better known to management, and management's financial situation is well known to the union. So they know how much flexibility there really is for management to act," he says. "The union is no longer trying to get everything possible from the company, with the company trying to knock the union down."

Phase Two Begins

The drop in sales marked the end of employee ownership's first phase. When McCann resigned to run for Parliament, Ebelher, who was operations manager, assumed the presidency on an interim basis. The company began to look for a new president who could reinvigorate the business and help to develop a suitable exit strategy for the owners, some of whom were nearing retirement age.

In the end, they reached for a Coke. Ron Waldman had grown up in the bottling business, since his father Harold ran Beverage Central, which covered most of Saskatchewan for Coca-Cola and Canada Dry. It was the largest family-owned Coke franchise in Canada; as the parent company began to buy back franchises, it was a prime pick. However, that left Ron Waldman adrift at age 32, without what he had expected to be his life's work.

He was consulting on corporate governance and running his own investment-banking outfit when he was approached to take the helm at Great Western. It appealed to him because employee ownership had many of the features of a family business, and he felt this particular concern could be highly successful if the right strategy was put in place. But the shareholders also attracted him: "They seemed like very decent, hard-working folks, who had clearly leveraged a lot of their personal accumulated wealth to be involved in this enterprise. It was quite courageous, out-of-the-box thinking. I wanted to help where I could."

Sales were still dropping as he took over. The company had not been consistent in its product offerings and had overreached in the market, going in too many directions. It had lost the confidence of the consumer—not just the average beer-drinking denizen but also the key licensee operators at liquor board outlets and hotels that made large purchase decisions. "The challenge in the beer business is that generally you only get one shot at it with the consumer. From our perspective, we had to find a way to reinvent ourselves. It would almost have been easier to start over but that wasn't an option," Waldman says.

Because of the plant's high overhead—which had to be applied against a small-scale operation—it was clear the company couldn't save its way to success. It would have to grow, taking 10 percent of the market, if it could. "We had to rekindle our relationship with the consumer, one bottle at a time. To do that, you need time, money, and the ability to focus on and grow your branded business," says Waldman. But buried in that strategy was an important contradiction, since the time and money to grow the branded business would come only by finding non-branded opportunities to boost volume and revenues.

After eliminating a lot of underperforming brands and brews that offered no strategic advantages, they settled on three core brand propositions to compete selectively in the marketplace. The foundation was a series of popular brands, built around Great Western Ice, Great Western Original Gold, and Saskatchewan beer—as well as the licence they gained to brew and sell Pabst Blue Ribbon in Western Canada.

Supplementing those were two sets of premium and specialty beers, since everyone still believed they would be crucial for success. The first were meant to be regionally relevant and were dubbed the Brewhouse family, with Brewhouse Pilsener and Brewhouse Light kicking the series off. They didn't have Great Western's name all over them, making a pitch for newer, younger drinkers who wanted a premium beer. The final step in the strategy was to develop a new generation of Great Western products that were in the same vein as Moosehead and Oland—specialty beers that conveyed a traditional, small-town, quality flavour. The first two were Western Premium Lager and Western Premium Light.

"Brands are badges," explains Waldman. "In Saskatchewan and the Prairies, we have begun to position ourselves as Canada's Prairie brewery. Our brands—particularly Western Premium Lager and Western Premium Light, and others that will follow—resonate with that small-is-good, crafted-with-care, Canadiana feeling." That contrasts, he notes, with beers like Molson Canadian or Labatt Blue, which take a more national perspective. They wrap themselves in hockey or nationalism, bidding to be known as the quintessential Canadian brand. "There is all kinds of imagery involved. But from our perspective, we are just as much a part of the Canadian landscape but are trying to be more regionally relevant, tying ourselves to regional events and images, and trying to be the very essence of all good things in the Prairies," Waldman says.

To meet the overhead and buy time for those new brands to take hold, Great Western also greatly increased its contract packing for other brewers. It became a licensed distiller and also qualified as an organic brewer. It picked up a lot of contracts to produce everything from spirit-based lemonade drinks, to organic malt syrups, to beer for branded and private-label suppliers in both Western Canada and the United States.

It also entered into arrangements to represent other breweries' brands when selling to licensees. The intent was to transform Great Western from a lowly third brewer competing against Molson and Labatt to a brewing specialist. Practically, it meant a salesperson visiting an establishment could sell more than one company's brands, increasing the return for time spent.

That strategy helped the company turn the corner. Sales improved and market share increased, slowly but steadily. The change didn't come easily, however. Inevitably there were tensions. Indeed, one of the first acts Waldman needed to make on entering Great Western was to order an 18 percent wage cut to keep the operation afloat—in a company where just a few years earlier there had been a 15 percent wage rollback.

The Challenges of Employee Ownership

He believes the challenges of managing a business remain similar whether the operation is employee-owned or not. But greater anxiety occurs in employee-owned and family businesses, particularly in bad times. When things go well—as they have been lately—that anxiety is surpassed by the self-satisfaction and pride that envelops the owners, which becomes evident to all and can spread to all. But early in his tenure, when everything was rockier, Waldman was conscious of the embarrassment, aggravation, and disappointment in the employee owners, which also could be contagious.

"It takes a lot more emotional energy to manage an employee-owned business because you have to be sensitive to—you want to be *more* sensitive to—the issues and people," he says. It's not just the conversations during the working day, when employee owners expect more from the president they hire than an average worker, but also in off-hours. There will be calls at home in the evenings, or chance encounters at the supermarket that turn into lengthy business conversations. The president has to be approachable and accountable 24 hours a day, seven days a week, in a way that wouldn't occur in a non-employee-owned business.

The employee owner role was diminished on the board, with only one serving as a member of the five-person board. But the others take turns filling the two observer slots, getting a chance to sit in on meetings and see how the affairs of their business are being handled. Waldman is a director and the three other directors are outsiders, who aren't paid for their time but are covered by liability insurance.

When he joined, Waldman had stipulated that he would need the freedom to make decisions and not be second-guessed continually. "I had enough experience with governance to know that there had to be a process that when the decisions were made they stuck—or else I should be fired. I wasn't going to be in a situation where there were all kinds of manipulations," he says.

He views himself as formally accountable to the board and to shareholders only through that board. At the same time, under his tenure, management has raised the level of reporting to shareholders, issuing annual reports and providing detailed reports every two months to the board of directors, which can be shared with shareholders by their representative and observers. Quarterly town hall meetings are also held with all staff—not just shareholders—to report on performance, explain strategy and expectations, and receive feedback. But Waldman doesn't meet regularly with shareholders as a group, noting the formula he follows is similar to that of a public company, where the board meets once a year with its shareholders at the annual meeting.

That structure satisfies the shareholders, who have recently tended to meet only once a year themselves. Brenda Kitz, who represents the shareholders on the board, visits the plant most days—her own office is just two blocks away—and she'll meet with Waldman, discussing issues and communicating with the shareholders. "It's no different from any other business," Ebelher says. "The owners don't consider themselves as owners. It's more of an investment."

In the plant, he finds employees more conscientious than in the old days. To some extent, that results from ownership. But he also stresses it stems from the plant's vulnerability. They all know that they are small fish swimming with some big sharks. They have been through one shutdown and know that the market can turn against them again. "There is no large, mother company we can rely on to help us or can draw funds from. This is it," says Ebelher.

The company benefited initially with beer drinkers from being employee-owned and a small, locally owned operation. And it has run ads in the past stressing its unique ownership. But Waldman doesn't like that approach: "You can't market by obligation—especially with a product like ours, which is fun. You have to market by giving consumers reasons to buy your product." The products must be top-drawer and must appeal because of their quality and image. The best the company can hope for is that its ownership structure might be a tiebreaker, when its product is equally appealing with a competitive brew.

Waldman is mixed in his assessment of employee ownership. He feels it adds stress in bad times and strength in good times, since nothing is as exciting as feeling you are on a winning team. But for it to work, he believes more people have to feel they are on that special winning team, which means having broader employee ownership than at Great Western. The brewery's ownership, he notes, falls somewhere between a partnership and full-scale employee ownership. In a partnership, the owners expect to be treated differently; under broad employee ownership, people recognize that they are part of a team— that by working together they can increase the value of each other's stake in the company.

That attitude can help to get everyone in an employee-owned company aligned with corporate goals. Waldman has seen it happen at Great Western with the employee owners and wishes it would apply more broadly. "The mindset of an investor who is an employee is different. We don't sing songs together, exercise together, or hold hands and pray to reach unity. But we are cohesive," he says.

Ebelher believes the Great Western model can be applied elsewhere. One big plus he stresses is the quicker decision-making that resulted from having control of the plant in Saskatoon. People can get an answer to a question or solve a problem on site, with a colleague, rather than having to wait for a solution from corporate headquarters in another city. That also means employees are more likely to raise an issue, rather than keep silent, which in turn means that problems get addressed quicker.

He urges others facing a closure and considering employee ownership to make sure they carry out a strong feasibility study that outlines exactly where the money will be going and coming from in the new operation. "If you don't have that, you are dead," he warns.

Finding an Exit

A major headache for Great Western's owners has been the failure to find a way of selling their shares profitably and exiting the business. Some have retired already; others are conscious that retirement is nearing. The company has spun off dividends, and the wage settlement in the latest contract allowed employees to get back to where they were before the buyout—no great achievement, but an improvement. Overall, they have kept their jobs, raised total employment to an average of 55 people, and know that at some point they should be able to make a healthy capital gain by selling the business. But it has taken longer than everyone expected to realize that return on investment.

Ironically, when times were good in the first 18 months, Greg Kitz had championed the notion of having an initial public offering of shares. But some opposed him, wanting to wait for a better opportunity, and others were simply uncomfortable and unsure about the financial process itself. Finally, he was replaced as board chair over the dispute. "We had a chance to get more people involved then," he says. "Hopefully that will come back. But it was our window of opportunity. I was disappointed. They followed Brenda and me through thick and thin and then abandoned us."

The failure to raise capital hurt a few years later when the company wanted to buy kegs and the equipment for moving into that segment of the draft beer market. Finally, some of the owners and their friends—39 people in all—loaned the company money for the venture. Instead of reducing their exposure, the owners were increasing it.

Still, Ebelher is optimistic. "I don't feel trapped. I'm still working," he said in an interview a little over 10 years after his group took control. And others feel the same way. Liquidity has been introduced, with owners able to sell their shares to other people as long as they are not part of the brewing industry. But everybody has still been holding on rather than selling. And with shareholder value built up again, Waldman has been determined to find a buyer. "I think that any employee ownership that doesn't have an exit strategy is a very frustrating experience for the employees. They have no option but to ride with you," he says. Indeed, he feels that's the most important message he would pass on to others considering a similar ownership approach: "I salute those who do this but they have to go into it with their eyes wide open and they have to realize that an exit strategy must be part of the equation—and they have to have a time horizon for that to occur."

Exit Strategies

Companies embracing employee ownership need to think of an exit strategy for internal shareholders. Otherwise the employees may find their wealth inaccessible until they retire or quit. The company may also find itself hamstrung by such repurchase liabilities.

How did our companies handle this issue? Some went public and created an external market for the shares. Others sought a share swap with or an outright sale to a larger publicly traded company. How did these companies and their employees fare?

At Creo, the decision was to take the company public. The July 1999 initial public offering of shares put the company's valuation at $1 billion, giving the founders and early employees 160 times the hypothetical value of their first shares.

Others decided on various sale scenarios. Employee owners at Spruce Falls, who initially owned 52 percent of the company's shares, came to trust Tembec's leadership over a period of six years. It must have seemed natural to sell their shares to Tembec when it was allowed to increase its stake from 41 percent to full ownership in 1997, with an average employee investment of $10,000 at the end of 1991 turning into about $145,000. Frank Dottori observed that many employees were uncomfortable with share ownership: "They want job security so they don't have to wake up tomorrow and find themselves unemployed. But they don't like to be shareholders. Many will say, 'I can't sleep at night if I have $10,000 invested in Tembec and see it drop from $10 to $9, with me losing $1,000.'"

At Integra, the company took what Klingbeil called "the elevator ride of value." At Integra's worst moment it was worth virtually nothing. Two and a half years later, it was probably worth 10 to 20 times earnings, a significant value per share. However, economic cycles made the share value extremely volatile. Employee capital should theoretically be patient capital, but many employees find it difficult to be patient. So Integra employees chose to be bought out by the Scott Pickford Group rather than continuing as an independent company, swapping their shares for shares in Scott Pickford's parent and reaping 10 times their original investment. Most kept their shares in the publicly traded company, rather than cashing them in after the lock-up period expired.

At Revolve, the employee owners, who split their holdings across their two business lines, had a long and complicated journey to a safe exit. In November 1997, SKF bought a 40 percent stake in the company. But SKF wasn't interested in the gas seal business, so Revolve had to sever that operation off. The seal business was owned 100 percent by family, friends, and business associates. The magnetic bearings business—which quickly grew to become the large operation—was 60 percent owned by those same family, friends, and business associates, with SKF holding the other 40 percent. Employee owners had to wait six months more to sell their remaining interest to SKF and to another partner firm.

SFG also found a strategic buyer—after employees there also experienced the elevator ride of value—and became an operating division of Cayenta. Some long-term, senior employees found the value of their shares worth as much as $400,000, while relatively new junior employees got a few thousand dollars.

Some of these exits weren't as much strategy as luck. And some employee owners are still waiting for their opportunity as at Great Western Brewery.

In that sense, employee ownership must mirror venture capital and investment banking deals, where everyone recognizes that at some future date the company will evolve to a different structure. "They shouldn't look at it as forever and a day. They have to look for ways that this structure can add value and then move on to the next structure," he says.

In Hollywood, stories always end up with everyone living happily ever after. However, in employee ownership, Waldman argues, it can't be forever. For Great Western Brewery, the script is therefore still being written. The early draft had its deeply romantic and heartwarming moments. And recently there have been many pleasant vignettes, with employment up to 75 people during parts of the year and sales on the rise. But with that critical final scene—the exit—not written, the short, blissful feature has turned into an epic of longer duration than anybody expected, and with far more drama and moments of despair than had been hoped. Now, everyone is awaiting the final, happy ending.

Spruce Falls

๏๏

The 15 Percent Competitive Edge

"You get a 10 to 15 percent edge with employee ownership. It can be zero if I don't get them involved. But if I can get them involved and motivated, and they believe, I've got a 10 or 15 percent edge. Absolutely."

—Frank Dottori, President and
CEO, Tembec Inc.

When Dennis Turcotte returned from the town hall meeting of employees in September 1990, the hallways were buzzing as everyone came to grips with the dismal news just dumped on them. The Spruce Falls mill in Kapuskasing, Ontario, had been on the block for many years, and a deal had seemed in the offing with Kruger Inc. But management had just announced that Kruger was backing away from the tentative agreement, and the joint owners of the mill, Kimberly-Clark and the *New York Times*, still seemed intent on getting rid of the operation.

The 29-year-old Turcotte, who had both an MBA and an engineering degree and was then holding down an entry-level management job as supervisor of maintenance planning, was as baffled by events as anyone. But Joan Pope, a secretary in their department, had long thought that since the mill was the lifeblood of their town, it was only logical that it be owned by the people of the town and the employees, with the fruits of their labour returning to them rather than being siphoned off by large American corporations. When others didn't pick up on her idealistic notions, she turned to Turcotte: "You have this new fancy business training. Don't employees buy companies in situations like this?" Everyone chuckled—except Turcotte. "Don't laugh, guys. This kind of thing happens. It has happened in Canada and the United States. Yeah, it's possible," he said.

A decade later, the laughter has turned to pride. The employees and townsfolk of Kapuskasing did buy themselves a paper mill—putting up big chunks of their own cash. They got back even bigger chunks of cash—about 14 times what they put in, on average, in about half a decade—and the worn-out mill they were operating is now one of the most productive in North America, after a carefully planned and implemented $350 million capital upgrade. And Turcotte is no longer a first-level supervisor: He's an executive vice-president of Tembec Inc., the company they partnered with in the buyout, overseeing not just Spruce Falls but also Pine Falls Paper Company, a Manitoba mill that was picked up in a similar employee buyout.

Even after Turcotte supported Pope in that bull session, the others dismissed the idea as fantasy. But he returned to his office and couldn't get the thought out of his mind. So he decided to phone a friend in investment banking to kick the notion around. That friend was out but a colleague took the call. Just as Turcotte got started—and before he identified the mill the fellow said, however, "Stop right there. You're calling from Spruce Falls, I take it?" His firm represented the *New York Times*, he informed Turcotte, and therefore had a potential conflict. But he followed that by asking if a senior official at Kimberly-Clark knew about the call, and, after being informed no, affably suggested Turcotte phone a boutique-financing firm.

Turcotte was puzzled—and frightened. "I figured I'd get fired. I had meddled where I shouldn't. I decided to come clean right away," he recalls. So he headed off to talk to Maurice Hicks, the chief financial officer for the plant. "Maurice, I think I've done something stupid," he began. It was the end of the day, Hicks was supportive, and as they chatted the vice-president of engineering happened to wander by and join in the discussion of a buyout. Was it possible? Could they actually purchase the mill? The senior managers were curious and excited by the prospect.

The next day the regular management meeting was held. Turcotte was invited to drop in and make his pitch. Again he found receptivity—but to a point. Most of the managers felt it made more sense to simply try a management buyout. But Turcotte was insistent. "Being a very vocal person—whether I was junior or not, frankly this was so important I didn't give a damn what people thought," he says. The plant could be turned around, he argued, only with a change in employee attitudes. And that would come only if employees shared in ownership of the mill. Joan Pope's notion was starting to root firmly in his mind and interconnect with his value system.

Towards a Solution

At that point, however, his argument was theoretical. The managers weren't particularly interested, nor were the employees. The unions simply saw the company's announcement as a tactic aimed at delaying collective bargaining and winning concessions. They were confident Kruger would return with a new offer, or the company would locate another buyer. The managers formed the Phoenix Group to probe the possibility of a buyout but the unions stayed on the sidelines.

Kimberly-Clark and the *New York Times* had jointly operated the mill since opening it in 1926, with Kimberly-Clark as the managing partner and the *Times* as a major buyer of its newsprint supply. But in the 1980s, the Canadian pulp and paper industry hit a slump. Kimberly-Clark had decided early in the decade to withdraw from pulp and paper and concentrate on its consumer goods, like Kleenex, Huggies, and Scott paper products. That meant selling its Coosa Pines mill in Alabama, the Terrace Bay mill in British Columbia, and Spruce Falls.

In 1987, in response to a glut of newsprint on the market, Kimberley-Clark instituted an early retirement program at Spruce Falls. Over 180 workers with a combined experience of 6,400 person-years left, that loss of expertise contributing to already declining productivity and performance. Even more fundamentally, with its eye on selling, Kimberly-Clark was failing to make the major capital investments that were needed for the mill to remain cost-competitive over the long term.

Spruce Falls had owned the power rights to the nearby Smoky Falls hydro-electricity generating station since the mill opened, receiving about 50 percent of its power supply from that dam. In 1989, however, Ontario Hydro, which was considering a water diversion plan that would increase the dam's efficiency, bought the rights to the generating station for $113.5 million. The agreement guaranteed Spruce Falls its present consumption of electricity from the dam for 80 years at no cost.

That made the plant attractive to a purchaser and in June 1990, Kruger signed an agreement in principle to take over the mill. But the deal fell through over the summer when Kruger failed to get financing. Over the next few months the Phoenix Group developed a plan for a buyout but was unable to sell it broadly, because of the prevailing cynicism in the plant and its own role as management.

The mayor of Kapuskasing, Ted Jewell, and the town administrator, Matt Rukavina, eventually decided to bring the various players together and see if injecting top-level civic support could create momentum towards a local solution. The Purchasing Employees

Group was formed, although the unions were wary and didn't join initially. "Our goal was to get a collective agreement in place," says Norm Leybourne, who headed Local 256 of papermakers, and whose members were convinced Kruger would still buy the plant.

Darwin Smith, the president and CEO of Kimberly-Clark, tried to beat back such sentiment by sending a letter to Jewell in January 1991, stressing the seriousness of the situation. "No one having a stake in Spruce Falls should continue to believe that Kruger is a viable candidate to buy Spruce," he warned. The issue transcended financing, since Kimberly-Clark, angry at Kruger's about-face, was not prepared under any circumstances to sell the plant to the Montreal-based pulp and paper manufacturer. "I simply will not agree to cause either the stockholders or the employees of Spruce to be subject to their [Kruger's] irresponsible type of business conduct which has been demonstrated since we first commenced discussions with Kruger," Smith insisted.

Over time, the five unions joined the Purchasing Employees Group, with each providing two members and management supplying two representatives of its own. But it was still an uneasy situation. Leybourne's local, for example, made sure that its representatives realized they were not permitted to commit to anything—and were separated from the all-important contract bargaining team.

Darwin Smith's Video

Again, Smith tried to light a fire. The mill had lost $194,000 the previous year and his eagerness to jettison it had naturally heightened. On March 13, with the mill shut down for two weeks—providing the 1,500 workers with a taste of what could lie ahead—Smith had a video delivered to every employee's home in which he provided a detailed analysis of the mill's situation.

Smith began with a chart of possible owners, placing a large check mark beside "No" for three of them: Kimberly-Clark, the *New York Times*, and Kruger Inc. "Understand that the decision by Kimberly-Clark and the *New York Times* to discontinue ownership of Spruce Falls will not be changed. Understand also that Kruger Inc. is out of the running. It failed to live up to its June 1990 agreement in principle to buy Spruce Falls. The subject will never be opened up again with that company." That left checkmarks beside "Maybe" for two potential buyers: Spruce employees, or "an unknown third party."

To help employees, the company had already indicated it would give them the plant for free—along with the free power from the Ontario Hydro deal. But Smith insisted on a quick answer. And that was complicated by the fact that before any hand over Kimberly-Clark wanted to receive the proceeds of the Smoky Falls sale, some of which Smith pledged to funnel to the employee owners as assistance. However, at that point, that deal was being held up by Ontario Hydro, which was leaving it as part of a broad-based package of power issues to be considered by the government rather than pushing it through as a separate item. More importantly, a positive environmental review would be needed for the deal to be sealed.

Smith pushed for an early decision, noting that every month it was delayed, Hydro's cost of purchase was rising by $1.2 million. He suggested that the Ontario government, rather than the employees of Spruce Falls, assume the risk of a negative environmental assessment. "Perhaps the risk is acceptable when measured against the social cost of the loss of 1,200 direct jobs in Kapuskasing," he suggested.

Advising that time was running out, he then set out two options for employees to consider. The first was what he called the Rebirth Plan. In line with what happened to a mill in Amos, Quebec, the Spruce Falls operation would be dramatically downsized, discontinuing the production of wood and closing the chip mill, groundwood mill, magnetite mill, and three of the five paper machines. About 75 percent of the work force, or 1200 jobs, would be eliminated and the remaining work force would concentrate on the thermo-mechanical paper mill and a new de-inking facility to allow for the production of recycled paper.

The alternative, which he called the Survival Plan, was for employees to take over the mill. With employees as owners, he noted, that might facilitate the collective bargaining process—and the process of coming to grips with the economic reality of the plant rather than continuing to rely on the mill to play rich uncle to the citizenry of Kapuskasing. "The mill can never be cost-competitive operating the way it is unless labour costs are reduced and production increased. Perhaps employees would understand this better if they owned Spruce Falls," he said.

Before closing his presentation he posed three tough questions:
- "Are you willing to change the way you work?"
- "Are you willing to reduce costs?"
- "Are you willing to lay the 'Uncle Spruce' syndrome to rest?"

As he signed off the video, Smith said that he wished a less threatening way were available to put his ideas across, but he felt compelled to tell it like it was. Naturally, the employees didn't agree as they sat and watched the big boss impassively make his statement. Nobody was inclined to use the term "rebirth plan," let alone endorse it. They simply called it the Amos Plan, with disgust.

The Tembec Connection

A lot of effort was going into the struggle to save the mill, with the Purchasing Employees Group meeting every day, for long periods. But they weren't getting anywhere. Smith's April 30 deadline passed without any significant progress.

In late May, Leybourne recalls his members' becoming inflamed when they heard a rumour that Hicks and a few others from the Purchasing Employees Group had visited Frank Dottori, the president and CEO of Tembec Inc., and promised a major cut in wages and changes in the collective agreement if he would help to take over the plant. But if Leybourne's members were angry, they also weren't inclined to see their situation as particularly perilous. Senior employees didn't even view the drastic Amos Plan as a threat; they were confident they would still hold on to their own jobs. The general feeling was that the union should continue to focus on collective bargaining, where real security lay, rather than a buyout. "The message I was getting from my members was that it was still a red herring," he says.

Dottori had indeed been approached. For months he had been receiving entreaties from interested parties—including the federal government. It was a natural match, since if anyone understood what Spruce employees were potentially facing, it was Frank Dottori. He had stood in their shoes, nearly 20 years earlier, after a devastating plant shutdown—and with vision and courage, he and his fellow employees had triumphed.

At the time, Dottori had been a 32-year-old chemical engineer with Canadian International Paper in Temiscaming, Quebec, who had recently made an agonizing decision to commit his career to the Kipawa dissolving pulp mill. He had initially joined the company for a few years after university graduation, but, being rebellious and frustrated at the disorganization, eventually accepted a more senior position with mining company Texas Gulf. But he loved the people and area of Temiscaming. He returned, only to find the company still distressingly disorganized and to receive yet another offer to transfer to Texas Gulf, this time taking charge of a $250 million smelter that was being built. He knew he couldn't keep flipping endlessly between the two companies. After his boss at the mill pressed him to stay—telling him he had a great future and one day might even be president of the entire company—he decided over the Christmas holidays in 1971 to refuse the smelter job and remain in Temiscaming.

A month later, at a meeting similar to the one that had provoked Turcotte to action, the president of CIP read a one-page press release saying that the mill was being shut down. Dottori was stunned. He had a wife and three children and was now facing the prospect of being unemployed in a remote northern Quebec town. He rushed back to his office to call Texas Gulf to see if the position was still open, but learned it had just been filled.

"I'm one of those guys who don't get depressed; I get aggressive," he recalls. "I said of the shutdown, 'That's not the way you treat people.' It became a moral principle." He crystallized the idea of a company of people building their own future. He then went all over the mill gathering support, telling colleagues, "These jackasses don't know what they are doing. We are going to take over this company and make it work because we know what we're doing. We have a vision and we are going to get this thing done."

Faced with unemployment, people bought into his rather simplistic message and agreed to put their severance pay into a fund to purchase the mill and start it up again. In 1972, however, that was unheard of. And it wasn't as if Dottori had the background to make governments and the company willing to support his plan. He recalls, humorously, his first meeting with Guy Saint Pierre, the young, technocratic minister of trade and commerce in Robert Bourassa's government. When asked how much money they had, Dottori and his team replied none. The government officials responded, "Well, that's strike one." Then they were asked who was going to sell the pulp for them. After Dottori's team responded that they didn't know, the government officials declared, "Well, that's strike two." Next, they were asked whom they had found with credibility to run their organization. Again, the honest answer—nobody—was insufficient. "That's strike three."

But Dottori was still to get a few more swings. Given the government's concerns about marketing, he recruited George Petty, an ex-salesperson with CIP and former vice-president of international sales with International Paper in New York, to head up their effort. Backing him would be Jack Stevens, former vice-president of corporate planning for CIP, and Jim Chantler, an ex-plant manager and CIP's director of industrial relations. They became known in Tembec lore as "the Founders," and the next time Dottori returned to see the minister he let Petty do the talking. "He was like a bull moose, pushy and self-confident," Dottori later recalled in a case study for Ivey Business School. "He presented the plan in a 'you have a problem and I have the solution' style and we walked away with a cheque for $25,000 to complete a feasibility study."

The company wasn't eager to sell the plant to the employees; a Quebec law even prevented employees from serving on boards of directors. But the time was right for their plan. The Vietnam War, the student movement in universities, the recent overthrow of Allende in Chile, and the growing concern about American multinationals were fuelling left-wing sentiments in the populace. The unions backed the plan, as did the newspapers. "It became a crusade to let these poor helpless guys in northwestern Quebec create their own mill and company. Why should government and big business prevent that?" he recalls.

When the feasibility study found the idea was financially viable, negotiations began with the company and government. It was to be a rugged fight, with the company—sensing leverage—trying to block the deal unless it received a better deal from the government on pollution controls for its other Quebec operations, while the government threatened expropriation. In June and July of 1973, the townspeople even blockaded the Ottawa River to prevent CIP transporting logs from the region to its other mills downstream. But that seemed to break the negotiating logjam; in August of that year, the new employee-owned company, Tembec, took control of the mill.

Originally, there had been no sophisticated model in Dottori's head. He just saw a bunch of people working together—without making any distinctions between union people and non-union people. But as the unions got on board, that distinction became important. Talk then grew of a co-op, which he resisted. "I'm a small capitalist. I believe in competition and that all people should be treated equally, but not all people are equal. I believe everybody should get something—but after that the harder you work, the more you get," he says. In the end, the managers bought 44 percent of the mill, the employees 44 percent, and the government 12 percent.

Tembec proved to be a slick operator. It invested wisely in capital improvements and expanded production. It also developed what became known as the Tembec model of employee participation. And it became profitable, with Dottori rising from his initial position as production manager to head the company. When Tembec went public in 1983, many of the employees took advantage of the healthy stock price over the next few years to cash in. Those who had invested $1,000 a decade earlier got $100,000 back—100 times their investment.

So Dottori was seasoned in buyouts and turnarounds when the calls to assist Spruce Falls streamed in. But he was reluctant to get involved, fearing that he would be accused of trying to steal the company. Finally, after six months of consideration, he agreed to meet for three days in February 1992 with the Purchasing Employees Group to offer advice. He reviewed their business plan and suggested alterations to make it workable.

He also told them that if they couldn't swing it on their own and needed a partner, he would be willing to help. But at that point, he would switch from being an advisor into being an investor. And he listed some tough conditions that needed to be met. He would have to be granted an exclusive opportunity to put the deal together and a chance to own 50 percent of the company. As well, employees would have to contribute cash—matching his company's investment dollar for dollar—since to his mind that was essential to get them behind any plan. "They almost got indigestion—and went off," he recalls.

But the pressure continued to mount, on everybody. Darwin Smith didn't stop with his video. He flew to Kapuskasing to meet the Purchasing Employee Group several times. He was pushing for an employee buyout, but was insisting they develop a realistic financial plan for capital expansion that could take the company into the future, not wanting to be accused someday of saddling them with a venture that had flopped. He also wasn't confident in local management's ability to run the new operation and was urging the employees to find a partner. When Dottori's name surfaced, Smith was enthusiastic. "He knew we needed an entrepreneur," says Turcotte. "We didn't need some guy in a blue suit to come in and start managing from a paperwork point of view. We needed a guy who would roll up his sleeves and get in, who knew the paper industry, who was committed to it, and who didn't just want to take out cash from this business."

The Ontario government was also pushing for partnerships in its evolving strategy for the buyouts that were occurring on the lip of the recession. To Peter Tanaka, who was overseeing the process as head of the Strategic Investment Group, Tembec's own history of building itself up from a humble beginning seemed an ideal model. And Dottori seemed the kind of dynamo to make it all work out. "It was the right company with the right attitude, style, and culture," he says. "If they had teamed up with a traditional firm, it wouldn't have worked as well."

The Final Stages

Finally, Dottori, in Toronto on business, got a phone call inviting him to meet again with the purchasing group. They wanted to deal. And two important things happened at that crucial meeting. First, Dottori noticed a fellow who had been present at the initial meeting but had taken a back seat to the more senior officials. This time, as that individual spoke, it became clear to Dottori that he was the brightest of the bunch, somebody who intuitively understood what needed to be done. He asked somebody who that fellow was. "Dennis Turcotte." What does he do? "A maintenance manager." Dottori was astonished at the low-level position—and impressed at the talent: "He reminded me of when I was younger and starting out. We started to develop a relationship and he started to become the dominant leader with the employees, playing a key role in getting people organized there."

The other important element of the meeting was that they began developing a workable plan for joint ownership. Dottori ditched the financial advisors, figuring his people knew how to put together an employee buyout, having done one before. The big issue, however, was how to finesse the problems raised by the Smoky Falls deal. The government was resistant to taking the financial risk for what might come out of the environmental assessment. Indeed, on June 28, two days before the deadline Smith had set for an agreement—and with the employees and Tembec having now forged a deal between them— the Ontario government announced it was withdrawing from the proposal because of the U.S. owners' refusal to share any responsibility for the environmental risk.

Instead, the government proposed two alternatives for Kimberly-Clark and the *New York Times* to consider. In the first, they could collect one half of the revenue from the sale of the Smoky Falls facility immediately and collect the other half pending a favourable assessment of the dam. The second option involved Kimberly-Clark making a loan to the Purchasing Employees Group that would be repaid upon a positive environmental assessment of the dam. Smith turned both thumbs down, calling the suggestion that the owners share in the risk "naive and preposterous."

Leybourne remembers the government's withdrawal as devastating. So that stalemate had at least one positive effect: it made all employees realize their jobs were indeed in jeopardy. But the situation was to get worse before it got better. After Kimberly-Clark made another offer that the government quickly rejected, despair set in. The Purchasing Employees Group broke apart in frustration, with Smith no longer willing to deal with it. A new group formed, under Rene Piché, publisher of the Kapuskasing *Northern Times* newspaper: KAP, for Kill Amos Plan. Again it brought together business people, employees, and other spokespersons from the community, trying to keep open communication lines with all the parties.

About 150 residents of Kapuskasing camped at Queen's Park for four days to draw attention to the situation and held a mass rally at the legislature while KAP leaders met with Premier Bob Rae. The protest drew lots of media attention—and from Peter Tanaka, lots of admiration. "It was amazing. If I had any cynicism developed over the years, it evaporated. I was amazed by what people do when they band together and put their will into it," he says.

A new deadline of August 15 was set. KAP was dissolved and a fourth committee formed, the Employee Ownership Group, led by the man who, with Joan Pope's assistance, had started it all: Dennis Turcotte. This time, it was to prove successful. All the unions were now full participants in the process, working in tandem with their managers and Tembec to forge a deal. Nothing could be decided without full consensus, as everybody buried past differences for the greater good of Kapuskasing. "It took the crisis of government walking away for people to believe it was real," says Leybourne.

Whereas the Steelworkers had driven the Algoma deal, here the community was now driving it. Finally, solidarity existed between management, unions, and the citizenry. "They were of one mind," says Tanaka. It was also NDP territory. The government had to respond.

On August 13, two days before the final deadline, all parties came to an agreement. The mill would be given to management and the workers for $1. As a further gift from Kimberly-Clark, the employees would be handed 20 percent of the shares in the new company that owned the mill, part of them allocated equally and part according to seniority. Tembec would invest $12.5 million in shares of the new company and supply an additional $12.5 million as a loan—as well as promising $15 million more for capital investment in the following three years. The employees and residents of Kapuskasing would try to match Tembec's $12.5 million share investment, thereby splitting the remaining 80 percent of the company evenly.

Ontario Hydro would pay close to $140 million to Kimberly-Clark and the *New York Times* for the Smoky Falls power plant and dams. But instead of guaranteeing 80 years of free power, the utility would provide $34 million cash to be used for mill modernization, as well as 10 years of free power. The Ontario government committed itself to reimburse Ontario Hydro for up to $274 million if the environmental assessment was unfavourable. Finally, Kimberly-Clark supplemented the cash being raised for capital investment by pledging $60 million in loans at low interest rates.

Often in the scramble to put together a buyout, the new company is formed with only minimal financial resources to meet the future. Heeding Dottori's and Smith's instincts, this new company was being armed with a war chest to reinvest in productivity improvements. And Dottori insisted on a provision preventing dividends to shareholders—his own company, included—for seven years. The intent was to build, not milk.

A new labour contract was also now negotiated, with the concessions that had been feared. But the atmosphere had changed and if employees were not happy at least they were committed to the broader mission. The wage package was cut by $3.50 an hour and vacations were trimmed from a maximum of seven weeks for senior employees to just two weeks. However, pay increases were scheduled for 1992; of 3 percent for woodlands employees and 4.3 percent for mill employees, with an across-the-board 5.5 percent hike in 1993.

Employees voted 88 percent in favour of the new labour contract, although the unpopularity of the vacations cutback led to a compromise: employees could take time off work without pay, that unpaid vacation varying according to seniority. But the bigger issue now was to persuade employees and citizens to buy shares, so that they, rather than Tembec, could keep control of the company. At first, that seemed in doubt, as everyone wavered, hesitant to commit. With the business plan calling for labour force cutbacks, the unions were also cautioning members in the grey area of the potential layoff list not to invest until they were sure of their financial status post-buyout.

When it appeared that only a few million dollars might be raised, the government suggested that Turcotte and his team meet with a new provincial heritage fund to see if money could be raised there. But in the last few days, cash poured forth. With the town dependent on the mill's future, banks figured it was better to loan money to local citizens and employees rather than have a flood of mortgage defaults in the event of a plant closure.

On November 13, two weeks before the deal was to be consummated, only $2.4 million had been pledged towards the $12.5 million sought. On November 26, at 12:30 p.m., the fund hit the $12.5 million target; by the end of the day, it settled in at about $16 million. The average investment was about $10,000, as 1,024 employees put in $10.2 million and 636 local investors put in $5.8 million. Together with Tembec, they were the proud new owners of the Spruce Falls Acquisition Corp., with Tembec taking 41 percent of the shares, local residents 7 percent, and employees 52 percent.

However, Tembec was to be the managing partner. Dottori would become president and CEO of the company, with the authority to name his senior lieutenants. Among them was Turcotte, now clearly Dottori's protégé, who became production manager and within seven months was named vice-president of the operation. Tembec took three slots on the board of directors, one of them for Dottori. The employees also received three members: the union coalition leader became an automatic representative, and unionized and non-unionized staff jointly elected two others. Finally, three independent directors were named, one of them to be drawn from the local area. That honour went to the town administrator, Rukavina, who was just retiring and was to become a source of sage advice in coming years.

One final hurdle had to be overcome, however, before the agreement could be completed. The new company and its investment advisors petitioned the Ontario Securities Committee to exempt the deal from the extensive "know your client" suitability requirements for investors. Under normal circumstances, the investors would all have to complete personal information forms and send them to Wood Gundy stockbrokers, who would then be required to check their suitability for such an investment and also warn them it was high risk. After a hearing, the commission decided that only those investing more than $16,000 would have to go through those procedures.

A New Company Begins

The new company immediately began a dizzying series of capital investments that continued steadily through much of the next decade. Kimberly-Clark had been milking the operation, investing the minimum required to keep the plant in good condition and producing reasonably efficiently. It hadn't spent the kind of money that was needed if the mill was to be a core asset—and now it was a core asset, for a town, a new company, and its employee owners.

The two immediate linchpins were a de-inking facility, to allow the mill to catch up with the growing thirst for recycled paper, and a new thermomechanical pulp mill that would produce pulp from wood chips through the use of mechanical refiners. At the same time, the plant spent $35 million on new secondary treatment facilities for liquid effluent, to meet new federal standards. To extract more value from the logs that were cut, Spruce Falls set up a chipping mill and a sawmill, which provided chips for the new thermomechanical operation at a lower cost. An important side benefit was that more jobs were being created in the sawmill and in the woodlands area itself, since they needed to cut more wood because a portion of that harvest was being shipped out as lumber while the plant still needed the same amount of chips. Those projects cost $52 million.

Another $25 million was spent on a variety of quality improvements to the paper machines. And in an employee-owned plant, money was invested in making the environment more comfortable to work in, such as $3 million to improve ventilation. From early 1992 to the end of the program in 1999, the new company spent $350 million in capital improvements of about $40 million to $50 million annually.

The company had started life with about $110 million from various sources and in the next 18 months raised another $80 million through private placements. Spruce Falls was also generating funds for investment through its operations, despite the soft market conditions. The business plan had forecast that the discounts prevailing in the industry to lure purchases would average a painful 27 percent within the first two years of operations. In fact, that was wrong: it was worse, with discounts ending up troughing at about 42 percent. In 1993, they experienced a dead-cat bounce—just as the market started to pick up, it collapsed again. It wasn't until 1995 that a recovery began.

Still, in 1993 and 1994 they managed to average about $16 million in net earnings, and that shot up to $50.9 million in 1995 and $83.1 million in 1996. Production was climbing, as the capacity of the plant expanded, and new markets were being secured in Asia, where buyers were paying high premiums for paper. Efficiency also soared. When the buyout occurred, Spruce Falls had the reputation of being the lowest-productivity mill in North America, running at 7.1 person-hours per tonne. By the end of the decade, it was running under 3 person-hours per tonne and was one of the most productive, low-cost operations anywhere.

Staff was trimmed, both in the search for economies and as parts of the mill were shut down while the new facilities were being built. Among those who lost their jobs was Joan Pope, who had originated the idea of the buyout. She was re-employed again briefly but then again laid off once more in a further cutback, never to return.

In general, the philosophy was to try to minimize the pain of restructuring, not just by early retirement packages but also by hiring laid-off employees for the various construction projects, either directly or by insisting that outside contractors use them to the extent they could. The rule became that employees would be considered for construction jobs—and local businesses for all supply contracts—as long as they were no more than 5 percent higher than competing alternatives.

Defining Values

The co-operative spirit that had marked the final days of developing the deal was translated into new joint committees, in line with the Tembec model. At the start, Tembec insisted a committee be formed of five of the most senior managers and the five union presidents and vice-presidents. It met initially on a weekly basis and then shifted to once a month, discussing all aspects of the operation and in particular the relationship between the parties. "We'd look at: Are we changing our management approach? Are the workers changing—are they becoming more flexible and productive? Are they willing to change their ways? Are the managers leading in a different, more participative way? It was great. It was full of conflict. It was full of discussion and debate," remembers Turcotte, who believes that debate is productive rather than a source of concern.

Those talks were essential because the perspectives had shifted. In the buyout, everyone had a common goal. Now management was asking the unions to change 180 degrees from their normal preoccupation and join in the crusade for productivity, efficiency, and higher profits. At the same time, managers were also being asked to change dramatically—to be less authoritarian, more open and more flexible. "There was a need for both parties to change, but the objective wasn't so common anymore," Turcotte says.

Indeed, he recalls getting a stark reminder of that the first week after the takeover, when some routine maintenance was being carried out. The employees had ratified a new contract allowing greater flexibility in work assignments so that if, say, a welder could do pipefitting as well as his or her normal work, it wouldn't be necessary for two people to be called out for repairs. The language didn't reach as far as Turcotte had wanted: full flexibility. But it had moved in that direction—on paper. A maintenance supervisor, however, rushed into Turcotte's office to give him the reality on the shop floor: they were facing a work stoppage in the magnetite area because a millwright was refusing the foreman's request that he also handle pipefitting on a job. "We had to threaten to terminate the guy," says Turcotte. "That's the kind of conflict that comes up when you try to change."

Tembec's Four Pillars

- Employee Ownership: Tembec encourages employees to become shareholders. In some cases, it's a condition of employment.

- Profit-sharing: The company shares its wealth through profit-sharing with every employee.

- Participation: The company provides a simple industrial democracy structure that allows employees to contribute to the running of their plant and company.

- Open Communications: Open meetings and communications are held to establish mutual respect and trust at all levels and build a long-term commitment from employees. "However, we do not like complainers," stresses CEO Frank Dottori. "Our philosophy is 'put up or shut up.' Constructive people build the world. Complainers create misery."

Many people had also assumed that the plant would be run with the same consensual spirit that marked the last days of the buyout. But management didn't consider that feasible. Instead, Tembec is built on four people-oriented pillars.

The first is employee ownership itself: the value of having employees own shares. The second is profit-sharing, which runs throughout Tembec and is based on the simple concept of sharing the wealth with all the employees. Four percent of gross profits go into a pool and are divided equally amongst employees, providing they earned a certain salary over the previous year. "The employees want fair treatment. They will accept less during a crisis if they can share in the good times," says Dottori. "They object to owners who pay themselves dividends and bonuses during good times and then 'claw back' from employees during the tough times. Employees want respect and fairness. Profit-sharing is an important element if you want to develop a partnership."

Next is participation. Tembec tries to keep it simple, with joint union-management committees at all levels as well as the employee representatives on the board of directors. "Most companies talk about participation. Every CEO today must say 'employees are my most valuable asset'—that's the standard line. But the question is: Who does it? We do it," says Dottori.

At the company's various sites, the union president can participate in meetings of the all-important operating committee. The union president also joins in the annual strategic planning meetings, where the five-year plans are reviewed and objectives for the following year are developed. To allow for effective representation of employees in such meetings, the union president is paid by the company to work full time on union and corporate matters.

When Spruce Falls joined the Tembec fold, it also immediately established committees with representatives of management and the union to deal with a range of issues, from discipline to donations. A tech change committee considered the various capital expansion programs, and a training committee prepared employees for the challenges ahead.

Before the buyout, all donations were at the discretion of the president. Now a donations committee with a decidedly non-management bent—it's composed of one representative from each of the five unions and one staff representative—evaluates all proposals and is given authority to decide on any donation under $5,000. Turcotte, as president, can involve himself if he adamantly disagrees, but the intention is that those matters shouldn't come to him. Beyond the $5,000 ceiling, the committee takes the first cut at the proposal and makes a recommendation for the president or the board of directors, depending on the magnitude of the donation. The committee recommended a $350,000 donation to add a wing to the local hospital—which was approved—and was also a driving force behind the decision to commit $450,000 to expanding the local sports complex.

The composition of committees varies with the situation. On discipline, separate committees are set up for each union's jurisdiction with equal representation by management and the union. However, those committees don't work very well: by the time the matter comes to the committee, the human resources staff has already taken a tentative decision, and the union, of course, feels bound to defend its member unless an extreme violation of the rules has transpired. "It's a very difficult committee to make work," notes Norm Leybourne. Invariably, the discipline committee will fail to reach consensus on a decision, which then bounces back to management to decide—and the union to grieve, in the time-honoured fashion.

Employees Join the Board

Employee representation on the board has been very successful. Management meets with the employee representatives before board meetings to ensure that they have understood the material sent out beforehand. Leybourne—who served a stint as union coalition president after the buyout, spent a year in management trying to train front-line supervisors, and now after returning to the mill floor is an employee representative on the board of directors—notes that the other board members are very patient, unwilling to proceed with an issue unless it is thoroughly understood by all. But Turcotte stresses that the representatives are no slouches, since most have been union leaders, a job that requires intelligence and leadership ability: "These guys are smart guys. They have vision. They have good thinking ability and common sense. They bring a healthy perspective to the board. If I was with any company, I would want some type of union leadership on the board of directors."

Leybourne says he didn't find it very difficult to join the board because he had already been grappling with many of the issues during the buyout. A bigger step was moving from being the coalition president to being an employee representative on the board, since he felt he had to extend his scope now that he was representing everyone. But in both roles, he stresses, your position has to be softened by the fact you are a director of the company and have broad fiduciary responsibilities. The key skill for an employee representative on a board of directors, he believes, is "the willingness to learn and adapt to the new environment you are in, rather than trying to do things at a confrontational level."

The board, he feels, is a crucial place for employees to be represented since it's where they can have significant influence on the overall policy and direction of the company. The greatest input comes at the financial level, where employee representatives can ask questions that probe inside the operating numbers. Then, at later meetings, they can return to ask vital questions about implementation. "Maybe management comes in $2 million under budget on something but they haven't accomplished what we set out to accomplish," he notes.

Similarly, employee representatives can remind board members of previous commitments. There had been, for example, agreement that woodlands operations wouldn't be contracted out as long as costs were kept in line. As midline managers started pushing towards contracting out anyway, employee representatives were able to remind board members of the pledge and push instead for new equipment to boost productivity.

Dottori sees another advantage to having employees on the board: "At times management tends to forget, because they earn a hundred grand a year, what an extra $3,000 means for a person earning $40,000 a year with a kid or two going to university. Employee representatives bring that realistic perspective onto the board. They bring constructive ideas—instead of doing one thing, they present an alternative we can consider. They talk to their members and come up with things. It's a valuable contribution."

Open Communications

The fourth pillar in Tembec's participative approach is open communications. Meetings are held between senior management and the union executive every six weeks to discuss any issues that surface, from financial results to operations to marketing. The intention is not to resolve grievances but to keep employees informed and allow feedback. General managers hold similar meetings at the division level with employee representatives. And, of course, weekly bulletins are issued to provide information beyond union reps to all employees.

Employees are encouraged to bring their ideas forth. If their supervisor doesn't listen, they are urged to pursue the issue with higher authorities and guaranteed no repercussions will occur. The procedure is for the employee to send a letter telling the supervisor he or she is not satisfied and wants the site manager to consider the issue. Any supervisor who then threatens or punishes an employee is removed.

If the employee doesn't receive satisfaction from the site manager, there is another level of appeal: Dottori. The only guideline is that the process should be constructive, rather than antagonistic. When asked how many appeals he gets, Dottori laughs: "We have 7,000 employees. Probably half of them don't believe they can do it." But on average, he receives one to two letters a week.

He reaches to his desk to pick one that just arrived: An employee argues that the 15 filter bags in the mill don't need to be replaced weekly but could remain in place for a month. At $500 per bag, that would save $7,500 a week—or $22,500 a month if three filter changes were eliminated. The employee raised the matter with the supervisor, who told him to mind his own business. His letter to Dottori concludes: "I think he's wrong and the situation should be corrected."

Naturally, the CEO is intrigued. "I think that's constructive. There's a lot of money here, if he's right. What I'll do is phone the guy or have someone call him and get more details. Then I'll phone the supervisor and say, 'How come this guy came to me? It looks like a pretty practical idea. What's your version of events?'"

In 99 percent of the cases, he prods the supervisor to schedule another meeting with the employee and resolve the situation. With the filter bags and other situations where the supervisor has erred, he goes even further: "I'll suggest to the supervisor that this type of stuff shouldn't happen—the employee having to come to me—and it indicates there could be a problem here. They should start holding employee meetings, pick up on good ideas, and carry out the corporate philosophy better. Here's a guy wanting to save us a quarter of a million bucks and he has to write the president of the company. So the supervisor will get a hint that it's better to start listening to the employees."

The process doesn't take a lot of Dottori's time, and he considers it time well spent: "This case with the filter bags—I guarantee you I'll never see another one coming out of that department. They don't like the president calling. The guy—the operator—will go out and tell all his friends, 'I called the president of the company and he listened to me.' That gives other people more confidence to be participative. So it's a good process—and this letter here on the bags, I love it. If I had ones like this every week I could earn my keep by just doing this."

He stresses that it's an exceptional suggestion—most aren't that potent. And in some cases, he has to deal with people who have what he likes to call "the X factor" in their personality, always tangling with colleagues and becoming convinced the world is persecuting them. Dottori gently suggests that maybe they need to look in the mirror, since the world isn't always wrong.

But overall, the four pillars boost productivity markedly. "You get a 10 to 15 percent edge with employee ownership. It can be zero if I don't get them involved. But if I can get them involved and motivated, and they believe, I've got a 10 or 15 percent edge. Absolutely," Dottori says.

Defining Participation

How much people believe, as even Dottori acknowledges, can be open to question. And an even bigger issue at Spruce Falls has been *what* they believed. After the buyout, an expectation of co-management had taken hold in the work force and its leadership. But in fact Tembec had operational control. "Reality crashed in quickly," recalls Leybourne. And even the joint committees are tilted towards management, he argues: "It's a joint committee as long as management agrees with the committee members. If a disagreement occurs, it gets kicked up a level and the management makes the decision."

In the first three years, the high-level committee of management and union leaders thrashed that out, again and again, even bringing in a consultant to help them find a solution. During the buyout, the rule for the local group had been: If everybody didn't agree with a proposal in the negotiations with Tembec or Kimberly-Clark, it wouldn't be pursued. But now, in running a company, management—led by Dottori and Turcotte—was arguing that a full consensus approach wouldn't work. Says Turcotte, "I don't believe, in the long run, that consensus decision-making is sustainable. I don't think you can run any organization that way, profit or non-profit."

Instead, management was arguing that participation meant varying degrees of employee involvement, depending on the circumstances. Involvement could be as little as receiving information, which was dramatically stepped up from the Kimberly-Clark days. Next came consultation: managers consulting with employees but making decisions at the end of the day, because they were responsible if things went awry.

Finally, there could be full participation, with employees deciding within the context of their jobs. "That's what I am trying for in all our operations," Turcotte says. "We should move away from the approach where the managers tell the employees not only what they want done but how to do it. Within the context of that employee's work, he should be trained and have the tools and the authority to make his own decision on how to do his job."

Practically, as the letters that flow to Dottori illustrate, achieving full participation—even in the limited area of the mill floor—is very difficult. The front-line supervisors at Spruce Falls who are in place today mostly came into their posts during the Kimberly-Clark era, which had a very traditional management approach. Their job, as Turcotte notes, also places them at the pinnacle of conflict: "It's one thing for me at the buyout, full of new ideas and fairly open-minded— I would like to think—to embrace this participative thing. But here is a guy who is 50, saying, 'Hey, I have been doing it this way for 30 years. I tell the work force what to do and how to do it. Never mind this coddling-them bullshit.'"

In retrospect, he feels it was unfair to expect them to change. He wishes management had transferred at least 60 percent of its supervisors into individual contributor jobs, where they could use their experience and expertise to solve technical problems. Then others who were more naturally aligned with a participative style could have replaced them. Of course, that assumes management could have found the right people, which even today, he admits, would be difficult.

Leybourne remains disappointed at what has resulted. He acknowledges the openness and the attempt to allow greater participation. But he feels it's not enough: "In the buyout, we had a revolution. Since then it has been an evolution. It's hard to change 100 or 200 years of labour relations overnight."

Gerry McMeekin, a longtime union leader who wasn't a part of the buyout but returned to lead his local in the mid-'90s and became coalition leader as discontent grew with the new regime, is somewhat bemused by the debate over consensus. "You mention consensus to Dennis and his hair stands on edge," says McMeekin.

The coalition leader recognizes that the mill is considerably different from the way it was under Kimberly-Clark. Doors to management are more open and much more information is available to all workers. But McMeekin is not sure it's realistic to expect much more than that, as in fact employees can't run companies. "I think that things are slightly better than under Kimberly-Clark—but only slightly better," he says. "The reality is managers run companies."

While the economic fortunes of Spruce Falls have improved over time, Turcotte notes that, conversely, employee involvement in running the enterprise has ebbed over time. Asked to rate that transformation on a 1 to 10 scale, with 10 high, he puts the situation in 1990, under Kimberly-Clark, at 2. At the peak of the negotiations, he calls it a 10, with everybody working together, under consensus, in a team. But then it declined to about a 5, not just with time but also as management became too preoccupied with other matters and these issues slid to the bottom of their agenda.

Another crucial factor was Tembec's full purchase of the company in 1997, giving employees a chance to recoup the money they had invested. "A lot of people claim that owning shares doesn't change the way a person looks at his company. That's totally false," Turcotte says. While acknowledging that it varies with each individual, overall he found interest dwindling as employees sold off their shares. That was particularly true, he feels, for the 5 percent of employees who tend to be undesirable employees. "You would hear a lot of rhetoric about how now that I don't own a lot of stock, maybe it's time to go back to the old ways," he says.

Whether they went back to the old ways or not, the investors all made a sensational return on their investment. While the exact amount varied according to the percentage each individual received of the 20 percent of shares Kimberly-Clark gifted to employees, the average investment of $10,000 at the end of 1991 turned into about $145,000 about six years later. In a town where the average home costs about $75,000, it was like collectively winning a lottery. "Everyone is putting on additions to their home and buying new vehicles. The prosperity is all around," says Rukavina, who like many, adds regretfully, "I wish I had invested more."

Some employees kept their money invested in Tembec, but those shares went through a period of high volatility that only encouraged them to bail out when it recovered. Indeed, although it's a Tembec rule that all employees must own shares in the company and a handsome loan program has been established as an incentive towards that end, Dottori estimates that only 20 to 30 percent of employees actually own shares. "Employees are not entrepreneurs and risk takers. You can see it happen at Tembec, Spruce Falls, and Pine Falls. They want to go to work. They want a good job. They want job security so they don't have to wake up tomorrow and find themselves unemployed. But they don't like to be shareholders. Many will say, 'I can't sleep at night if I have $10,000 invested in Tembec and see it drop from $10 to $9, with me losing $1,000,'" he observes.

Spruce Falls and its parent are committed to a strong environmental program that is rooted somewhat in its employee ownership philosophy. By 2005, the company wants its operations to have "zero impact" on the environment—or, to be more precise, zero negative impact. It also has launched a Forever Green program in woodlands operations, to ensure that the forest is managed in an optimum manner to ensure a source of pulp fibre forever.

The zero-impact program drew criticism from peers, because when it was announced in 1995 the technology wasn't available to make it a reality. But Turcotte says that's simply Dottori's way: he inspires by setting very high expectations. And he places a high value on a clean environment.

So do the citizens of Kapuskasing. While Dottori is one of the main reasons for the environmental effort, Turcotte stresses that it also emanates from the fact employees and local investors in the company were concerned about the environment around their mill. Many have homes downstream from the plant and a lot enjoy hunting and fishing, bringing them close to their environment. "We don't drive logs down the river anymore and we have secondary treatment for effluent. The river smells better and people are swimming in it now. There's more fishing. It's a natural thing we are all concerned about," he says.

Turcotte Shines

While Dottori presided over the company in its early days and was on site at least one day a week, Turcotte was the man he turned to for implementation. "The guy who bought the strategy, the concept, the whole thing was Dennis. He was a bit of a young fellow so he ran into a few heartaches in the initial period and almost got buried a couple of times because this was a big operation. We had to help him out— send in some people at times—but basically he executed the plan," says Dottori.

Turcotte moved steadily up the ranks, becoming executive vice-president of Spruce in 1996 and then later replacing Dottori as president, while his boss remained chairman of the board. After the

Turcotte's Lessons

Dennis Turcotte has four main pieces of advice for other companies that embrace employee ownership.

1. **Stakeholders must establish very clearly at the start what their values are and what their expectations are upfront.**

   That is tough to do, because subconsciously everyone fears being too overt as they are working together to save their company and don't want to create any discord. But Turcotte believes people must be honest and transparent. "The values, objectives and principles from each party's perspective must be nailed down upfront," he says.

2. **The parties must drill down deeper and discuss the value system of the combined entity after the buyout.**

   In practice, what will happen when trade-offs are faced? What will flexibility in the work force mean? What does productivity mean? Is the operating premise to employ as many people as you can or not one more person than necessary? Where on the continuum from extreme capitalism to communitarianism will this new company try to end up? "At the end of the day, for any relationship to get stronger and flourish, the fundamental values of each of the participants have to be aligned enough—and aligned in critical values perfectly—to make that relationship thrive," Turcotte says.

3. **The organization must develop a clearly defined leadership system.**

   Spruce Falls was lucky to inherit the Tembec system. But every employee-owned company must develop its own leadership system.

4. **All parties must realize that at the end of the day a business must maximize its returns and business performance.**

Other issues and values are important, of course, and must be part of an overall guiding philosophy. But he insists that if a company—particularly one in a commodity business—doesn't seek to maximize returns, at some point competitors who have that goal will surpass it.

purchase of Pine Falls in 1998, he became executive vice-president for Tembec's newly formed Publishing Papers and Newsprint Group, while retaining the presidency of both mills. In 1999 he was also assigned responsibility for organizational development and strategy.

"Dennis just shone. His true colours came out in this," says Rukavina. "He is just duplicating what Dottori did in 1973. Dottori keeps challenging Dennis to bring out his ideas. They are a good pair." Leybourne is also impressed: "Dennis has changed for the better—at least 500 percent. At the start I would have termed him a small businessman not giving a shit about the employees if he got his end goal. Now he tries very, very hard to understand and address concerns that are raised. To me he has come a long, long way."

Turcotte was troubled when one of his friends—Mike Micallef, an electrician at the plant, who served on the board of directors—mentioned to a mutual friend that Spruce Falls had become too concerned with business. "It's not the way they thought it would be," Turcotte admits. "But when you look at what we've got, I think we've got something great. I'm frustrated that other people don't see it. I don't think I'm being naive, either. I see it for what it is. It's nowhere near where I want to be and it's not Utopia but when I look at it compared to other mills I go into—and I go into a lot of mills—they are miles ahead at Spruce Falls. But it's not what they wanted it to be. As Mike says, we are too focused on business. Unfortunately we are in one of the toughest businesses on the planet, a commodity business, making a product that is under attack by the Internet and changing demographics, with the price continually dropping. We need to focus on costs, we need to restructure, and we need to continually assess: Do we have one more person than we require, because if we do we need to lay them off. We are being very aggressive. But it's not too aggressive. It's as aggressive as the environment our business is in dictates."

Those matters don't affect Joan Pope as much, as she watches from the outside now. It hurts to have been laid off—in effect, she is one of those "one people too many." But at the same time, she believes her vision was right—and she's overjoyed at what has resulted. The town is economically healthy, rather than devastated by a shutdown or implementation of the Amos plan. In fact, there are more employees today than in the Kimberly-Clark days, as operations have expanded. Her husband, like so many other people in Kapuskasing, is employed at the plant and making good money, the work force having caught up in the last labour agreement with similar mills. And having invested in the company, they got a sufficient return despite having only one income to pay off the mortgage and help their children attend university. "It was necessary to save the place," she says. "You may not have your job, but you have the town and you have your house."

The Analysis

The Analysis

&❧&

Lessons from Our Cases

To Raffi Amit, employee ownership has only benefits and no drawbacks. A professor of entrepreneurship and strategy at the University of British Columbia and early investor in Creo, he believes that once employees feel like owners there is much less of a financial risk for other investors and that returns for the business inexorably increase. The advantage arises through what he calls the "hidden action of employees"—the things that they do daily that managers can't see. "Employee ownership gets them to behave so I don't have to worry that they will shirk," he says.

Amit knows from experience that it's not automatic—a truism backed by all the cases in this book. Indeed, our profiles of companies have illustrated many problems and drawbacks experienced with employee ownership—as well, of course, as many benefits. We set out to present an honest, warts-and-all portrait. We felt it was important to highlight the difficulties these companies experienced, so they could serve as lessons for other companies or groups taking the same general path.

The key questions that we need to answer are:

- Does employee ownership confer an advantage on companies, and does it result in superior returns to employees?

- If so, will it work under all circumstances, or are there some key conditions that need to be fulfilled before employee ownership will generate superior results?

- Does employee ownership need to be combined with employee participation to be effective?

- Does employee ownership work better in non-unionized companies?

- What are some of the important issues or design options that a company should think about before embarking on employee ownership to make the implementation smoother?
- Finally, what are the key lessons that emerge from this study?

Does Employee Ownership Work for Companies?

Previous studies have generally shown that employee ownership has a positive impact on profitability, growth in revenues, and productivity. Our case studies show that employee ownership has meant this and more.

Employee Ownership and Companies in Crisis

For the companies in crisis, employee ownership has been a decisive factor in their survival, return to profitability, and continued growth. Of the ten companies we studied, five were in severe crisis at the time employee ownership was proposed, and four of those are still in business. Of that quartet, Spruce Falls and Great Western Brewery can be called success stories; Algoma showed positive signs in the very tough steel industry before difficulties getting its new Direct Strip mill onstream took a toll in 2001, with the company forced to seek protection from its creditors; and Provincial has been bought and folded into a large corporation.

So all in all, employee ownership helped preserve corporate value, and shareholders and creditors received returns they would have lost otherwise. Furthermore, some communities that otherwise would have experienced severe dislocation were saved. All five of these companies were in "old economy" sectors in which a high failure rate and consolidation have been rampant. Employee ownership helped these companies—and towns—to beat the odds.

Employee ownership helped turn the Spruce Falls mill from an obsolete, underperforming and overstaffed operation to a streamlined and modernized venture, when many other Canadian newsprint mills had to close their doors. In 1992, Tembec embarked upon a reinvestment strategy, which resulted in dramatically improved earnings and productivity. Profits averaged $16 million in 1993 and 1994, then rose to $51 million in 1995 and $83 million in 1996. From one of the lowest-efficiency plants in the industry, it went to being one of highest—from 7.1 man-hours per tonne to three.

At Provincial Papers, productivity improvements were not made under employee ownership, although the plant began to make its first modest profit in five years after employee ownership. It took a new investor, Rolland, to buy out the employees' investment and to introduce efficiencies, before the plant really got back on its feet. Rolland downsized the union workforce by 20 percent and the management ranks by 25 percent. It streamlined the operation, introduced discipline and computerized operations. Revenues improved almost immediately and the plant can look forward to a badly needed modernization program for its outdated equipment.

Great Western's business results have fluctuated over the period of employee ownership, but are now steady and seem sustainable. Immediately after the buyout, demand soared and market share in Saskatchewan rose to 20 percent instead of the 5 percent forecast in the business plan. But then its major competitors introduced new brands and Great Western's market share slid back down to 8 percent. At the end of three years, the brewery was running at less than 50 percent capacity. However, a new strategy based on specialty beers has revitalized the company and made it a major player in the Prairies, enabling it to capture 1.5 percent of the entire Western Canadian beer market.

Algoma's results have also been erratic, following the cyclical nature of the steel industry in Canada. However, employee ownership was a deciding factor in its continued survival through the 1990s and in several years of excellent financial results. From a loss of $185 million in 1990 under Dofasco management, Algoma in 1993 realized a net income of $7.1 million, total sales of $889 million, and cash flow from operations of $62.7 million. This was indeed a dramatic turnaround. Algoma went on to post profits of $209 million in 1995. However, not all of these results can be attributed to employee ownership. Algoma's restructuring efforts, an improved economy, strong demand for steel, and an improved product mix also played their part. After the peak year of 1995, profits dropped in 1996 and 1997; the company posted losses of $59 million in 1998 and $82 million in 1999, as demand for steel weakened across North America. By contrast, Dofasco, a major competitor, showed profits of $173.6 million in 1998 and $260.2 million in 1999. Clearly, while Algoma has gained time—nearly a decade of work for its employees, and a new management style before once again finding itself facing court-supervised restructuring—its challenges continue.

Only CPET—or Interlink, as it became known—did not survive, despite earning $600,000 in profits in its first full quarter of operations. Although wages were rolled back, the company could not overcome its long list of disadvantages, including initial undercapitalization, a long and expensive buyout negotiation, the loss of its American partner, and being behind in adjusting to deregulation and severe competition. When it filed for bankruptcy, the company had $51 million in assets and only $27 million in liabilities, but it was losing money and there was no sign that could be turned around.

Startups, Spinoffs, and Privatizations

For the five companies not in crisis at the start of employee ownership, the picture is even brighter. Four have generated superior returns for their shareholders; the other, which has no external market for its shares, is turning in a very profitable performance. The five started out as small entrepreneurial companies, and employee ownership has helped them to avoid the high failure rate typical of such companies. They were able to retain valuable employees, bootstrap growth, attract investors, and expand rapidly, while facing and overcoming the inevitable crises of their growth curve and life cycle.

One of them, Creo, has become an international success story and was for a period a stock market darling. The company experienced accelerated revenue growth of about 40 percent a year since 1996. Employee growth has been almost as fast-paced, growing from just 40 in 1989 to over 1,800 before its merger with Scitex (which, in turn, took it to 4,400 employees). And its stock price rose from the initial IPO price of $30, hitting a high of $75, before settling back down into the $50 range by early 2000 and then, with the bad markets for technology and some concerns over the company's ability to handle its merger, sliding further, to the mid-20s in 2001.

The Integra story reads like a rags-to-riches-to-rags-to-riches story. Profitable as a small company, it was unable to cover its overheads when under the Landmark banner. After the employee buyout in 1994, it grew rapidly and added more employees, then started to lose money again in 1995. When the three top managers put in more capital and some layoffs took place, it again became profitable in 1996. Forecasts looked bleak once more in 1997, so the remaining 15 shareholders decided to join forces with competitor Scott Pickford to expand and raise more capital. The company continues to do well financially under the new banner Integra Scott Pickford.

SFG also experienced ups and downs throughout its life as a small entrepreneurial employee ownership company. It grew from about 30 employees in 1990 to approximately 110 at the end of 1999. After an ill-fated U.S. expansion, it had to sell 70 percent of the firm to venture capitalists, which diluted employee shares dramatically. However, by 1999, the company was back in the black with roughly $13 million in revenues and a profit of about $2 million. The sale to Cayenta meant that SFG could also now target larger utilities as clients, taking it to the next level of growth and holding out the promise of another gain for the employee shareholders when Cayenta goes public.

Armed with a gold-plated agreement from former parent Nova, Revolve Technologies performed well right from its first year as an employee ownership company in 1992, earning $1.7 million in revenues and $50,000 in profits. In its second year of operations, sales increased to $2.7 million. The company's work now continues, profitably, within the two different companies that bought the different arms of the business.

PRT grew steadily from its birth in 1987. In the first four years alone, it added 325,000 square feet of greenhouse space and ran the entire operation efficiently. But keeping up with the latest technologies and expanding PRT's markets takes capital, and so in 1997 the company transformed itself into an income trust. With this cash infusion the company plans to take over more government-run nurseries in other provinces as well as many small mom-and-pop operations. Then it intends to expand further into the United States.

Our case studies, therefore, show better-than-average results for struggling companies that used employee ownership as a turnaround strategy. Of the five companies in crisis at the time employee ownership was initiated, four are still in business. The future of Algoma Steel is still in question, and Provincial would probably have failed if not for finding a buyer with deep pockets in Rolland. The other two are in good to excellent shape—in all, not a bad turnaround record.

For companies in crisis, clearly employee ownership can assist in realizing rapid and effective improvement. For spinoffs and startups, it provides a stable platform upon which to build profit, growth, and expansion to global markets. We believe that, used properly and in combination with other wise choices, employee ownership is a winning strategy for companies in various sectors and circumstances.

Does Employee Ownership Work for Employees?

For employee owners at the five startups and spinoffs, the story is very positive. At Creo, the founders and early employees realized 160 times the hypothetical value of their first shares at the July 1999 initial public stock offering. This was a spectacular return for those present when the company was founded in the early 1980s. For those who joined later, the return was still excellent. In the early 1990s, for example, a share was worth $1. At the time of the IPO, after a stock split, that share was worth $70, a 40 percent appreciation per year.

Other employee owners at the startups and spinoffs have not fared quite as well, but they certainly have no cause for complaint. At Integra and SFG, the two other companies with an external market for their shares, returns to employee owners have ranged between good and great. Employees at Integra got back ten times their investment after four years when the company sold out to Scott Pickford—a home run by any venture capitalist's scorecard, as major shareholder Mark Klingbeil noted. At SFG, 12 years of struggle were rewarded when Cayenta acquired its shares. Shares that could be picked up for five cents were suddenly worth 50 cents; some long-term employees got windfalls of up to $400,000.

Revolve, through some strategic mistakes, failed to hit a home run and employees didn't fare as well as they might have from investing in the average mutual fund during that period. Original employee owners at PRT, however, got more than 34 times their original investment back when it held a public offering and became an income trust. For original investors, it was about a 40 percent return per year. With the exception of Revolve, then, employee ownership has been very profitable for employee owners at these companies. Clearly the potential for home runs is there—but you can also strike out.

At the five companies in crisis, results were not as good, except for Spruce Falls. When after five years of successful operations Tembec purchased most of the employee shares, employees were able to cash in admirably on their investment. The average investor who bought $10,000 worth of stock at the end of 1991 saw this investment rise to about $145,000 in six years.

At the other paper mill, Provincial Papers, employees have not benefited as much. When they sold their 75 percent share to Rolland, senior employees got about $30,000, roughly making up for the lower wages they had endured due to the pay cut. Rolland also introduced a profit-sharing plan and adjusted some of the wage rates upwards. But they still lag behind industry averages by $8 to $10 per hour. On the other hand, 600 jobs were saved and the mill continues to operate successfully, albeit with a smaller workforce.

At Great Western Brewery, results were similarly mixed. Employees had taken two large wage cuts to help the company survive, but were able to keep their jobs and regain those wage concessions. The company has experienced fluctuations in market share, but fortunately it is now on a positive trajectory. As for the 16 employees who invested from $50,000 to $100,000 apiece in their new company, they hope at some point to make a healthy capital gain, but the major obstacle is finding a way of selling their shares profitably and exiting the business.

Algoma employees accepted wage and benefit rollbacks in 1993 in return for a 60 percent stake in the company. By 1995 they had regained these concessions and were allowed to withdraw up to 300 shares from their trust. Those who sold stock then did well, but others watched the shares fall from $12 to about 30 cents in Spring 2001. However, the new Algoma survived and even returned a profit in several years since the employee buyout. And it has done so despite the combined disadvantages of a difficult location, a sub-optimal product mix, and outdated equipment.

Finally, CPET, or Interlink, did not survive and so a large number of employee owners found themselves unemployed after struggling to turn the company around. However, during its four years of operation, 250 people retired on full pensions and employees earned over $300 million in wages. Some believe that it came within six months of succeeding. Probably it was a case of too little, too late. Interlink had too little time to adjust to the harsh realities of deregulation and competition from U.S. firms that had already prepared for cross-border operations.

It's important to restate, however, that these were companies in crisis. All five might well have closed their doors without employee ownership. While the returns—other than Spruce—haven't been stunning, the companies other than CPET are operating, paying salaries, and, depending on the situation, some employees have also seen dividends or capital gains from selling stock.

Employee Ownership in the Canadian Pulp and Paper Industry

The pulp and paper industry is the largest manufacturing industry in Canada, in terms of total employment, both direct and indirect. As well, its work force is highly unionized, with approximately 82 percent of workers belonging to a union. So the shift to employee ownership by some companies in the industry during the 1990s is of special economic and social importance.

Back in 1985, Canada produced 15 percent of the world's wood pulp and 32 percent of the world's newsprint. In 1988, there were 144 operating mills controlled either directly or indirectly by 76 firms whose sizes ranged from 20 to 16,000 employees. As well, 38 percent of these mills had some proportion of foreign ownership.

Because the industry exports approximately 80 percent of its production annually, it provides Canada with a source of foreign currency and also reduces the deficit in the current account of the balance of payments. The industry contributes greatly to revenues of all levels of government in Canada, through taxes and other payments.

The industry fell upon hard times during the global recession of the early 1990s when the demand for pulp and paper products plummeted. Newsprint production suffered the largest losses in this period, as Canadian production capacity declined from 27.8 percent of the total world production in 1991 to 25.6 percent in 1993—more than 2 percentage points in just 2 years. Dependent on exports, the Canadian industry profits when demand is great or when the Canadian dollar depreciates against other foreign currencies. However, in recessions the higher-cost Canadian pulp and paper suppliers can be in serious difficulty because they have higher fibre and transportation expenses. Also, Canadian mills tend to be smaller, older, and more inefficient. Finally, the industry is subject to a number of government regulations, including environmental impact legislation, which decrease the flexibility with which producers may make investment and operational decisions.

Over the years, Canada has lost market share to U.S. pulp and paper mills, which generally operate at a higher capacity than Canadian mills. This has been an important factor in Canada's economic position as a marginal or "swing" producer. Foreign government regulations have also posed difficulties for the Canadian pulp and paper industry. The European Economic Community, for example, uses a combination of tariffs on Canadian newsprint and fine papers and non-tariff barriers such as environmental labelling to restrict Canada's access to European markets.

Furthermore, the trend towards using recycled newsprint also affected the Canadian industry. The high cost of transporting recycled newsprint encourages companies to move closer to the sources of waste newsprint in the United States instead of Canada.

The result of all these unfavourable trends was that smaller Canadian towns in isolated locations have been doubly threatened with mill closures and layoffs. In 1993, Price Waterhouse warned that the Canadian pulp and paper industry would become smaller and more competitive by the end of the 1990s, resulting in the loss of between 15,000 and 20,000 jobs. Single-industry pulp and paper mill towns were most at risk.

One solution tried by several of these mills was employee ownership. A first wave of employee buyouts had occurred in the United States in the mid-1970s, mainly when conglomerates attempted to divest unprofitable or non-core businesses. For the most part, those companies were financially viable. By the early 1990s, a second wave of buyouts in both the United States and Canada hit financially troubled operations. Many of these buyouts needed large capital investments before they would be able to compete in the increasingly global marketplace. This second round included many plants where whole communities were at risk. It was common for jobs to be saved through a combination of bank loans, wage and benefit concessions, downsizing the workforce, and the infusion of worker equity and government grants and loans. Significantly, governments were a crucial player—in an era when corporate handouts were increasingly frowned upon—to avoid the social and political costs of plant shutdowns.

Comparing Spruce Falls and Provincial Papers

Spruce Falls and Provincial Papers, both in the same difficult and cyclical industry, turned to employee ownership at approximately the same time to solve the same problem. They were not generating enough returns, and their parent companies wanted to divest these non-performing assets. But the stories diverge there. Spruce Falls went on to generate superb returns to its employee owners and it became one of the most productive and profitable mills in Canada. On the other hand, Provincial barely stayed alive until Rolland bought it out in 1997. Whereas Spruce employee owners realized a profit on their stock of about 10.5 times its initial value, Provincial employee owners just realized enough from the sale of stock to Rolland to make up for wages lost in concessions. What can companies considering employee ownership in similar crisis situations learn from these two examples, so their results are closer to the outstanding outcomes of Spruce Falls?

Spruce Falls had many disadvantages to overcome, including but not limited to outdated equipment, isolated location, dependence on a few powerful customers, and a cyclical industry. But Spruce Falls was able to exploit the opportunities afforded by employee ownership and the strategic alliance with Tembec to create a productive and profitable operation.

First and most important, Spruce Falls employees formed that strategic partnership with Tembec. Tembec brought experience both in the industry and in the buyout process to the partnership. It also provided three experienced managers to guide the changeover at Spruce Falls. Not that Spruce Falls was on the brink of collapse—the main reason for the buyout was that returns were low and the owners wanted out of the newsprint business. It needed a management team to come to Kapuskasing and run the company "hands on," rather than from U.S. headquarters. And in Frank Dottori, Spruce Falls gained a sophisticated and dynamic CEO. Dottori knew how to steer a turnaround, find internal talent, and manage the relationship with both the union and the employee owners as individuals.

When Dottori came to Kapuskasing his cost management ideas were already formulated. Implementation started immediately. This quick pace of change generated hope and enthusiasm, and with early success it kept the momentum going. Furthermore, Dottori's strategic plan made sense in light of the price-sensitive markets the mill faced. His first priority was to cut costs, because Spruce Falls' production was almost $150 per ton greater than the lowest-cost producer in North America. The goal was to catapult Spruce Falls into the top 10 percent of mills, with respect to cost effectiveness, by 1994. The increased cost effectiveness was to come from organizational restructuring, a new labour contract, modernization of facilities, and a decrease in number of employees. The company also made a commitment to high-quality production, an expansion into some specialty grades of paper, and a focus on markets in the Northeastern United States.

The capital investment plan involved expenditures of nearly $130 million to improve pulp yield. Nearly $30 million would be spent on the environment to clean up the waste the mill was putting into the river. Finally, $50 million was put towards upgrading and modernizing the newsprint machines to enhance quality, efficiency, and customer satisfaction.

A second plank in the business plan was a reduction in labour costs. Indeed, the workforce was cut dramatically, but early retirement was used as much as possible to downsize the workforce in a sensitive way. A new labour contract included reductions in the wage package worth about $3.50 per hour, as well as a cut in paid vacations. The downsizing took place in a climate of union-management consensus, in which the union was willing to make wage concessions that contributed to a payroll reduction of between $6 million and $7 million each year.

Overseeing the implementation of the business plan was a board of directors comprising representatives of the employee shareholders, Tembec, and three independent directors jointly selected by Tembec and the employee committee. Dottori was also able to develop internal management talent. He found an able successor in Denis Turcotte, who installed Tembec's people-oriented management program. This potent combination was able to see the company through downsizing and concession bargaining with a high level of co-operation.

The Spruce Falls buyout also had strong local support. Finally, the new Spruce Falls adopted many principles and structures in line with what two researchers with the National Center for Employee Ownership called a "Theory O" type of company. The Ownership Theory of management is one in which employees not only have ownership but also the information and avenues to participate in running the company. The Tembec operating model is founded on four pillars: employee share ownership, profit sharing, participation, and open communications. Many joint union-management committees were formed at various levels, including a senior operations committee. Employee representatives on the board of directors rounded out this structure, giving employees a voice in decisions of all types. However, participation didn't mean co-management. Even joint committees were tilted towards management.

The Tenets of Theory O

1. The person at the top of the organization is committed to the concept.

2. There is a written set of values embodying the commitment to employee ownership.

3. Attention is given to symbols indicating the importance of employee ownership.

4. Decisions are made at the level where there is the most relevant expertise.

5. Training in technical and participative skills is given.

6. The sharing of information from the bottom up as well as the top down is practised.

7. There is a realization that participative decision-making takes more time but is often more effective.

8. The combination of methods used to implement Theory O is unique to each company, since what works for one company will not necessarily work for another.

At Provincial, by contrast, there wasn't the same community involvement and the new management provided much less of a strategic advantage. Nor did Provincial recruit a senior team of the quality built at Spruce. The two experienced managers from Abitibi-Price left the company shortly after the buyout. While the new CEO, Ian Ross, had experience in the pulp and paper industry, his depth of knowledge was not comparable to that of Frank Dottori. Neither Ross nor any other senior manager at Provincial had significant employee ownership experience.

Furthermore, Ross did not move to Thunder Bay and manage the many onsite challenges. Boosting sales and bringing on some new products was his priority, so he personally sold to major clients at large companies and shed some customers who were too expensive to serve. He also recruited new sales and marketing managers, overhauled the sales force, and reduced the scope of new product development to two lines that could be produced on the idle machines. The New Provincial Papers mill's strategy would be to move away from the production of low-grade products, into higher-grade speciality products such as beer labels and wallpaper, which provide a high return and have generally less competitive markets. While many parts of this strategy made sense, it did not match the breadth and depth of Dottori's business plan. If the mill could not produce to the standard and price required by the sales strategy, then Provincial would not succeed.

All in all, at Provincial Papers, employee ownership seemed to intensify the divisions between union and management, but it also often pitted union against union. Management met regularly with the unions to get input, but then the rank and file started to think union reps were in cahoots with management. This feeling was exacerbated by the fact that employee board members often couldn't report on critical matters because of confidentiality requirements. At Spruce Falls, the employees also suffered downsizing and benefit concessions, but pay increases were scheduled soon after the buyout and helped to restore confidence.

Participation at Provincial was confined to meetings between management and the union coalition and to union representation on the board of directors. Provincial failed to take the advice from Spruce Falls, which had gone into the process earlier, or to adopt any of the pillars of management put in place by Tembec. Little or no provision was made for employee participation. In addition, profit-sharing was not considered and communications were far from open.

Indeed, even the commitment to employee ownership was shallow at Provincial, where the strategy had always been to try and turn operations around and sell the plant. The five unions had formed a "mill council" to discuss issues with management and studied the Spruce Falls buyout, but they remained skeptical of employee ownership. As one manager put it: "They didn't want anything to do with employee ownership. They just wanted a job." This was in contrast to Spruce Falls, where the five unions, although initially skeptical, worked with managers to bury past differences.

Furthermore, the buyout process itself at Provincial was not transparent and only heightened distrust between management and the union. Rather than building an alliance and coming to consensus about many of the details of how the new company would be managed under employee ownership, the deal was rushed and many details were missed. At Spruce Falls, Dottori had participated in similar deals before and made sure that the conditions for success were set up in advance. He also ensured that employees invested real money in the new shares; at Provincial, shares were traded for wage concessions. This 20 percent pay cut was traumatic for employees with families and remained a sore spot thereafter.

Provincial never seemed to make any progress towards improving the plant's operations or its culture. New work systems were tested, but the company wasn't fully committed to them, perhaps because there was too little trust to go further. The "new suggestions" plan petered out. Even after a team visited other employee ownership companies for good ideas, no changes or improvements were made. The plant just seemed to operate much as it had in the past with a low productivity and a high conflict culture.

In crisis situations, companies have much less time or patience to set the stage for success after the buyout. But it is probably even more crucial for them to get it right quickly than in cases where there is no immediate danger of closure or bankruptcy.

Nevertheless, as the Provincial case illustrates, employee ownership can help a company survive until a new corporate owner can be found. Table One summarizes the contrasts between Spruce Falls and Provincial Papers going into employee ownership and illustrates why the Provincial Papers buyout had little chance of being as successful as the one at Spruce Falls.

TABLE ONE:

A Comparison between Spruce Falls and Provincial Papers

SPRUCE FALLS	PROVINCIAL PAPERS
New management team skilled and experienced in employee ownership and in the pulp and paper industry. Development of internal management talent. Highly involved on-site leadership	Management team inexperienced in employee ownership and less experienced in the industry. Some internal managers felt left out. Senior leadership managed from a different location
Tembec owned 41 percent of shares, local residents 7 percent and employees 52 percent initially. Tembec held three seats on board, employees three and three were independents (1 from community). Authority vested in management	Employees owned 75 percent, management 25 percent, but partially tied to performance. Five directors—three independent, two union. Management right to manage under direction of the CEO who responded to the Board *cont'd*

Partnership with Tembec, a successful player in the industry	An "orphan" plant, making it more difficult to compete and secure sales
Appropriate business plan and turnaround strategy based on capital investments to improve productivity and cost position, and to process recycled paper	Strategy based on product line changes and improvement of sales organization
Strong community support and actual dollar investment in the plant by both employees and townsfolk	Weaker community support and no community dollar investment. Employee investment limited to wage concessions
Rapid implementation of the business plan, which reaffirmed customers' and employees' faith in change	Slower implementation characterized by stops and starts
Four pillars of management philosophy installed: Commitment to employee ownership, profit sharing, participation, and open communications	Weak commitment to employee ownership itself. Management philosophy was not harmonized with employee ownership
Relatively calm employer/ employee relations in the past. Co-operation of the five unions with management and among the unions themselves	More difficult employer/ employee relations not improved during the employee ownership process. Adversarial relationship with the five unions scarcely improved. Inter-union distrust
Viable company to start off with	Less successful plant to start off with
Ontario government committed to reimburse Ontario Hydro for up to $274 million if the environmental assessment was unfavourable	Ontario government offered $6.5 million direct loan and $11.5 loan guarantee; also ensured a 20-year supply of wood fibre *cont'd*

Five unions, initially resistant, but did join the buyout group. Unions slow to believe the mill was in peril, but in the end worked with managers to forge a deal and buried past differences	Five unions formed a "mill council" to respond, but were resistant to employee ownership
Ten years of free power, low interest loans, and cheap wood chips from local wood lots. Wage and benefit concessions by employees	Employees took 20% pay cut and 112 jobs cut. Employees did not put up real money for shares. Abitibi Price provided $15 million to fund operations

Although Spruce Falls started off with many advantages not shared by Provincial Papers, the question remains whether Provincial could have improved its results by attention to those things it could control. We believe the answer is yes. Onsite management with a philosophy similar to the four pillars at Spruce Falls; a more detailed turnaround strategy; a better-rounded management team; and more attention to the relationships among employees, the union, and the management team could have helped achieve a better return to stockholders and employees. Nevertheless, again it has to be stressed that Provincial Papers did find a good buyer in Rolland, and jobs and community stability were saved. Employee ownership can largely be credited with enabling the plant to survive until the new buyer could be found.

Great Western versus CPET/Interlink

The contrast between Great Western and Interlink can also help us to understand how employee ownership can work for companies in crisis. Both enterprises were facing closure by their parent companies in a climate of severe competition and downsizing. Both struggled with employee ownership, but only one survived.

TABLE TWO: **A Comparison between Great Western and CPET/Interlink**	
GREAT WESTERN	**CPET/Interlink**
Same management team right after the buyout, experienced in the business, but inexperienced in employee ownership. Later brought in a CEO from a different industry. Highly involved onsite leadership	New senior management inexperienced both in the business and in employee ownership, although some board members had employee ownership experience. Highly involved onsite management
Sixteen employees invested from $50,000–$100,000 apiece, in return for 100% ownership. Originally board had several employees but now only one of five is an employee rep. (Employees can send two observers.) There are also three outsiders and CEO on the board	Five classes of shares were issued with different governance rights. Unionized employees owned at least 66.6% of the company. Three reps from the union, three from management, and five independents sat on the board, but board meetings were not productive, partly because the union felt left out of the loop
"Orphan" plant with no large distribution network	Lost its U.S. partner very soon after employee ownership, largely abandoned by CP
Appropriate business plan and turnaround strategy based on brewing quality specialty beers and appealing to people of Saskatchewan. Difficulty responding to competitive response by big breweries	No coherent business plan, dabbling in too many segments; inadequate understanding of the pricing and profit mechanisms of the industry. Undercapitalized, yet continued to make large investments, further straining the financial situation *cont'd*

Strong provincial support for the local beer. Actual dollar investment in the plant by a small group of employees and relatives	No identifiable community interested in its fate. Employee investment limited to wage concessions
Fast implementation of original business plan, more difficulty adjusting after competitors regained market share with the introduction of new brands	Relatively fast implementation, but business plan lacked focus
Management committed to being "approachable and accountable 24 hours a day, seven days a week." Commitment to employee ownership but low employee participation, no profit-sharing.	Weak commitment to employee ownership itself. Management philosophy was not harmonized with employee ownership
Relatively calm employer/employee relations in the past going into the buyout	Very difficult employer/employee relations, distrustful and adversarial
Government involved and contributed both development money and loans to the new company	Government not involved
Union was receptive to employee ownership. President of the union local attended the weekly owners' sessions and also chaired union meetings	The union was receptive to the idea of an employee buyout, but the deal was difficult for the union to sell to members and the vote on ownership was not unanimous. Afterwards, the union felt excluded from important issues
The 29 employees agreed to take a 15% wage cut. Relatively efficient plant to start off with	Relatively inefficient operation to start off with

From those two sets of contrasting case studies, it appears that the common factors uniting the successful cases include the following:

- management expertise (at least in the industry);
- an appropriate turnaround business strategy, implemented fairly quickly;
- an employee stake in the stock that goes beyond mere wage concessions;
- better employee relations going into the buyout and getting the union on board; and
- a commitment to employee ownership and to some form of employee input in decision-making.

Leadership and management expertise should not be underestimated, especially in a crisis situation. Employees and investors alike are looking to the leadership team to save them from financial catastrophe and are more likely to accept direction from credible leaders. While the Great Western leadership team did not have the experience of a Frank Dottori with employee ownership, it was experienced in the beer business and had run a very efficient plant in the past. The leadership team remained on site, and remained very involved and committed to the success of the plant. In contrast, at CPET/Interlink, the new senior management was inexperienced both in the business and in employee ownership. This situation posed a double risk, not because the senior managers could not learn to run the business well but because the time frames were too short and the situation too desperate to allow for mistakes and learning.

The lesson here is to ensure the senior leadership team knows the business and shows its commitment by hands-on local management as a minimum requirement. Even better, the new team should have had some experience with employee ownership—at least with a highly participative management style. In a crisis, there is not much time to experiment.

At Great Western, a clever "underdog" appeal to the beer drinkers of Saskatchewan created an early success. This strategy was implemented quickly and gave the company much-needed breathing room and capital to respond to the next competitive threat. In comparison, CPET/Interlink demonstrated no coherent strategy—frustrating a bold plan by the CEO (though it may or may not have been the right course)—and ended up trying to be all things to all segments. The strategy of aggressive investing in the face of financial vulnerability and without a clear understanding of the profit mechanisms of the industry proved fatal in the tight window of opportunity facing the company.

At Great Western and CPET/Interlink alike, employees had a large stake in the success of the company. Great Western was 100 percent employee owned, although only by 16 employees who invested real dollars, while they and their colleagues took a 15 percent wage cut. At CPET/Interlink, employees owned two-thirds of the company in return for wage concessions, but none put up real after-tax dollars. It is interesting to observe that in the clear success stories like Spruce Falls and Great Western, more than wage concessions were on the table. Perhaps this real and present investment exerts more psychological pressure over the long term than the wage concessions.

Better employer-employee relations and a greater sense of trust, such as at Great Western, can act as the glue that cements the whole effort together. A good relationship eliminates all the second-guessing and foot-dragging that can slow down the transformation effort, as seemed to be the case at CPET/Interlink.

Finally, for employee ownership to work, companies would be wise to follow the tenets of Theory O—namely, to promote commitment both to employee ownership and to some form of employee input in decision-making. The lack of both until near the end may have been the most decisive nail in CPET's coffin. While union representatives sat on the board, the union still felt isolated from the real decisions. By comparison, at Great Western, management was "approachable and accountable" even though other forms of employee participation were largely absent and there was not a demonstrable deep commitment to the concept of employee ownership itself.

Employee Ownership in the Steel Industry: The Case of Algoma

The steel industry is another vital element of the Canadian economy facing continual competitive pressures, so it's worth paying special attention to our example from that area. Canada became a large steel-producing nation during and after the Second World War. By 1995 it employed approximately 31,600 people and generated $10 billion in sales. However, that employment was down nearly a quarter from just eight years earlier: over 10,000 workers were laid off between 1988 and 1996, mostly because of productivity initiatives.

It wasn't just a slash mentality at work. Between 1988 and 1993, the Canadian steel industry invested more than $2 billion in quality training, improved management techniques, and business restructuring, which translated into a 35 percent increase in productivity. Still, profitability remained unstable and margins thin. Of the big three steel producers in Ontario, Dofasco has usually turned in the best results, with Stelco second and Algoma struggling in last spot.

Like the pulp and paper industry, the Canadian steel industry began to suffer in the early 1980s with the beginning of a recession. Increased production from Japan, east bloc countries in Europe, and newly industrializing countries led to an oversupply and sharply decreasing prices. However, at that time, Canadian suppliers still had an advantage over U.S. producers in that they had been early adopters of mini-mill and other technologies and enjoyed a favourable dollar exchange rate.

Most Canadian steel mills returned to profitability at the end of that recession, and it was at that time that Dofasco acquired Algoma in order to secure a supply of rolled steel for its production lines. But in the early 1990s when the next recession hit, Canadian producers faced an overvalued Canadian dollar and revitalized U.S. competitors. Dofasco responded partly by divesting the troubled Algoma plant. Without Dofasco's backing, Algoma was left ill-prepared to face the recession, and it turned to employee ownership as part of its adjustment and survival strategy.

Algoma had fewer advantages going into its period of adjustment to employee ownership than Spruce Falls, as Table Three shows. For one thing, Spruce Falls had the advantage of the Tembec partnership, with its employee ownership experience, and was able to draw some of its senior management from Tembec. By contrast, at Algoma only the union had experience with employee ownership through some of its U.S. experiments. Furthermore, while Spruce Falls joined an alliance with a large successful company, Algoma became an "orphan" plant in an isolated location. And while the new management team at Spruce Falls hit the ground running with a turnaround business plan immediately after the buyout, Algoma had to wait six months before hiring an appropriate CEO. Al Hopkins knew the steel business and was predisposed to employee participation, but he hadn't developed a sophisticated management philosophy congruent with employee ownership similar to Tembec's four pillars.

The provincial government offered financial assistance and moral support for both companies in their buyouts. But the whole community of Kapuskasing got behind Spruce Falls, with townsfolk and employees alike investing real after-tax dollars in its stock, whereas at Algoma the employee investment was in the form of wage and benefits concessions only. There was less on the line for them.

In comparison to Provincial Papers, the New Algoma did implement employee ownership more carefully and completely, and its results were initially excellent. The company turned its first profit in years right after employee ownership, even if it has been struggling more recently. While employee ownership helped the company survive, it cannot by itself outweigh the disadvantages of poor location, severe competition, the pricing dynamics of a commodity product in a cyclical industry, and outdated equipment and product lines.

Still, let's stress it again: employee ownership appears to have helped Algoma overcome poor union-management relations and achieve a degree of viability in a very turbulent market. The question remains whether Algoma can survive in the long run. Even the strong commitment of managers and employee owners may not be enough.

TABLE THREE: ALGOMA STEEL

Advantages and Disadvantages of the Algoma Steel Buyout

ADVANTAGES	DISADVANTAGES
A new management team consisting of both outsiders and insiders, led by Al Hopkins, an experienced and skilled steel executive. Development of internal management talent. Highly involved onsite leadership	Long time lag between the buyout and time new president and CEO was named (six-months). No managers with buyout expertise on staff but use of skilled consultants during the initial phases. Steelworkers had expertise developed in the U.S.

cont'd

Employees got 60% of shares, creditors 40%. A mutual trust and respect developed that enabled the board to reach consensus on difficult issues	Board confidentiality prevents the union directors from keeping the constituency fully informed. Board members initially felt uncomfortable in their role
No partnerships with other steel industry players, but a strong partnership between Steelworkers union and management	Severing of ties with Dofasco, for which most previous production was destined
Appropriate business plan and turnaround strategy based on capital investments to modernize equipment, improve productivity, and change the product mix	Algoma behind its competitors, the other integrated steel producers, and facing severe competition from mini-mills
Sault Ste. Marie had a lot to lose if the plant closed and so gave moral support to the buyout	Weaker community support than Spruce Falls and no actual dollar investment in the plant by employees (wage and benefit concessions in return for stock)
Skilled implementation of the business plan	Slow start to implementation because senior management was not in place right after the buyout
Congruent with Theory O: commitment to employee ownership and employee participation in terms of joint committees and participation units	Salaried Advisory Group felt left out. No profit-sharing, and philosophy of open communications not as strongly supported as desirable *cont'd*

Steelworkers more disposed to employee ownership than many other unions and brought together a team of experts to help develop the deal. Union and management able to co-operate after the buyout	Turbulent employer/employee relations in the past
Ontario Premier Rae became heavily involved. Province gave $90 million loan guarantee and provided other significant con-tributions	Government didn't want to become the banker and did not want others to walk away unscathed. Government viewed employee ownership as a short-term solution on the way to finding a suitable owner
Financial restructuring meant the new Algoma started out with a better balance sheet and lower costs. Union took a per-manent wage cut (14.5 percent equivalent), decreased holidays, and downsized workforce of 1,600 over five years	Algoma still had high trans-portation costs and an inferior cost position. Customer skepti-cism about viability and relia-bility of Algoma as a supplier. Trade barriers limited access to the nearby U.S. steel markets

Employee Ownership in Startups, Spinoffs, and Privatizations

The other companies in our sample tended to be small, and employee ownership was not driven by the desperate lack of other alternatives. They were either startups, like Creo and SFG, or spinoffs. Employee ownership in a spinoff or startup may have its frightening moments for those involved at the outset but it appears to be an easier situation to manage; all were successful to some extent. They generally have more time, less anxiety, and a smaller size than the larger companies we studied, which may help to overcome even some big initial missteps.

However, all those we studied faced challenges. A summary of the major circumstances of their employee ownership follows.

TABLE FOUR:

Comparisons of Employee Ownership Circumstances

	Creo	**Integra**	**SFG**	**Revolve**	**PRT**
Results	Excellent	Good	Good	Fair	Excellent
Management skilled and experienced in employee ownership	No	No	No	No	No
Ownership	Stock options determined by contribution to company. Employees elect one of nine directors	18 of 21 employees invested, but key managers bought 48%. Employee reps on board	Generous stock options. No voting rights for employees	Employees had to invest in shares. Voting rights on some decisions	Key execs own over 50% but all employees must purchase shares. No voting rights for employees
Management skilled and experienced in the industry	No	Yes	Yes	Yes	Yes
Highly involved onsite leadership	Yes	Yes	Yes except for U.S. period	Yes	Yes
Partnership with a large, successful player	Yes	No— bought out	No— bought out	Yes	Yes
Actual investment by employees	Yes—stock options but some stock granted	Yes	Yes—stock options	Yes—some funded by salary reductions	Yes
Commitment to employee ownership	Yes	No	Yes	Some	Yes
Employee participation	Yes—unit presidency and 360° feedback	Some and open book management	Little	Some	Some

cont'd

Government involvement	No	No	No	No	Privatized operation —no special deal for former employees
Union	No	No	No	No	Unions reduced flexibility

No clear success pattern emerges from our examination of the circumstances and conditions surrounding these companies. We classified two of the five as excellent employee ownership results—Creo and PRT—based on the high returns they generated for the employee owners, profits, growth, and their continuing to remain employee ownership companies with the potential for continuing good returns to employee owners. Revolve ended up not being financially successful as an investment for the employees, but did allow them to continue to develop their technology and stay employed without interruption. The others had good results.

It is interesting that none of the companies started off with experience in employee ownership but that did not appear to impede success. Creo did not even have experience in the industry it chose, but even that did not have a negative effect. Neither had a partnership with a big player originally. As for the presence of a union, PRT achieved excellent results while having to negotiate with several.

What seemed to distinguish these two was the combination of commitment to employee ownership and good employee relations. That was combined with intense input and participation from the employee owners at Creo and moderate participation at PRT. They fell, therefore, in line with Theory O—predicting superior returns from a combination of both employee ownership and participative management approaches—and the findings from many U.S. studies.

But while our study is consistent with that theory, the degree of participation needed remains very much a question, especially from our findings with the small entrepreneurial firms. Furthermore, the Algoma story shows that this combination of employee ownership and participation cannot by itself ensure excellent performance. It may well be that the management philosophy of the company and how that effects participation is more important than merely installing some participative mechanisms such as representation on the board or other committees.

A closer examination of the differences between Creo and SFG might help explain some of the synergistic effects of commitment to employee ownership and the management philosophy. Both companies were startups in a high-tech industry, and both had a strong commitment from the senior management to employee ownership.

At Creo, founders Gelbart and Spencer espoused the goal of having the company one-third owned by employees, one-third by the founders, and one-third by outside investors. They made a commitment to sharing both the risks and returns with everyone in the company. At SFG, founder Elliott introduced employee ownership in 1988 because it fit the flat, empowered, team-oriented organization that he wanted to nurture. He also felt that the company would create a lot of wealth and thought it was reasonable to share that bounty. But Creo remained an employee ownership company, whereas SFG sold all its equity to Cayenta. It is true that employees did well in this sale and were given stock options in Cayenta, but the entity SFG no longer exists. At Creo, by contrast, employees not only realized a spectacular return when the company went public but also retain ownership and control of their company—and have been transmitting this pattern, as if in gene therapy, to the employees of Scitex. They also remain strongly attached to their company and committed to its success. What gave Creo that extra edge?

We believe it is the management philosophy—which is so inextricably woven into the fabric of Creo—that distinguishes it from most of the other employee ownership companies and that makes it such an attractive workplace. The Creo Philosophy is based on ownership, employee participation, trust in colleagues, profit-sharing, self-management, decision-making rules, and stock options based on peer assessment. This is a sophisticated, interdependent system, much broader than just employee participation. It has helped Creo to create an unusually low turnover rate within the technology industry; an unusually high level of morale, despite the stress of rapid growth; and a strategy for attracting, paying, and keeping talent without having to pay astronomical salaries. Given the parallel between the Creo Philosophy and the four pillars of management at Spruce Falls/Tembec—and the great success both companies have achieved—it suggests such an approach might be the most important factor in creating superior value in an employee ownership firm. It is also extremely hard to imitate, so implementing such a philosophy may confer great competitive advantage.

No such clearly articulated and internally consistent philosophy existed at SFG. In fact, the employee shares at SFG did not even come with any voting rights. Elliott wanted to avoid having to obtain shareholder approval from too many people. Viewed by some of his employees as somewhat autocratic, he also wanted the lines of authority clear.

The unanswered question remains whether a management philosophy closer to Creo's would have helped avoid some of the near-fatal decisions that occurred over the years and whether growth, profits, and returns would have been better under such a management philosophy.

The Relationship between Employee Ownership and Participation

Theory O states that superior growth and profits come from a combination of employee ownership and employee participation. While that may be true, our study also shows that good growth and profits may be realized without high employee participation. We have only to look at the large returns to employees from their shares when SFG sold out to a strategic buyer to realize that the relationship is not a simple one. While it is true that SFG had its ups and downs, the same can be said of most small entrepreneurial companies. As a matter of fact, our employee ownership companies had a much higher survival rate than most, even though not all were highly participative on all the Theory O elements. Furthermore, it's worth stressing that a combination of employee ownership and participation cannot overcome poor odds to ensure long-lasting success, as demonstrated by the Algoma story.

Nevertheless, the best returns and the longest life seemed reserved to those companies that made a commitment to employee ownership and that had a detailed and integrated management philosophy that combined a number of participative approaches. If we were to predict which of our employee ownership companies would thrive as employee ownership enterprises into the future, our bets would definitely be on Creo and Spruce Falls/Tembec.

It may not be just employee participation, but a coherent mixture of participative approaches, that really makes the difference. The four pillars at Spruce Falls and the Creo Philosophy are examples of interdependent processes that amplify each other and together make a potent brew to sustain motivation, commitment, and loyalty on the part of employees.

In summary, to sustain superior returns and to maintain broad ownership for the long run, what's needed is the combination of employee ownership and a management philosophy that goes beyond employee participation to actually match the spirit of employee ownership. In the short run, employee ownership alone may help a company survive and grow, but employee owners lacking a degree of control and participation are often eager to sell out to a larger player in order to find a safer haven. If they cannot control their own fate and doubt the prospect of large returns from ownership, then it seems better to throw in with a successful company that provides a respectable salary and less risk.

Employee Ownership and Unions

Faced with difficult economic times and relentless competition, many companies in the "old economy" have revisited the union-management relationship to see if a higher degree of co-operation might help the parties work jointly towards the survival of their company. Many companies have restructured and downsized in a quest to remain competitive and have found that is not enough. Those that want to survive the new business realities will have to become more flexible and adjust quickly to changing times. A more co-operative partnership between management and unions can help channel the energy, knowledge, and experience of employees toward cost management, productivity improvements, and creative solutions to business problems. Employee ownership has the potential to create that type of co-operative union-management environment.

Traditional labour and management relations have been based on the assumption that employers have a direct interest in decreasing the cost of labour in order to maximize profits. Employees, on the other hand, have a direct interest in increasing the price of labour, which can negatively affect company profits. Under those belief structures, there is little motivation for employees to exert extra effort or contribute their ideas for improvement. This win/lose mentality assumes constrained resources and a fixed pie to be divided, and it underlies the basic adversarial climate so prevalent in many unionized companies.

Employee ownership has the potential to explode these assumptions, to help both parties bake a larger pie and to divide it more evenly. However, old attitudes die hard, and changing these ingrained beliefs is not without its challenges.

Our sample included six unionized companies; of those, three—Spruce Falls, Great Western, and PRT—were successful after adopting employee ownership. Of the other three, CPET/Interlink went out of business, but Provincial Papers achieved a partial turnaround and Algoma has had some successful years that suggest an infusion of financing and its new strip mill it might be a viable operation. The question is whether differences in union-management relations and attitudes contributed to those different results, or whether other factors were at work.

The attitude of the union towards employee ownership at the beginning of the buyout seemed not to be the crucial factor. For example at Spruce Falls, a key union was initially opposed to employee ownership and dragged its feet in negotiations, whereas at Algoma it was the union that drove the buyout initiative. And whether or not trust between union and management was high going into employee ownership does not appear to be the deciding factor either, as trust was low at most of the companies. Joint union-management initiatives were undertaken at both Spruce Falls and Algoma, yet results were different.

It seems, therefore, that employee ownership can succeed under a variety of initial union-management scenarios, and that other factors may be more important. However, if we are looking for an improved union-management relationship under employee ownership, the contrast between Provincial Papers and Algoma is very instructive.

At both companies, the union-management relationship had been difficult for a long time. But Algoma's union got behind employee ownership, took control of much of the buyout process and started co-operating with the company to achieve its end of preserving jobs and union membership. A key element of the union plan was the proposed framework for governing an employee ownership company. This framework helped the parties anticipate and resolve many future difficulties before they became severe. It also provided a statement of values that the new company had to live by—values that the union strongly endorsed. After the buyout, union and management officers addressed gatherings of staff together, symbolizing the new way of running the company. Joint committees at all levels were put in place, and much effort went into gaining employee input into decisions. Indeed, one of the union officers later became the human resources vice-president. None of this co-operation prevented the difficult decisions to cut wages and jobs at Algoma, and both of the parties had to share in the pain. However, this pain did not seem to poison the new relationship.

At Provincial Papers, on the other hand, the five unions were not enthusiastic about employee ownership and did not take charge of the process in the same way. Furthermore, a significant number of members insisted right up to the end that Abitibi-Price had been bluffing about a plant closure and that employee ownership was unnecessary. Management, for its part, seemed reluctant to share power with the new employee owners, and union officers felt they had to battle for every bit of information or influence. Whereas employee reps on the Algoma board of directors were able to make an important contribution, at Provincial Papers they were not effective. Furthermore, the broader union membership lost confidence in their reps when they couldn't report on confidential matters. Despite having studied the Spruce Falls buyout, the parties at Provincial Papers seemed unable to understand or implement any of the joint structures, participative initiatives, or a philosophy congruent with employee ownership. They could not let go of their old adversarial attitudes and beliefs. For many, it was a blessing when Rolland purchased the company and re-instated a traditional management hierarchy. At Provincial Papers, neither party was willing or able to make the transition to a union-management relationship that could have sustained employee ownership.

Role Confusion and Design Options

Let's move on and look at two other important issues that emerge from our study: the confusion that can arise under employee ownership between the role of the owner and the role of the employee, and the design options that employee ownership must consider.

Role Confusion

One of the major challenges at Revolve was implementing the shareholders agreement, which demanded unanimous approval from all employees for any major decisions. The process was not only inefficient and frustrating but jeopardized Revolve's ability to do business. With time, employee owners realized they would have to give over more control to their managers and concentrate on their own jobs, especially if they wished to access venture capital for expansion. Eventually, the company evolved a delegation of authorities guideline that identified which levels of the organization should make various types of decisions. Employees began to separate their roles as shareholders and employees both in their minds and in their work life. Things settled down after that and Revolve went on to find a multinational investor to help it expand internationally.

At Integra, by contrast, this issue was sorted out at the beginning. Their shareholders agreement restricted the conditions under which unanimous approval had to be obtained for issues related to shareholder ownership. Employees started out with the exclusive right of electing a board of directors, and operational decisions were delegated to management. Thus it was agreed that the owners' role would be distinct from the employee role, and share ownership became more of a way for employees to participate in the risks and benefits of ownership.

When employees also are major owners of the company, their interests can be more aligned with those of management than in the traditional enterprise. Both have a vested interest in the continued success of the company. However, the role of owner often conflicts with that of employee, especially when tough decisions must be made, such as layoffs or major expenditures that affect the bottom line negatively. The challenge under employee ownership is to reconcile these competing interests, or at least to reach an acceptable balance between them. This balance requires reaching a clear understanding and consensus around the delegation process and determining which decisions fall within the authority of the employee owners and which rest with management. Companies embarking on the employee ownership adventure would be wise to discuss this issue thoroughly and resolve ambiguities before they cause problems.

Design Options

Researcher David Toscano identified eight design areas that employee ownership companies must decide, preferably before setting up their employee ownership plan. Examining the companies in our study with the best results from both the crisis and non-crisis cases may help determine whether a clear superiority exists for any design option, or combination of design options.

Toscano's first criterion was the role of shares. Shares can, in fact, play three roles: they may reflect the market value of the company; they may entitle the holder to a portion of the profits; and they may give the shareholder formal power in direct relation to the amount of stock held.

The second criterion is the method of share purchase or acquisition. Employees may acquire shares directly at market value, or through a purchase option that offers the shares at lower than market rate. The choice may be to award shares at no cost to employees in accordance with their remuneration or seniority.

The third criterion is the manner of shareholding. Shares can be held individually or by a company or union trust, which releases them to employees over time. In those cases, the employees often have limited voting rights and are prevented from selling their shares while employed by the firm.

The fourth criterion is the provision for the sale or transfer of stock. In cases where employees may sell their stock freely to outsiders, employee ownership may erode over time. On the other hand, if a company must repurchase the stock from retiring employees, a large appreciation in the stock price may cause a financial drain on the company.

The fifth issue is the extension of ownership to new employees. Should they be required to work for a minimum time period before becoming eligible for ownership? Should all employees be forced to own shares? Should the accumulation of stock be determined by years of employment or some other criterion? In situations where a trust is set up to distribute the shares, should new employees have to work for a number of years before their ownership is "vested"?

The sixth consideration is the share concentration. If distribution is based on seniority or on salary, management may end up with a larger proportion of shares.

The seventh criterion is the role of outside investors. If ownership plans do not limit the amount of outside investment, employee ownership can become diluted, especially in successful companies.

The last design factor concerns control. In the conventional capitalist firm, legal control lies with the shareholders, whereas day-to-day control actually rests with top management. It's legitimate to question whether or not this control pattern should be altered, especially when employees are the majority owners. Control also depends on the type of shares held by different groups. In some cases designated employee groups may receive "non-voting" shares, whereas in other cases shares also confer influence and voting rights over major company decisions.

TABLE FIVE

Design Options at Creo, PRT, and Spruce Falls

Design Option	Creo	PRT	Spruce Falls
1. Role played by shares	Stock price reflects market valuation of the company, entitles employees to share in profits and elect a board member	Stock price reflects book value of the company and stock entitles employees to share in profit, but confers no voting rights	Stock price reflects market value of Tembec, entitles employees to reps on the board
2. Method of share purchase	Stock options are given annually—determined partly by contribution to the company, as set by the peer review process. A minimum is awarded to all	All employees encouraged to buy some stock. Shares issued annually at first. Tried to maintain the relative stake of managers and employees over time	Initially employees had to buy stock, matching Tembec's investment. Now loan incentives are provided to encourage share purchase
3. Manner of shareholding	Shares held individually	Shares held individually	Shares held individually
4. Provisions for the sale or transfer of stock	Prior to the stock being listed, company ran an e-mail exchange, which regularly listed blocks of shares that were up for sale, ensuring excellent liquidity. Now can sell freely on open market	Initially no external market for the stock. Employees required to start selling back their shares at age 60, so company had to ensure sufficient funds to repurchase. Now public market for shares in the income trust and employees can buy shares in the holding company	Tembec went public in 1983 and most employees cashed in a majority of their stock. Now employees can buy and sell shares on the open market

cont'd

5. Extension of ownership to new employees	Stock options granted to new employees under same terms as longer-term employees (performance-related)	Stock issues available to new employees under same terms as longer-term	Stock can be purchased by new employees under same terms as longer-term
6. Share concentration	Employees owned 20 percent and founders and senior managers held another 20 percent	Key executives owned just over 50 percent of the stock	Initially, Tembec owned 41 percent of shares, local residents 7 percent, and employees 52 percent. Now Tembec is majority owner and only 20–30 percent of employees own stock
7. Role of outside investors	Now stock available to outside investors through open market	Now stock available to outside investors through income trust	Now stock available to outside investors through open market
8. Principles of control	Employee control on board restricted to one rep. However, authority shared broadly in daily decision-making	Originally PRT appointed one employee to the board, but discontinued. Control largely management driven with some employee input	Employees had three reps out of nine on board, given training. Control based on four pillars of employee ownership, profit sharing, participation, and open communications

Table Five illustrates how these options played out at three companies. Firms should pay special attention to the common design choices made by our three very successful employee ownership companies. First, in all three cases, employees owned their shares individually, rather than in an employee trust. That makes ownership more immediate and compelling and so can have a greater motivational effect. Second, all three opened up share ownership to the broader market, which created an outside pricing mechanism and allowed employees to realize a profit on their shares. Third, new employees were allowed into the plan on the same terms as the original employee owners. While they would not have as many shares and could not reap as many rewards over a shorter time period, this did create a level playing field, and probably also reinforced the notion that everyone was in the venture together.

Finally, some level of employee input and control was encouraged. In two of the cases, employees had representatives on the board of directors. In such situations, however, the company will probably have to train reps if they want them to be fully involved and motivated members.

Further Lessons from the Case Studies

For companies in crisis situations

For companies in crisis, needing a swift turnaround, employee ownership can help your company survive, but our study shows certain factors can raise the probability of good results for both the bottom line and employee financial outcomes:

- Ensure that the new senior leaders of the company have expertise in the industry. Experience with employee ownership is also an asset.
- Force employees to make an actual dollar investment in the stock, even if it is not large—and even if downsizing and wage and benefit concessions are also necessary.
- Work with the union and help the union leaders to look good to the membership.
- Make sure that the turnaround strategy makes sense for the industry the company is in and that it is implemented fairly quickly.
- Work to create and maintain good employee relations.
- Make a commitment to employee ownership as a philosophy.
- Encourage employee involvement and participation, at least to a greater extent than prior to employee ownership.

For small entrepreneurial firms

For small entrepreneurial companies facing uncertain futures, our study suggests employee ownership can help overcome many of the hazards of the organizational life cycle by helping to retain valuable employees, to enable growth without giving away the company to venture capitalists, to attract investors, and to expand more rapidly. Here's how:

- Make a commitment to employee ownership as a philosophy.

- Supplement that with a management philosophy that goes beyond mere employee involvement and consider some elements of Tembec's "four pillars" system or Creo's unit presidency concept.

- Encourage employees to continue investing in the company's stock in some way.

- Think of an exit strategy for internal shareholders, be it an initial public offering of stock on the open market; an internal repurchase plan funded from internal sources (which is riskier for the company); or a strategic alliance with (or outright sale to) a partner.

- Encourage good employee relations and participation from the union, if there is one.

- Make sure senior leadership is highly involved and on-site.

- Make sure employees hold the shares individually.

- Keep the playing field as level as possible for new employees.

Conclusions

Our study started through a chance remark about honesty, employees, and ownership. After looking in depth at ten companies, it's clear that employee ownership is much more complicated than that chance remark allowed. But at the same time, our study shows the truth of the basic element of that statement—that employee ownership can change employee behaviour for the better.

Whether as stated by Frank Dottori, it's truly worth a 15 percent competitive advantage is, of course, debatable. But the case studies show that employee ownership, when designed appropriately, can be a powerful mechanism for survival, profit, and growth in a variety of different types of companies and industries. It can be a new source of competitive advantage. We hope more managers will become familiar with the concepts of employee ownership and will seriously consider implementing it in their firms. We hope more unions will consider employee ownership as a positive force, whether in a crisis situation or not, and will co-operate with management to make it a success. Finally, we also hope that governments, both federal and provincial, will take a closer look at employee ownership and enact more legislation to encourage employee ownership and remove some sources of red tape restricting its growth in Canada.

Appendix

Appendix

The EO FILES

ॐ

After analyzing our cases it's also worth looking at the extensive literature on employee ownership and at various government initiatives. That search—call it the EO Files—begins with a deceptive question: What is ownership?

Traditionally, ownership has been a right conferred upon an individual, by the perception of others that a legitimate relationship exists between that person and certain property, be it land or a social object. Indeed, as Raymond Russell (1985) noted in *Sharing Ownership in the Workplace*, "ownership is never an unmediated relationship between a human subject and an object of value. It always involves the judgement of other people." Ownership grants the right to use the property, to enjoy and profit from its use, and to dispose of that property.

Since the seventeenth century, society has acknowledged a much broader notion of ownership than just property: a person owns his or her own labour. But the Industrial Revolution changed that yet again, unleashing the notion of employment, which allowed a worker to sell his or her own labour, thus relinquishing the property rights to the new owner. The worker was now separate from the fruits of his or her labour.

The Categories of Ownership and Possible Designs

Ownership, then, has evolved significantly over time. Employee ownership can involve various different arrangements, of which four stand out:

- Social ownership, whereby people in a community or society, including employees, have an ownership stake in the organization;

- Worker co-operatives or producer co-operatives, in which employees are the exclusive owners;

- Employee Stock Ownership Plans (ESOPs), in which employees participate in ownership in the firm, perhaps to the extent of being majority or exclusive owners. Ownership in an ESOP is frequently held by an employee ownership trust established by the company on behalf of its employees.

- Direct share ownership, whereby employees purchase stock in the company that employs them.

Worker co-operatives are dramatically different from the other three versions. The most famous example is the highly successful Mondragon co-operatives in Spain, which are based on democratic self-management and equality, and are an eye-opener to those who doubt such arrangements can be effective. Producer co-operatives in Canada have a long history in farming communities, notably in the West. Worker co-operatives tend to be more prevalent in Quebec than other provinces, although obviously they are a rarity in the business landscape.

Employee ownership can also be categorized by the design options available in such ventures. David Toscano (1983) identified eight criteria when he tried to develop a topology of employee ownership. They remain central today, as our case studies and analysis showed:

- the role played by the shares;
- the method of share purchase or acquisition;
- the manner of shareholding;
- the provision for sale or transfer of the stock;
- the extension of ownership to new employees;
- share concentration;
- the role of outside investors;
- the principles of control.

Shares can play three roles in a capitalist organization. Generally—although not always—they reflect the market value of the company. They may entitle the holder to a portion of the profits, although again that doesn't apply in every case and to every category of shares. And they may give the shareholders formal power, in proportion to the amount of stock held.

In a producer co-operative, by contrast, shares do not fluctuate to reflect market value. Instead, the share price is established by the co-operative itself to enable each new employee to purchase shares. In our sample, interestingly, some of the companies evolved from being privately owned and having some of the characteristics of a producer co-operative to a more public form of shareholding, with an IPO and a presence on the stock market.

Employees may acquire shares directly at market value or through a purchase option, which offers the shares at lower than market rate. Alternatively, as in some of our companies and in many ESOP programs, shares may be awarded at no cost to employees in accordance with their remuneration or seniority. While employee-owned companies like employees to own shares, they generally don't make such ownership mandatory. In co-operatives, however, employees are normally required to purchase a certain number of shares (although usually just one) in order to work in the organization, participate in decision-making, and receive a portion of the profits.

Shares can be held individually or by a company or union trust, which would release them over time. When the shares are held in a trust, this can—as at Provincial Papers—reduce the stake employees feel in the company. In such situations, employees often have limited voting rights and are prevented from selling the shares while employed by the firm.

How shares are sold or transferred is a crucial design consideration, as our case studies demonstrate. In companies where employees may sell their stock freely to outsiders, employee ownership may erode over time, as at Tembec and Spruce Falls. On the other hand, if a company must repurchase the stock from retiring employees—as at PRT—it can cause a financial drain, particularly if the stock price appreciates.

An ownership plan must also consider how to handle new employees. Should they be required to work for a minimum time period before becoming eligible for ownership? Should all employees be forced to own shares as a matter of employment or should stock ownership be restricted to some defined group? Should the accumulation of stock be determined by years of employment or some other criterion? In situations where a trust is set up to distribute shares, should new employees have to work for a number of years before their ownership is "vested"?

Share concentration is also an important consideration. With the exception of some producer co-operatives, shares are normally distributed unequally, even in situations where unions are involved. If distribution is based on seniority or on salary, management can end up with a larger proportion of shares. This may be problematic, as at Integra, and can lead employees to see the company as somebody else's. Or it may be beneficial, as Chris Worthy believes it was for PRT, and ensure stable direction.

The designers of an employee ownership plan must also decide on the role of outside investors. In co-operatives, by their nature, outside investment is prohibited. These days, start-ups are eager for outside investment, as a rite of passage to the big leagues in an era when scale and first-mover status are prized. But as Revolve Technologies demonstrates, employee ownership can become diluted by this outside capital, especially in a successful company.

The last design factor concerns control. In the conventional capitalist firm, legal control lies with the shareholders, whereas day-to-day control actually rests with top management. As our examples show, that division between legal and day-to-day control remains in many employee ownership firms and can create powerful tensions. It's reasonable to ask whether this control pattern should be altered, especially in situations where unionized employees have majority ownership. And if so, what kinds of control mechanisms can be erected to ensure the company runs smoothly and effectively?

The U.S. History

The first ESOPs in the United States were a creature of the Employment Retirement Security Income Security Act of 1974, which set out their basic design. Under an ESOP, in contrast to a direct share purchase plan, the company transfers shares to employees. The shares are held in an Employee Stock Ownership Trust and the trust often votes on behalf of the employees. So employees have limited voting rights. The shares are also distributed on the basis of seniority, salary, or some other formula, resulting in an unequal allocation. Typically, employees are prevented from selling their shares while employed with the company.

Since the original legislation, variations of the ESOP have sprung up. One is the stock bonus plan that allows a company to contribute a portion of the employee payroll—usually up to 15 percent—to the employee stock ownership trust, for which it receives a tax deduction. The company must then redeem the employees' shares with cash when they retire or leave.

A second version, the leveraged ESOP, is commonly used in U.S. buyouts because of the significant tax incentives it provides for both the company and the lending institutions, and the ease with which an ESOP can borrow money. Here's how it works, as described by the National Center for Employee Ownership (1992):

1. The employees set up a shell corporation, which in turn sets up an ESOP.

2. The corporation goes to a bank or other lender (sometimes the parent firm) and seeks a loan to buy the assets of the company being purchased. Instead of borrowing the funds directly, however, the company has an ESOP borrow them, something only ESOPS, among all employee benefit plans, can do.

3. The ESOP then buys the assets and exchanges them for all the stock of the newly created company. The ESOP now has stock. The company guarantees the bank that it will make contributions to the ESOP sufficient to repay the loan. The assets are used as security, although sometimes a government guarantee is involved as well.

4. The contributions the company makes to the ESOP are fully deductible for the entire interest portion of the loan and for up to 25 percent of the total payroll of the participants in the ESOP for the principal portion.

5. Finally, the bank or other commercial lender making the loan can deduct 50 percent of the interest income it receives on the loan. The law was modified in 1989, however, to limit this interest income exclusion to ESOPs owning over 50 percent of the company's stock and passing through full voting rights on shares allocated to employees and acquired by the loan.

The final type of ESOP is the Payroll-Based Stock Ownership Plan, which owes its existence to the 1975 Tax Reduction Act's stock ownership plan. It's unlike the original ESOPs designed by lawyer Louis Kelso and has been criticized by some ESOP supporters (see for example Blasi, 1987) as little more than a personal attempt by Kelso's partner in promoting employee ownership, Senator Russell Long, to increase the tax credits given to corporations rather than an effort to promote employee ownership. Under it, firms receive a dollar-for-dollar tax credit with an upper limit determined in relationship to their annual capital investment or payroll. That results in an employee benefit at virtually no cost to the company.

All of these ESOP plans were originally designed to promote investment in company securities, while at the same time allowing the company to use this capital until the employees leave or retire. In addition, however, these plans encourage employee ownership even if there is a lack of knowledge about the concept or a lack of funds to launch such a program. They also create a method of establishing employee ownership in firms where stock is not publicly traded.

The Canadian History

In Canada, the federal government has created few incentives for employee ownership but it has established two kinds of profit-sharing plans: the Deferred Profit-Sharing Plan—which is often used as a type of pension plan, notably in small companies—and the Employee Profit-Sharing Plan. Only the deferred plan is structured to encourage employee ownership, but it is not a strong incentive. It allows the employer to claim tax exemptions, which include both the company's contribution to the plan and the annual earnings of the trust until the employees receive the benefit.

A later amendment, however, set a threshold on the tax deduction, limiting it to the employee's RRSP contribution level. As well, employees who are "significant" shareholders were made ineligible. Richard Long (1992), of the University of Saskatchewan's Industrial Relations and Organizational Behaviour department, notes that the amendment was an attempt to prevent "top hat" plans for which only senior management would be eligible. In 1990, the federal government passed another amendment, which gave some additional tax incentives to employee owners. For example, any appreciation in the value of the shares was now treated as capital gains rather than income.

The provinces have been more active than the federal government in promoting employee ownership in Canada. Quebec was in the forefront, creating the Quebec Stock Savings Program in the 1970s; later, the Quebec Federation of Labour set up its solidarity fund. Two further programs in the 1980s acted as vehicles for employee ownership, the Régime d'Epargne du Québec and the Société de Placements dans l'Enterprise Québécoise.

By contrast, Ontario was slower to promote employee ownership, first enacting legislation in 1988, under Premier David Peterson's Liberal government. They wanted Ontario's ESOP to promote co-operation and participation in the workplace and to open up a new source of equity capital for small- and medium-sized businesses. Employees who bought shares in a registered ESOP could receive a cash grant of 15 percent, up to a maximum of $300 a year. Corporations and employee groups could also receive modest grants to offset the costs of setting up an ESOP. But the small size of the incentives, combined with the red tape required to set up the plans, resulted in only eight registrations in the first three years of the program. And the program, modest as it was, fell victim to government cutbacks under the Rae government, to be replaced later by the Ontario Investment and Employee Ownership Program, sparked by the high-profile corporate resuscitations detailed in earlier chapters.

Instead of the cash grants that were available under the previous program, this employee ownership program provides Ontario personal income tax credits for individual employees up to a maximum of $4,150 annually. There is also a maximum lifetime limit of $150,000. As well, the program offers crucial help in getting started in employee ownership ventures, by subsidizing the development of business plans. An employee group may receive financial assistance of up to 50 percent of the cost of engaging private financial help to evaluate the feasibility of an employee ownership plan, with a maximum grant of $12,500. If the plan is considered feasible, the employee group will receive additional financial assistance up to 50 percent of the cost of developing a full business proposal by a private professional.

Under the program, employees must hold shares for a minimum of five years or any tax credits claimed will be taxed back. Exceptions are allowed, however, for death, retirement, involuntary retirement where there is no cause, or permanent disability. To ensure a significant employee stake, the existing owners of a company using this employee ownership program must be prepared to sell over 50 percent of the equity in the company to its workers. If an outside investor is involved, the company must sell at least 40 percent of its equity to employees and the combined investment of the outside investor and the employees must reach 50 percent, or more, of the company.

The program requires an employee group to submit business, investment, and human resource plans to an Employee Ownership Board. If the board likes the proposal, it is passed to the provincial cabinet for approval. The employee group then prepares a disclosure document containing detailed information from the plan for consideration by the employees, with an independent advisor appointed by the government helping them to assess the proposal. An employee vote is conducted under the supervision of the Ontario Labour Relations Board. If approved, the corporation is registered and shares can be sold to employees.

B.C.'s plan—the Employee Investment Act of 1989—was designed to encourage employees to make equity investment in British Columbia companies for the purpose of job creation, job protection, and participation in ownership. It encourages three types of employee investment, of which the ESOP is one.

That program gives eligible employees a provincial tax credit of 20 percent of the amount they invest in a registered ESOP, up to a maximum credit of $2,000 per year or $10,000 in a lifetime. Employee or employer groups receive financial assistance of 50 percent of the costs of establishing an ESOP over two years, up to a maximum of $10,000. Eligible companies cannot exceed 150 employees, must have total assets worth less than $500 million, and must pay at least 25 percent of their wages to B.C. residents. In addition, the shares must be fully participating, voting shares; the plan must establish a method for share valuation; and share liquidity must be ensured by a redemption plan if no outside market for the shares exists.

What the Research Shows

Reliable statistics about the extent of employee ownership in Canada are, unfortunately, sparse. A study of 821 firms listed on the Toronto Stock Exchange (Benefits Canada, 1987) found that 554, or 63 percent, had at least one form of employee equity program in place. The most popular were stock option plans, instituted by 54 percent of the companies, while 24 percent had share purchase plans. In 1987, the Conference Board of Canada reported that 61 percent of companies with publicly traded shares had stock purchase plans (Booth, 1988).

Both those studies, of course, were geared to larger companies. Richard Long surveyed a representative sample of 626 Canadian firms between May 1989 and June 1990, discovering that profit-sharing was much more common than employee ownership (Long, 1992). Only 7.5 percent of the firms surveyed had employee ownership plans, whereas 17.3 percent had profit-sharing and 2.4 percent had both. Both employee ownership and profit-sharing were more widespread in the primary sector. When examined by type of firm, 37.3 percent of public corporations had some form of employee ownership, compared to 3.8 percent of private corporations.

Long concluded that "well over a fifth (22.4 percent) of Canadian firms employing at least 20 persons had broad-based profit-sharing, employee ownership, or both." He indicated that although profit-sharing was more common, employee ownership was actually growing more rapidly at the time. He also concluded that Canadian firms were adopting ownership plans for reasons other than tax incentives, which in any case were much lower than those available south of the border.

An earlier survey (1978a) had looked at views towards employee ownership. Workers believed the major advantage was the chance for monetary gain. That was followed by the satisfaction of working for yourself; greater influence in decision-making; a chance to benefit from your own efforts; being part of something; and a better understanding between managers and employees.

Managers also listed monetary gains atop their list of advantages. But then they saw employee ownership improving their ability to manage the enterprise. They cited improved communication between management and employees; more conscientious staff; more co-operation from employees; more co-operation amongst employees; and more freedom to make decisions. They felt the company could reap improved performance and achieve more commonality on goals.

Disadvantages cited by employees included that the firm would expect more work from the workforce. As well, because a strike could harm a company's financial performance, they feared a strike threat by employee owners might not be taken as seriously, thereby reducing their leverage with management. As for managers, they worried about a loss of authority. They were apprehensive that employee owners might overrate their own importance to the firm; that management might have difficulty viewing—and treating—employee owners as workers; and that they themselves might have to perform better in order to please this new class of owners.

Other disadvantages pointed out by Corey Rosen, founder and executive director of the National Center for Employee Ownership in the United States (Rosen and Quarrey, 1987), include the high legal and accounting costs demanded by the requirement for annual valuations; the dilution of ownership as new shares are issued; and the expense of repurchasing the shares of departing employees in private companies. Media commentators have highlighted the fact that some employees might put their wealth at risk through employee ownership since their investments wouldn't be sufficiently diversified, and if shares declined in value employee owners might become demoralized rather than motivated.

Kelso, the visionary who started the employee ownership movement in North America when he wrote The *Capitalist Manifesto* (Kelso and Adler, 1958), saw it in broader terms than that. He was troubled by the high concentration of wealth in the United States and saw employee share ownership as a way to democratize capitalism and attack a major cause of poverty, the failure to own an adequate holding of capital. In The *Ownership Solution*, Jeff Gates (1998), a lawyer and investment banker who worked as counsel to the U.S. Senate Committee on Finance during the 1980s, echoed that concern 40 years later, noting that the net worth of the top 1 percent of Americans exceeds that of the bottom 90 percent. He argued that conventional capitalism can only make those patterns worse, because financing growth comes from only four sources: retained earnings, depreciation, debt, and new equity. Individuals who already own capital are the largest beneficiaries of those four sources, and breaking into this "closed system" is difficult for those who lack savings. Thus he advocated employee ownership, as an alternative source of equity financing, along with a host of other innovative proposals to expand ownership and the number of capitalists in society.

In the United States, where there has been a significant public debate on employee ownership, conservatives generally give a similar rationale for supporting the option: it will strengthen the capitalist system. On the other hand, liberals are motivated by the opportunity to increase employee involvement and control, as Jon Pierce and Candace Furo (1990) observed in Organizational Dynamics. The labour movement, traditionally to the left of liberals on the political spectrum, has been split. While some unions have begun to support the notion of employee ownership, on the whole they have remained fairly skeptical, worried about workers' being co-opted by management or the union role being devalued. On the far left of the political spectrum, advocates of employee ownership see it as a step towards the longer-term goal of economic democracy in which control of the economy would be returned to the people.

In Canada, of course, many of those same arguments are heard. But there's an extra one: employee ownership, and in particular stock options, could help to stop the alleged "brain drain" from Canada to the United States. Perry Phillips, president of ESOP Builders, a Mississauga-based consulting firm, and author of *Employee Share Ownership Plans* (Phillips, 2001), surveyed 1,200 high-tech firms in Canada in 1999 and found that 90 percent of those with ESOPs reported that their packages had helped to attract employees and 70 percent said they has been a factor in retention. The small response rate of the sample—4.25 percent—means it would be risky to draw any definite conclusions from those results, but clearly high-tech companies are increasingly depending on employee share ownership to recruit and retain employees.

There is no sign that employee ownership has made a significant impact on the distribution of wealth in society, which isn't unexpected given how limited the programs are in number and scope. Wealth is still highly concentrated in the United States and Canada. Rutgers University Professor Joseph Rafael Blasi (Blasi, 1988) has highlighted specific aspects of ESOPs that tend to prevent them from reducing wealth differences:

1. Employees excluded from the plans tend to be non-professional, non-managerial, younger and/or unionized, with lower incomes.

2. Many ESOPs are essentially government-subsidized stock plans for workers with high salaries.

3. The wide practice of allocating worker ownership according to salary level skews stock ownership even in ESOPs that include all employees.

But a study conducted in 1986 by the National Center for Employee Ownership of 140 ESOP companies in the U.S. was more optimistic (Rosen and Feldman, 1986). It showed that the average employee in such plans—earning the median wage of $18,000—would accumulate $31,000 in stock after 10 years and $124,000 after 20 years. The study concluded that for employees in companies with such plans, ESOPs "have been successful in accomplishing the central purpose for which they were established—to create a more equitable distribution of wealth." A more recent study by the same group, in 1999, estimated as well that employees in ESOP companies received 5 percent to 12 percent higher wages and had three times the assets in their retirement plans as employees in non-ESOP companies.

Attitudes, Participation, and Ownership

There has been a significant amount of research on the effects of employee ownership on job attitudes, with mixed but intriguing results. The Worklife Report (1986–88) reported that in general employee owners were proud to own part of a company and were also more interested in its financial success. At the same time, the report found that employees were less likely to see their ownership plans "as having an impact on their day-to-day work experience and job satisfaction, on their feelings of ownership, or on their sense of participation in the company." Significantly, education levels were negatively related to satisfaction levels: the lower the education, the more satisfied workers were with their ownership stake. Other factors associated with satisfaction were the amount of information given to and actually read by the employee about the plan; the employee's annual contribution and accumulated savings; degree of voting rights; and the level of participation. Where participation in the ownership plan increased above 20 percent of the work force, the attitude ratings increased significantly.

Richard Long attempted in two studies to separate the effects on job attitudes of share ownership and participation in decision-making (Long, 1978a; Long, 1978b). He concluded that share ownership had a significant impact, independent of participation, on employee involvement and commitment. Ownership also seemed to increase motivation for all employees, through peer pressure. Still, of the two factors—share ownership or participation in decision-making—the greater impact on job attitudes came from participation.

In a later study, Long (1979) measured employees' job attitudes before and after the conversion of a Canadian firm to employee ownership. He found that employee ownership did not have a positive impact on job attitudes in that instance; participation in decision-making had a large impact.

Less optimistically, a study by Raymond Russell, Arthur Hochner, and Stewart Perry (1979) found evidence that employee-owned companies have a tendency to degenerate into imitating the hierarchical practices of conventional capitalist corporations and exploiting the non-member employees. For these non-members, employee ownership can take on an oppressive character.

Even the idea that employee ownership will automatically increase the desire of employees to participate has not been proven. A study by Tove Hammer and Robert Stern (1990) of Cornell University concluded that employees in an employee-owned company still viewed their managers as the real owners of the company and themselves as financial investors rather than partners with management. That was particularly true if the work force was older, had longer tenure, was accustomed to a traditional division of labour, and, more surprisingly, had invested a great deal in the firm. Employee owners may believe that delegating decisions to expert managers is the best way to protect their investment.

Those findings were also supported by a longitudinal study of a Canadian electronics firm by Long (1981) before and after its conversion to partial employee ownership. He concluded that employee ownership did not increase the desire for worker participation amongst either managers or non-managers and did not significantly affect the amount or distribution of influence within the firm. His research seems to suggest that employee owners perceived their ownership as an investment and were not interested in taking an active management role in the company, unless poor management threatened their investment.

Katherine Klein (1987) probed further, trying to trace psychologically what elements of employee ownership produce increased commitment to the company. Would it be the simple fact of ownership, or what she called intrinsic satisfaction, that sparks greater commitment? Would increased influence in decision-making lead in turn to greater commitment to the company (what she called an instrumental satisfaction model)? Or would the trigger for greater commitment be external—greater financial rewards from employee ownership increasing commitment (which she labelled the extrinsic model)? Her results found the psychological sense of ownership by itself did not produce greater commitment, but there was evidence for the other two channels of increased commitment.

A study by Aaron Buchko (1993) of Bradley University adds to that research thread, finding greater evidence to support the instrumental view of employee ownership rather than the extrinsic perspective: "Perceived employee influence from ownership has more of an impact on employee attitudes than financial value." However, while those two studies delineating the power of the individual elements are useful, they may obscure a central point: the bulk of the evidence suggests that employee ownership and participation exercise a stronger influence on job attitudes when combined. You don't want just one element; preferably, you seek both.

Advocates of employee ownership, of course, contend that by itself it leads to improved corporate performance. When employees become owners, they become more concerned about quality and costs. That concern leads to higher productivity and better financial results for the company. As well, employee-owned firms may attract higher-quality employees and may allow employees to change policies more easily or to contribute ideas to improve their work.

While those specific steps remain to be proved, a series of studies reports that companies with employee ownership display greater corporate performance. The Toronto Stock Exchange, in a 1987 study (Benefits Canada, 1987), found more profitability and more productivity in companies offering employee ownership plans than those who do not. The profitability differential was 24 percent. Employee-owned firms also had reported a 95 percent higher profit in the most recent fiscal year; had a 123 percent higher profit growth rate within the previous five years; had a 92 percent higher return on equity and a 66 percent higher return on capital; and had a debt-to-equity ratio that was 32 percent lower.

Michael Conte and Arnold Tannenbaum (1978) examined 30 companies from the United States and Canada with employee ownership plans and concluded that employee-owned companies were 1.5 times more profitable than comparably sized companies in the same industry. Those results were not statistically significant because of the small sample size, but they do suggest that employee ownership may be associated with increased profitability. The study also found that the higher the percentage of employee ownership the more significant the impact on profitability.

Corey Rosen and Katherine Klein (1983) examined 108 U.S. companies with employee ownership plans. They found that companies with employee ownership plans over a three-year period averaged an annual employment growth rate of 2.78 percent higher than comparable conventional firms. Another study by the National Center for Employee Ownership in 1987 found that after an ESOP had been in place for five years, the annual employment growth rate of the companies was 5.05 percent higher than in the comparison firms (Quarrey and Rosen, 1993). As well, sales growth was 5.4 percent faster—and 73 percent of the companies in the sample significantly improved their performance after the ESOP was in place. Yet another study, in 1999, found that ESOP companies had a return on assets 2.7 percent per year better in their post-ESOP period as compared to their pre-ESOP period (Quarrey and Rosen, 1993).

A 1987 Center study that tried to delineate the drivers of the improved performance suggested that it was participation more than employee ownership (Quarrey and Rosen, 1993). "ESOP companies that instituted participation plans grew at a rate three to four times faster than ESOP companies that did not," it noted. A further study drew similar conclusions, namely that ESOP firms do not show improved profitability or productivity without higher levels of participation. There are numerous other studies that add to that evidence (Quarrey and Rosen, 1993).

In 1986, Michael Quarrey (Quarrey and Rosen, 1993) assessed the effect of various factors on corporate performance. He found that two measures of participation were significantly related to corporate performance: perceived influence and actual participation. None of the other factors he studied—which included ESOP contribution levels, management philosophy, communications about the ESOP, percent of equity owned, the features of the ESOP plan, voting rights, board representation, and company size—consistently predicted corporate performance without the presence of a measure of participation.

In terms of stock price, an index of public companies in the United States with at least 10 percent employee ownership grew 214 percent from 1992 to 1999, compared to 181 percent for the S&P index over the same time (Quarrey and Rosen, 1993). Scott Pittendrigh, in a study at the Queen's University School of Industrial Relations, compared the stock price performance of Algoma Steel, Spruce Falls, Tembec, and MDS Inc. with a number of similar companies that didn't have employee ownership. He found that the ESOP firms demonstrated superior stock price performance over the non-ESOP firms (Pittendrigh, 1998).

But again, it must be stressed that the preponderance of evidence suggests that employee ownership by itself will not necessarily increase satisfaction, motivation, organizational commitment, or corporate performance. A combination of a significant percentage of ownership and some form of employee participation appears to be the key to realizing the financial and attitudinal benefits of employee ownership, according to studies.

Theory O

That is in line with Theory O, developed by Karen M. Young, associate director and co-founder of the National Center for Employee Ownership, and Corey Rosen (Rosen and Young, 1991). Young was compiling a list of the traits common to companies with the most committed and satisfied workers, while Rosen was putting together a list of the features consistently occurring in financially successful companies based on a corporate performance study. Their two lists dovetailed and became the basis for the Ownership Theory of Management, or Theory O.

It sets out the following prescription for success:

1. The person at the top of the organization is committed to the concept.
2. There is a written set of values embodying the commitment to employee ownership.
3. Attention is given to symbols indicating the importance of employee ownership.
4. Decisions are made at the level where there is the most relevant expertise.
5. Training in technical and participative skills is given.
6. The sharing of information from the bottom up as well as the top down is practised.
7. There is a realization that participative decision-making takes more time but is often more effective.
8. The combination of methods used to implement Theory O is unique to each company, since what works for one company will not necessarily work for another.

If participation is key to employee ownership, as the studies tell us, then Theory O must be the map that companies use as they set out on their journey. In many cases, of course, that journey begins suddenly, with a forced buyout, and again the Center has developed a road map for that specific situation.

First of all, since time is a critical factor, employees must carve out a sufficient period to organize, conduct a feasibility study, create a business plan, obtain financing, and negotiate the deal. Rushing through the process too quickly can lead to design flaws, with serious repercussions later on. Second, the employees and the community must be mobilized and ready to support the employee buyout. It is important that this support come from diverse groups: elected officials, local business, labour, local churches, the media, as well as grassroots support from local citizens.

The viability of the firm being purchased is crucial. Prospective owners should satisfy themselves that a market exists for its products and that it can succeed against competitors—current ones and those that might emerge. Equally crucial is financing for the venture. Sources can include employee groups, the divesting company, local governments, provincial governments, banks, trust companies, credit unions, and local investors.

To make a smooth transition, resources must be committed, the current owner should be co-operative, and financial backing must be available to the company in the future. Supporters of the buyout and the local governments or groups should make technical assistance available. As well, entrepreneurial and managerial leadership is essential, as Robert Stern and Tove Hammer (1978) suggested in their 1978 study. In fact, they would argue that such leadership is the most crucial success factor of all in an employee buyout. Finally, closing the circle, the parties should agree upon a viable organizational structure that will facilitate participation in decision-making by employee owners—Theory O in action.

References

๛

Benefits Canada. December 1987. "TSE Releases ESOP Study," p.5.

Blasi, Joseph Raphael. 1987. "Employee Ownership through ESOPs: Implications for the Public Corporation." *Work in America Institute Studies in Productivity:* vol. 48.

Blasi, Joseph Raphael. 1988. *Employee Ownership: Revolution or Ripoff?* Massachusetts: Ballinger Publishing Company.

Booth, Patricia L. 1988. "Employee Involvement and Corporate Performance," *Canadian Business Review*. Ottawa: Public Conference Board of Canada, vol. 15–16, Spring, pp.14–16.

Buchko, Aaron A. 1993. "The Effects of Employee Ownership on Employee Attitudes: An Integrated Causal Model and Path Analysis." *Journal of Management Studies:* vol. 30, July, pp. 633–55.

Conte, Michael and Arnold S. Tannenbaum. 1978. "Employee-Owned Companies: Is The Difference Measurable?" *U.S. Monthly Labor Review:* vol. 101, July, pp. 23–28.

Gates, Jeffrey R. 1998. *The Ownership Solution: Toward a Shared Capitalism for the Twenty-First Century*. Reading, Mass.: Addison-Wesley.

Hammer, Tove Helland and Robert N. Stern. 1980. "Employee Ownership: Implications for the Organizational Distribution of Power." *Academy of Management Journal:* vol. 23, pp. 78–100.

Kelso, Louis O. and Mortimer Adler. 1958. *The Capitalist Manifesto*. New York: Random House.

Klein, Katherine. 1987. "Employee Stock Ownership and Employee Attitudes: A Test of Three Models." *Journal of Applied Psychology:* vol. 72, pp. 319–332.

Long, Richard J. 1978a. "The Relative Effects of Share Ownership vs. Control in Job Attitudes in an Employee-Owned Company." *Human Relations:* vol. 31, pp. 753–763.

Long, Richard J. 1978b. "The Effects of Employee Ownership on Organizational Identification, Employee Job Attitudes, and Organizational Performance: A Tentative Framework and Empirical Findings." *Human Relations:* vol. 31, pp. 29–48.

Long, Richard J. 1979. "Desires for and Patterns of Worker Participation in Decision Making after Conversion to Employee Ownership." *Academy of Management Journal:* vol. 22, pp. 611–617.

Long, Richard J. 1981. "The Effects of Formal Employee Participation in Ownership and Decision Making on Perceived and Desired Patterns of Organizational Influence: A Longitudinal Study." *Human Relations:* vol. 34, pp. 847–76.

Long, Richard J. 1992. "The Incidence and Nature of Employee Profit Sharing and Share Ownership in Canada," *Relations Industrielles:* vol. 47, pp. 463–486.

Phillips, Perry. *Employee Share Ownership Plans*. John Wiley & Sons Toronto, 2001.

Pierce, Jon L. and Candace A. Furo. 1990. "Employee Ownership: Implications for Management," *Organizational Dynamics:* Winter, pp. 32–34.

Pittendrigh, Scott. 1998. *Employee Stock Ownership Plans and Firm Stock Price Performance in Canada*. Kingston, Ontario: Queen's University.

Quarrey, Michael and Corey Rosen. 1993. *Employee Ownership and Corporate Performance*. The National Center for Employee Ownership.

Rosen, Corey and Katherine Klein. 1983. "Job Creating Performance of Employee-Owned Firms." *Monthly Labor Review:* vol. 106, July, pp. 15–19.

Rosen, Corey and Johnathon Feldman. 1986. "How Well Do ESOPs Reward Employees?" *Pension World:* vol. 22, February, pp. 35–39.

Rosen, Corey and Michael Quarrey. 1987. "How Well Is Employee Ownership Working?" *Harvard Business Review:* September–October, pp. 126–129.

Rosen, Corey and Karen M. Young eds. 1991. *Understanding Employee Ownership.* Ithaca: ILR Press, Cornell University.

Russell, Raymond, Arthur Hochner, and Stewart E. Perry. 1979. "Participation, Influence and Worker Ownership." *Industrial Relations:* vol. 18, Fall, pp. 330–341.

Russell, Raymond. 1985. *Sharing Ownership in the Workplace.* Albany: State University of New York Press.

Stern, Robert N. and Tove Helland Hammer. 1978. "Buying Your Job: Factors Affecting the Success or Failure of Employee Acquisition Attempts." *Human Relations:* vol. 31, pp. 1101–17.

The National Center for Employee Ownership. 1992. *The Buyout Handbook: Using Employee Ownership to Help a Distressed Company.* California: National Center for Employee Ownership.

The National Center for Employee Ownership, 1994. *Employee Ownership Report.* California: National Center for Employee Ownership, January/February, vol 14.

The Worklife Report. 1986–88. "Employee Share Ownership in Canada," vol. 5, pp. 8–9.

Toscano, David J. 1983. "Toward a Typology of Employee Ownership," *Human Relations:* vol. 36, pp. 581–602.

Index

ᏽᏽ